Collaborative Leadership in Action

Collaborative Leadership in Action

Partnering for Success in Schools

EDITED BY

Shelley B. Wepner

Dee Hopkins

Foreword by David Berliner

Teachers College, Columbia University
New York and London

Published by Teachers College Press, 1234 Amsterdam Avenue, New York, NY 10027

Library of Congress Cataloging-in-Publication Data
Collaborative leadership in action : partnering for success in schools / edited by Shelley B. Wepner, Dee Hopkins ; foreword by David Berliner.
    p. cm.
  Includes bibliographical references and index.
  ISBN 978-0-8077-5146-6 (pbk. : alk. paper)
  ISBN 978-0-8077-5147-3 (hardcover : alk. paper)
  1. Educational leadership. 2. Educational innovations. 3. Teaching teams.
I. Wepner, Shelley B., 1951– II. Hopkins, Dee.
  LB2805.C595 2011
  371.2'07—dc22   2010030296

ISBN 978-0-8077-5146-6 (paper)
ISBN 978-0-8077-5147-3 (hardcover)

Printed on acid-free paper

Manufactured in the United States of America

18 17 16 15 14 13 12 11   8 7 6 5 4 3 2 1

Alone we can do so little; together we can do so much.
–Helen Keller

This book is dedicated to our families for helping us develop our repertoire of collaborative abilities through their candid and loving feedback during easy and difficult discussions and negotiations.

For Shelley: To my husband, Roy Wepner; daughters and sons-in-law, Leslie, Marc, Meredith, and Judd.

For Dee: To my best collaborator, Robert Neeb, and the McKinney, Texas, tribe—Julie, Rob, Ian, Matt, and Paige.

Contents

PART III: COLLABORATIVE LEADERSHIP

Foreword

Successful leadership is not easy to achieve. Irrespective of your training and personality, despite your experience and record of past success, regardless of the lessons you have learned from analyzing past failures, and no matter how many of the myriad (and often silly) books you have read about how to be an effective leader, many who try to lead still fail. Other leaders do not fail completely but, instead, make a little progress on one front while suffering a small setback on another one, producing a mixed record overall. They are supported by some in their organization but found to be wanting by others. This is common.

Taking what one knows and applying it as a leader is so terribly difficult because contexts, cultures, resources, networks of communication, and economic issues outside of one's immediate control (such as the current recession) all conspire to make each setting and each time period for leadership quite different. Even the ordinary events of group life—an illness, a divorce, a drug or alcohol problem for a key person, or a scandal involving someone far from the leaders offices—will affect the perception of a leader's effectiveness, both within and outside of their organizations.

At different sites and at different times, a variety of context-specific solutions are needed to successfully lead complex organizations. School systems, both preK–12 and higher education, especially large ones, are remarkably complex organizations, and when they work together the complexity just multiplies. This makes leadership within those systems a highly creative endeavor, relying, as it must, on problem-solving in situations that have not occurred in precisely the same way before and are not likely to occur in precisely the same way again. The best a leader can do in these situations, given the vicissitudes of life, is to keep one's eyes on the few things that are important, no matter what else requires their immediate attention.

I would argue that awareness of goals is one of those few issues that transcends whatever else a leader does. Leaders must pay considerable attention to the small set of goals intended to guide their organizations and organizational sub-units. Leaders must monitor progress, provide resources, and remove the barriers associated with achieving an organization's goals. Only rarely should leaders impose these all-important organizational goals on others. It is much more desirable for the goals that will direct an organization to emerge from activities within and across sub-units of the organization itself. This yields a system in which many participants have collaborated in the development of the plans by which their individual success, and that of the organization, will be judged. This is a much surer and ultimately more satisfying, though usually slower and more frustrating, way to achieve commitment to organizational goals from those who will be doing the work.

Collaborative goal development is the first of many collaborative activities in which leaders must learn to engage, and many leaders are not well schooled in how this is accomplished. The authors of this book convincingly argue that collaborative activities require as much attention and nurturing as typically are spent on the organization's budget, and for the same reasons: The work of the organization cannot get done without both budgets and the personal investment of humans committed to fostering the organizational goals.

The focus of this book is the development of skills needed for developing and enacting successful collaborative activities within and between organizations. This book makes clear that collaboration is hard work that requires not just goal clarity and organizational intelligence, but also emotional intelligence. Successful collaboration, however, greatly eases the burden of leadership for two very important reasons. First, it automatically requires some sharing of the leadership role, making more people responsible for the organization's success. The theory of distributed leadership promotes the very sensible idea that the necessary skills for exceptional collaborative work need not be possessed by only one person or reside only in the organization's nominal leader. Second, engaging in collaborative leadership all but guarantees that potential problems with meeting organizational goals will be identified and understood more promptly, since many eyes are watching and evaluating the systems in which the participants work and in which they have a stake.

Collaboration within and across organizations and sub-units, especially school-university partnerships, is what this book is about. The authors teach us much of what we need to know about finding potential partners to achieve organizational goals, writing formal agreements and governance plans, sustaining relationships, celebrating successes, and handling damage control when public failures occur. This book has much wisdom that is based on lots of experience, and nowhere does that shine brighter than in the discussion about evaluating collaborative endeavors.

Evaluations cannot be only about achieving short-term goals or simple scores on standardized measures. Evaluators must be unusually creative in looking at whether the resources are adequate to the mission of the partnership and whether lines of authority are clear and governance structures are understood and followed. Also, there must be assessment of the degree of mutual respect between partners in the organization. Evaluators must interview and judge whether all the stakeholders in the project are involved enough to feel ownership, evaluators must worry about the lines of succession should personnel change in the organizations, and so forth. Evaluating collaborative efforts is an amazingly complex activity, and the wisdom provided for engaging in these activities is the great strength of this book.

Novice leaders of collaborative activities will surely enhance the possibility of organizational success and impact after they study this book. These readers are also likely to minimize the chances that such efforts will fail or be short-lived, which happens often, as is addressed in the very first chapter. Educators are lucky to have this resource available.

—David C. Berliner

Regents' Professor Emeritus, Arizona State University

Acknowledgments

Having spent much of our professional lives in leadership positions, we have had more than our share of great moments working with people and developing projects. Some of our most vivid memories come from our collaborative relationships with others. Looking beyond our own settings to work with others, who viewed the day-to-day quite differently than we did, we learned about new environments and re-envisioned our own environments through their eyes. We came to appreciate our partners' challenges in relation to their dreams as we worked together on the institutional "culture clashes" that affected us both. Most importantly, we realized that, with our partners, we could realize positive outcomes that were not previously imagined or expected.

We determined a few years ago that we wanted to develop a book about the unique qualities and challenges of developing and sustaining collaborative relationships. We also wanted to share our discoveries about leaders who were successful with collaboration.

It is one thing to have an idea that you think will work and quite another to find a publisher who shares your interest and conviction. Thankfully, Marie Ellen Larcada walked into our lives and spent the next several months working with us to develop a proposal that would allow us to share our ideas and, at the same time, appeal to the Teachers College Press readership. She worked with us at every stage to make sure that our coedited book would communicate a strong, coherent, and engaging message.

We also are especially grateful for the support of Carole Saltz, the director of Teachers College Press, who gave the go-ahead to publish this book and also helped to shape it so that it would be useful and enlightening. In addition, we thank Marie Ellen Larcada for her brilliant editorial abilities and unfathomable attention to detail.

Enormous gratitude is extended to our authors for sharing their expertise and insights about collaborative partnerships. In addition to having something significant to say about partnerships in general, they exuded the best of the collaborative characteristics described herein as they worked with us to prepare their chapters for publication. We thank our vignette authors, who so graciously shared their success stories in working with others. We also want to thank the tremendous partnerships throughout this country that are recognized within this book and the countless others that time did not allow us to mention.

We are appreciative of the work of graduate assistant Laura Josephson for spending what seemed to be endless hours conducting research, reaching out to our contributors for needed information, and providing yet another set of editorial eyes during various stages of the writing process.

Special thanks are extended to our families, friends, and colleagues who once again accepted that we could not necessarily pay attention to the details of life because we were obsessed with "writing one last sentence" or "editing one last paragraph." The "just five more minutes" plea that seemed to characterize our lives at home, on vacation, and at conferences was tolerated—even respected. We are forever grateful that we are surrounded by such caring and loving people.

Lastly, we thank anyone who reads this book for letting us know that, as with us, there is a deep and abiding interest in collaborating with others to inspire professional growth and promote learning achievement.

Introduction

Shelley B. Wepner
Dee Hopkins

We have heard so often that it takes an entire village to raise a child (African Proverb, n.d.). We like to say that it takes the entire profession of education, and then some, to provide that village for individuals of every age and ability so that they have the opportunity to learn. With chronic challenges in high-poverty schools and newfound challenges in increasingly diverse schools, collaborative leadership for creating that metaphorical village is more important than ever. This village comes from the partnerships that we develop with preK–12 schools and school districts, colleges and universities with teacher education programs, community and governmental organizations, and business communities.

Although it is easy to expect the creation of collaborative partnerships, there is a longstanding silo mentality of having separate structures for preservice teacher education, novice teacher support, and continuing professional development (Borko, Whitcomb, & Liston, 2008). Moving away from a silo mentality requires collaborative leaders who can promote a shift in thinking that the successful education of students is seen as a shared responsibility of both preK–12 and higher education faculty and administrators. Such leaders need to have the psychological, interpersonal, and financial wherewithal to create cross-institutional cultures that encourage teachers, professors, and administrators to partner to contribute to the knowledge base about teaching and learning by using classrooms, schools, and districts (Clift, 2008). Such leaders need to use their collaborative relationships to promote partnerships that ensure quality teaching and teacher education and, ultimately, lend dignity to the teaching profession (Borko, Whitcomb, & Liston, 2008; Clift, 2008).

Collaborative Leadership in Action is about creating partnerships and the leaders who make them happen. It discusses what is needed to move away from the silo mentality to develop, sustain, and evaluate collaborative relationships that enrich the preK–16 learning environment. This book is written for practicing and prospective school district and higher education administrators, teacher leaders, faculty leaders, and graduate students enrolled in educational leadership programs to help develop the collaborative know-how to cross boundaries to form successful partnerships and initiatives.

As the authors in this book have discovered from their own firsthand experiences, there are many challenges in forming partnerships: making connections with others, sharing a similar vision, forming a clear purpose, motivating others to participate, and knowing how to initiate and provide for sustainability. There also are certain attributes and strategies that collaborative leaders must possess to help others embrace the idea of reaching beyond their own contexts. While leaders in general might be quite skilled at navigating their own environments, they must now understand and succeed with the culture and climate of other organizations to succeed as collaborative leaders.

Collaborative Leadership in Action is unique because it speaks from the leadership perspectives of both preK–12 and higher education. It uses real-life examples to present theories and practices of collaborative leaders who have established and sustained successful partnerships with other organizations. It also provides specific guidelines for becoming a collaborative leader.

Unique features of the book include

- vignettes at the beginning of each chapter that describe a partnership related to the chapter topic,
- case studies interspersed throughout the book,
- vignettes written by school and district administrators collaborating with universities and by university faculty and administrators collaborating with schools. These vignettes of successful collaborative efforts are placed in each chapter alongside content that is relevant to the partnership.

Collaborative Leadership in Action includes three parts and eight chapters. Part I provides a theoretical and practical overview of partnerships. Chapter 1, by Dee Hopkins, defines the concept of a partnership and explains the importance, challenges, and components of collaborative partnerships. Chapter 2, by David M. Byrd and John McIntyre, describes the different types of partnerships and provides examples of each type of partnership.

Part II provides a realistic and practical discussion and description of ways to develop, sustain, and evaluate partnerships. Chapter 3, by Lee Teitel, focuses on developing partnerships that have the potential of becoming transformational. Chapter 4, by Diane Yendol-Hoppey, David Hoppey, and Ted Price, describes a dozen challenges for sustaining partnerships and provides lessons that collaborative leaders can use to keep partnerships afloat. Chapter 5, by Jerry W. Willis, explores how to evaluate partnerships in relation to the type of partnership formed.

Part III focuses on collaborative leadership. Chapter 6, by Shelley B. Wepner, describes essential characteristics and strategies for succeeding as a collaborative leader in either preK–12 or higher education settings. Chapter 7, by Jeffrey Glanz, describes ways in which collaborative leaders, especially principals, cross boundaries from their own institutions to other institutions in order to develop partnership opportunities. Chapter 8, by Shelley B. Wepner, closes the book with a set of considerations and guidelines for becoming a collaborative leader that reflects the ideas and recommendations from previous chapters.

There are two overarching premises to *Collaborative Leadership in Action*. The first premise is that preK–16 partnerships are an essential component of the education profession. Ensuring that teacher candidates are prepared properly, new teachers are better acclimated to their classroom situations, and practicing teachers are offered opportunities to continue to grow as professionals. The second premise, that collaborative leadership is critical for partnerships to succeed, assumes partnerships are as good as the leaders who initiate and oversee them. Even with the best of intentions, partnerships have come and gone as quickly as fleeting fads because of lackluster collaborative leadership between partners. Even though this book does not pretend to provide formulas for success, it begins to shed light on what we need to know about partnerships and ourselves to bring together the right people, ideas, plans, and resources to create something bigger and better than our own institutional realities. We hope that, as a result of reading this book, you find yourself more aware of what you have and what you need to form collaborative relationships that offer remarkable cross-institutional partnership opportunities for all different types of stakeholders.

REFERENCES

African Proverb. (n.d.). Quotes.net. Retrieved November 3, 2009, from http://www.quotes. net/quote/6994

Borko, H., Whitcomb, J., & Liston, D. (2008). An education president for the 21st century: Introducing eight letters to the 44th president of the United States. *Journal of Teacher Education, 59*, 207–211.

Clift, R. T. (2008). A letter to the 44th president of the United States. *Journal of Teacher Education, 59*, 220–225.

Part I

OVERVIEW OF PARTNERSHIPS

This first part of the book explains the value of collaborative partnerships for enhanced productivity across institutions.

Chapter 1, by Dee Hopkins, defines partnerships and collaborations, paying special attention to those most frequently found in educational settings. The chapter looks at the advantages and disadvantages of forming partnerships and provides real-life examples of the challenges individuals and institutions face as they attempt to create, implement, and maintain those partnerships. The critical components for successful collaboration, and the resultant partnerships that form, are also discussed.

Chapter 2, by David M. Byrd and John McIntyre, examines different types of effective partnerships—professional development schools (PDSs), community schools, and community-oriented PDSs—and research-based factors contributing to their success. This chapter discusses how foundations and businesses contribute to partnership work. It also describes the governing structures of effective partnerships.

These two chapters provide information on and offer insights into the benefits and challenges of different types of partnerships and different types of partners.

1

The Value of Partnerships

Dee Hopkins

This chapter

- defines and describes the types of partnerships and collaborations most common in educational settings;
- explores the advantages and disadvantages of forming collaborations;
- delves into the challenges partners face regarding commitment and responsibilities; and
- identifies the critical components of successful partnerships including how to implement, support, sustain, and assess them effectively.

* * *

When my daughter was 11, she was learning to play the violin. Every evening her screeches met me in the driveway. I began carrying cotton so that I could stuff my ears before coming in the front door. Julie had no sense of rhythm. She could not get the bow position right, and she had trouble balancing her instrument on her bony little shoulder. But she loved the violin and wanted to be in the middle school string orchestra. Julie wanted to perform. I continued to cringe. As weeks went by, Julie did not get any better. I wondered why someone at the school hadn't picked up on that—why they hadn't told her that she wasn't destined for a career as a concert violinist.

One night she met me with a big smile and splendid news. There was going to be a citywide performance by young people from the city and surrounding county school districts. Over 800 budding musicians would play. And guess what? Julie was to be one of the 800. I fretted for days. The longer she practiced the violin, the more I felt I should tell someone how bad she sounded. How could the school have missed it? What could the professionals have been thinking to bring 800 Julies together?

The night of the All City Children's String Orchestra arrived. Julie, in her white shirt and black skirt, took her place with the other 799 young musicians. The conductor took the dais and motioned for the musicians to lift their bows. I clenched my teeth, silently preparing for the caterwauling that would follow. The music began. Glorious! Glorious! Glorious! Alone, violinists struggled to find the right note; cello players stumbled through the melody searching for continuity. But together, the group made astonishing music. The music teachers knew it would be so. They worked with the children in their schools every day. They heard fragments become whole and trusted that knowledge—and their colleagues throughout the city—enough to expect their small-group success to be replicated when all of the groups were brought together. The feat required teamwork, a sharing of resources and talent, and it required trust. Every musician depended on the conductor leading. Each had to respond to the other musicians and blend his or her music with that of the group. The music directors had worked collectively for weeks selecting pieces to be played, agreeing on seating placement in the orchestra, and choosing who among them would conduct. Principals, many with cotton in their ears, had listened to sounds emanating from their building gymnasiums and music rooms every time they walked the halls. In spite of what they heard, they trusted their teachers and attended to the details that would get their school's children to the concert. The sound of 800 string instruments was divine. I was overwhelmed with relief—and joy.

* * *

Partnerships. Like that long ago concert, harmony can amaze us with its ability to create continuity in the midst of diversity. Each of us can make noise— and sometimes it is loud and sometimes people listen. Like each member of the orchestra, we can play the song alone. But it sounds better—and is more powerful—when played in harmony with others.

For years, a symbiotic relationship has existed between colleges and schools of education and the preK–12 schools. These primary partners are responsible for the education of our citizenry. Colleges and schools of education prepare tomorrow's teachers. During that preparation, the preK–12 schools provide placement sites—living laboratories—in which preservice teachers can learn by practicing their craft. They are assisted by knowledgeable classroom teachers and building administrators who offer guidance and instruction. In return, many of these same preservice teachers fill openings in the preK–12 schools upon graduation. Mutually beneficial, this relationship allows the education process to function effectively.

Developing a University–Community Partnership

Roberto Garcia

Antonio E. Garcia Arts & Education Center College of Education,
Texas A&M University–Corpus Christi, Corpus Christi, TX

The Antonio E. Garcia Arts and Education Center, in the heart of Corpus Christi, Texas, connects Texas A&M University–Corpus Christi (TAMUCC) to the community by providing educational programs, art exhibits, and cultural events. I became director of the Garcia Center in 2004, when the College of Education (COE) began overseeing the programming.

In 2004, the COE received funding from the Office of Juvenile Justice and Delinquency Prevention (OJJDP) to develop a program to reduce recidivism rates among juvenile offenders. We decided the Garcia Center was an ideal location to implement such a program. Working under the direction of the COE, we developed a program vision in which university graduate students would deliver services to the families of court-referred youth.

The program included a three-pronged intervention approach to combat the disproportionately high rates of school dropouts, alcohol and drug abuse, lack of parental involvement, and victimization of at-risk/court-referred youth. The three components were family connectivity, healthy interactions, and academic success. Family connectivity sought reduction of familial stressors by fostering family communication. Healthy interactions addressed participant and familial substance abuse, participant victimization, and inadequate coping skills by providing assessment, counseling, and prevention/intervention. Academic success provided youth with opportunities to participate in school/career related activities. Participants also received tutoring and mentoring.

The program was introduced to local justices and their case managers; high school counselors from Corpus Christi Independent School District (CCISD); and staff from Communities in Schools, a nationwide dropout prevention organization that provides services to CCISD students. This expanded group discussed the particular needs of the population and provided suggestions used to refine the curriculum. TAMUCC counseling graduate students, working under the direction of COE faculty, delivered the services. While honing their counseling skills and gaining invaluable experience, students received stipends to help them with their own school expenses. The community received much-needed services. At the request of local justices and case managers, we added GED classes, a leadership program, and conflict resolution classes. Since we began, more than 100 graduate students have benefited from working at the Garcia Center and more than 1,200 families have attended the program.

(continued on next page)

(continued from previous page)

By employing a similar model, the Garcia Center has made other programs available to the community such as academic achievement, health and wellness, art, and literacy. Approximately 80% of the programs offered at the center are staffed by university undergraduate and graduate students.

I attribute the success of the Garcia Center programs to the partnerships that have been established. Additional partnerships that have developed with agencies such as the local food bank, local businesses, and nonprofit organizations enhance the programs. As partnerships continue to grow, so will the possibilities for new programs for community residents and new hands-on experiences for our university students.

DEFINITION AND DESCRIPTION OF PARTNERSHIPS

So what exactly is a partnership and how does it differ from a collaboration—or does it? A partnership is a relationship. It can be two or more people or organizations involved in the same activity; two or more people or groups working together for a common cause; or an organization formed by two or more people or groups working together for some purpose. It often involves a formal agreement, sometimes written and signed by all involved, that delineates the purpose of the partnership and the responsibilities of each of the parties involved. A collaboration is the act of two or more people working together in order to achieve something. The terms are often synonymous and used interchangeably.

Describing the myriad partnerships that exist and relate to education is challenging; they are numerous and as varied as the partners participating in them. This book offers insight into the partnerships that are most dominant in education and into the characteristics of the leaders who pilot them.

The ivy-covered walls of academe are an archetype of the past. Today's partnerships—complex and extensive—bring collaborators together to improve education and expand beyond the boundaries of a campus. While colleges and schools of education are active members, other participants include businessmen and women, community members, university faculties from all colleges, community college instructors, educational service center trainers, and technologists. These diverse partners work together in varied and expansive relationships.

Technology has broadened the conceptualization of collaborating and allows us to work across boundaries that even a short while ago seemed impassable. Now that we have the capacity to create virtual teams, global collaborations are not only possible, they are occurring frequently (Wagner, 2008). A teacher in Morgantown, West Virginia, shared her fourth graders' experience connecting with their fourth-grade partners in Los Angeles, California, via web cams, email, Skype, and Facebook. Her students are discovering that there are real differences among people—even among those who live in the same country. The West Virginia students, excited about the start of hunting season, could not wait to tell their virtual friends about their guns, ammunition, and preparations for the big hunt. What they found was that their Los Angeles friends were shocked by their enthusiasm. They equated guns with gangs, drive-by shootings, and danger. The collaboration between the two classes is opening eyes to new knowledge and understanding.

Some types of educational partnerships are formed for specific purposes and involve few individual or institutional members. An example is grade looping in a preK–12 school. This type of collaboration allows teachers of consecutive grades, for example, second and third, to work with a group of children for a 2-year period and, then, to go back to the previous grade and begin again. Partner teachers in this situation must continually decide on curriculum delivery, distinctive assignments, and special needs.

At the university level, departments often pool brainpower and resources, permitting them to team teach courses. Educational leadership (College of Education) and business management (College of Business) faculties on many campuses have found ways to use one another's expertise in the delivery of administrative coursework.

Often partnerships are established out of necessity. Rural school districts across the United States, in order to stretch their resources, have agreed to share science, math, or foreign language teachers. Although these collaborations do not include a large number of participants, they do facilitate manageable teaching assignments for individuals who, in rural settings, are the sole individuals in their departments. By collaborating, two science teachers in separate rural districts—one with expertise in physics and one with expertise in biology—can exchange days, providing the high school students at both schools a more specialized view of each subject.

Numerous superintendents have had to utilize this model of instruction in order to conform to the requirement of No Child Left Behind to provide "highly qualified" teachers. Technology has made this type of partnering easier, but to have it work, participating districts have had to agree to common start times, block scheduling, and shared administration and assessment.

Educational centers are partnerships. Whether community based or university based, centers reflect the collaborative efforts of individuals with a common mission. Examples include centers for civic engagement, diversity, international affairs, senior citizens, and service learning. Many of these focused collaborations originate with a group of individuals who are willing to work together to realize a goal. These partnerships can last indefinitely if they serve a common purpose and have sufficient resources (see "Developing a University–Community Partnership" vignette by Roberto Garcia).

Some partnerships are statewide initiatives. Kentucky's Second Sunday is an example of a huge, effective, and expanding partnership. Second Sunday promotes family wellness and outdoor exercise. Major streets throughout communities are closed on designated Sunday afternoons so that families will have safe places in which to actively enjoy the out of doors. Biking, walking, playing tag, roller skating, pushing a stroller, all of these are encouraged. The University of Kentucky, chambers of commerce throughout the state of Kentucky, public officials, and extension agents have watched this push for healthy living grow from a conversation of concern regarding obesity in Kentucky to a statewide effort. Most recently, the statewide initiative has led to the promotion of a nationwide Second Sunday in October when streets across the United States would close on a Sunday afternoon for a few hours of family fun and exercise. For information about Second Sunday go to http://2ndsundayky.com/index 2.htm.

There are also national initiatives that lead to widespread collaborations within and among states. Texas, like many of the other 50 states, has been an active participant in statewide initiatives seeking to improve high schools including the national American Diploma Project Network. In 2003, the state, led by Governor Rick Perry and other elected officials, invested in a public-private partnership designated the Texas High School Project (THSP). The goals of the THSP were to boost graduation rates and to increase the number of high school students prepared for postsecondary education. Dedicated funds from the state, in the amount of $148 million in appropriated and federal funding, combined with the contributions of several philanthropic partners including the Bill & Melinda Gates Foundation, the Michael and Susan Dell Foundation, the Wallace Foundation, National Instruments, and the Communities Foundation of Texas resulted in a $260 million collaboration dedicated to improving Texas high schools (Hopkins, 2008).

One outcome of this alliance was the establishment of an early college–high school in South Texas. This collaboration between an independent school district and a university recognized the need for a new high school model. Conceptually, an early college–high school blends high school and college into a coherent educational program designed to allow all students to achieve up to 2 years of college while still in high school and earning a high school diploma. Study skills preparing students for college coursework begin in the middle schools, with emphasis placed on reading, writing, mathematics, science, and computer literacy. This seamless transition from preK–12 education to the university allows students to begin their college work when their performance shows they are ready (Hopkins, 2008).

RATIONALE FOR FORMING PARTNERSHIPS

Whether massive in scope like the evolving Common Core State Standards Initiative (CCSSI) being championed by the nation's chief state school officers or no bigger than a few colleagues at a small school who decide to become writing partners, partnerships are not easy to form or to sustain. So why do we do it? What is the motivation that urges us to plow through our differences and work together?

Impetus for Forming Partnerships

Sometimes our efforts are fueled by promises of private, state, or national financial support. Dollars are dangled in front of us with the caveat to work and play together, or go without. Unlike many education supporters of the past, today's grant funders are not as willing to finance a project in a single university, district, or school. Increasingly, their preference is multipartner collaborations focused on a common goal. Looking for "big picture" results, federal and state dollars also seem to be more and more available for partnered activity and research. Large consortia, because of their ability to produce substantial summative assessments, are seen as powerful levers of influence. As such, they tend to be supported more enthusiastically than collaborations involving fewer participants.

President Barack Obama's Race to the Top created an unprecedented clamor as universities and school districts strived to be among the once-in-a-lifetime recipients of the $4.35 billion in discretionary funds allotted for the redesign of public education. Secretary of Education Arne Duncan described the challenge as the inauguration of "a new federal partnership in educational reform with states, districts, and unions to accelerate change and boost achievement" throughout the United States (Duncan, 2009). Seeking innovation and a break from the status quo in today's schools, the Race to the Top competition encouraged governors to support (a) unified state efforts designed around ambitious reforms; (b) districts' reform efforts, including the identification of effective practices as well as the replication and dissemination of those practices, and holding districts accountable for outcomes; and (c) aligning American Reconstruction and Reinvestment Act funds and other funds to have the most dramatic impact. For more information go to http://www.ed.gov/programs/racetothetop/index.html.

The motivation to collaborate has often been fueled by legislation. The increased demand for content competency, heightened by No Child Left Behind, led to numerous new collaborations across the nation as school districts clamored to meet the high qualifications required of preK–12 teachers. As the call for the alignment of content knowledge to the preK–12 curriculum increased, new partnerships appeared on university campuses and in the field. Historically, content courses have been the responsibility of disciplines other than education. However, when the call for a national seamless pipeline came, it required pedagogy faculties and those responsible for content to work collaboratively. Off campus, these faculties expanded their collective activities to include community college colleagues and preK–12 teacher partners. Concerted efforts like the Regents' Initiative for Excellence in Education in Texas attempted smooth transitions for students from earliest preschool efforts to graduation from institutions of higher learning.

An outcome of many seamless-transition collaborations has been earlier and increased field-based experiences for preservice teachers. In many states, the increased time in the preK–12 schools is recommended; often it is legislated. This increase in field-based instruction has enhanced the presence of the university in the preK–12 schools. The role of university faculty is no longer that of dropping by to check things out once or twice a semester, but instead they are involved in frequent supervision and on-site teaching in the preK–12 schools. At the same time, community colleges, in addition to career preparation, have become more cognizant of their responsibility to ready young people for the university by shoring up those who need additional preparation or a more communal environment before taking the big step to the university.

The role played by preK–12 schools in the teacher education process has increased as well and is visible in several models of teacher preparation including professional development schools (PDSs), professional learning communities, and a number of field-based programs. The final link in this collaborative educational chain is the benefit that practicing teachers gain from the job-embedded professional development delivered and modeled in the preK–12 schools by their university and community college partners. In addition, most states have established educational centers to assist districts with the delivery of quality professional development. Some, like the Regional Education Service agencies in West Virginia, Regional Education Service centers in Texas, and Educational Service centers in Ohio, are located throughout a state and work most closely with their regional preK–12 schools. Others, such as the Center for Educational Partnerships at the University of California, Irvine, and Regional Professional Development Center focused on Special Education at Missouri State, serve their respective states. Partnerships have allowed more individuals, and more institutions, to be involved in the education process at all levels and with broader understanding.

Research on PreK–16 Partnerships

Research on partnerships is widespread and diverse. Studies have looked at the effectiveness of partnerships focused primarily on a specific type of partnership such as the professional development school model, or on a single distinctive partnership (Darling-Hammond, 1994; Rubin, 2002; Brandt, 2000; Sergiovanni, 1994; Ravid & Handler, 2001; Teitel, 2003). The short lifespan of many partnerships—even effective ones—does not produce many conclusions that can be made regarding their overall positive or negative effects. Too often major funders of educational collaborative initiatives like the Department of Education, National Science Foundation, Department of Health and Human Services, and National Institutes of Health demand data collection that is thorough and extensive for the life of the grant. Once the grant has ended, however, in many instances, collaboration is not sustained even though the partnership was viewed as successful.

ADVANTAGES AND DISADVANTAGES OF PARTNERSHIPS

The advantages of partnerships are many. Like the children's orchestra, together we can make beautiful music; alone, sometimes the best we can do is squawk. There is recognizable power in numbers, and partnering can provide noticeable sway. One voice suggesting restructuring of the school year can be easily ignored by a local school board. A collaboration of teachers, administrators, parents, and students, however, with data and a formalized plan for enactment of year-round schooling, is difficult to ignore.

Partnerships by their nature supply group support for the separate entities within them. Depending upon the makeup of the individuals or associations partnering, they may also provide the political clout needed to initiate change within a school, district, university, or state. One can enjoy the brainstorming of many bright minds upon a common topic. There is an excitement that is generated when sitting at a table surrounded by individuals with similar goals and passionate opinions. Listening to their suggestions and reflecting on possibilities, one can realize how much more productive a group is even at the initial discussion stage of a collaboration. Partnerships allow ideas to expand.

Generally, partnerships, even small ones, reach more people and have greater impact than one individual or one institution is able to produce. At a recent professional meeting, participants discussed the knowledge and skills essential for tomorrow's teachers at length. During the conversation, individuals expressed their fear that, without major transformation, today's teacher education programs are ill equipped to give tomorrow's teachers what they need to know and be able to do in tomorrow's schools. Dennis Van Roekel, president of the National Education Association, spoke at the meeting. He pointed out that numerous attempts to transform teacher education have occurred and many have been successful. But, as Van Roekel vividly expressed, those successes can be likened to campfires. Each attempt may have changed the terrain of a school or college of teacher education but was still contained in that one spot—like a campfire circle. "Instead, if we are seriously going to change the way we prepare teachers, the country doesn't need small campfires scattered here and there. What we need is a brushfire" (Van Roekel, 2009).

Partnerships develop team players: individuals who recognize the value of group dynamics and choose to be active participants. Those involved in a collaborative venture often discover skills that they have always had but have not developed or used. Some find that they are persuasive and learn to use this ability to convince others of a plan for school improvement. Others find that they are good listeners. Still others find that their sense of humor is a great tool for smoothing ruffled feathers; they recognize when people become frustrated and need a time-out, even if just to relax for a while and smile. Sometimes individuals in a partnership find they must develop new skills such as patience, leadership, direction, loyalty, and perseverance. As the partnership progresses, true collaborators also learn to give up certain negative attributes such as jealousy, selfishness, and self-aggrandizement.

Partnerships frequently develop new infrastructures that augment the existing frameworks of institutions and organizations, and allow change to occur. A district collaboration might lead to more school-based decision making, as teachers and principals work together to, first, decide what their schools need and, then, achieve common goals. Parents and community members frequently become active participants in a partnership of this type—if they are asked to belong.

Sometimes partnerships form unexpectedly and grow beyond expectations. In Whitwell, Tennessee, a small rural town in the Smokey Mountains, an associate principal heard a Holocaust survivor's speech at an inservice meeting and decided to teach the Holocaust to a predominately White, Protestant student population. At first the project was primarily a change in curriculum. Several new texts written by or about Holocaust survivors were added to the students' reading assignment. The new reading material led to new questions and a search for answers.

Trying to grasp the 6 million lives lost, one student suggested that the school collect paper clips, one for each Jewish life taken. Lena Gitter, a 94-year-old Holocaust survivor, learned of the project and alerted two German journalists. They traveled from Germany to the Smokey Mountains to visit with the children about the project. Once their stories began appearing in European and American newspapers, letters with paper clips enclosed began arriving, and the Paper Clip Project was born.

Originally intended as a unit of study for the eighth grade, the whole school became involved partners. Every letter received was answered; every paper clip was counted and documented. When the students decided to locate and actually purchase one of the cattle cars in which Jews were transported to the death camps, the whole town got involved. Partners across the sea assisted in the purchase and transport from Germany of the cattle car. It was then delivered by rail to Whitwell. Area craftsmen worked side by side with the students to refurbish the car, which had been sitting in a German rail yard since the 1940s. Students and teachers, parents, and community members turned it into a remembrance museum. The men of the town built a platform and stairway to facilitate entry. The women painted the outside and planted flowers and shrubs around it. Inside, on display were the 6,000,000 paper clips as well as the research projects completed by the students. Students at Whitwell continue to study the Holocaust; now they also give tours to students from other schools who are studying its impact on the world. A documentary film tracing the origination and growth of this school project that grew into a worldwide partnership is available at www.paperclipsmovie.com/. For more information about the Paper Clip Project and the children's Holocaust memorial, see http://69.8.250.59/homepage_pc.cfm?id=78.

Partnerships provide numerous advantages for getting things done. They can generate enthusiasm and give individuals collective hope that a shared goal can be reached. However, if the wrong individuals or institutions are sitting at the table, they can be ineffective, even destructive, with respect to accomplishing any goals, whether shared or independently held. That is one disadvantage in forming a partnership; there are others.

Remember when you were in seventh grade and the teacher assigned teams to complete a group project that went something like this: (a) read a work of historical fiction, (b) compare and contrast it to the historical period in which it was set, and (c) prepare a written report and oral presentation focused on how honestly the author portrayed the setting for his or her novel. It sounded exciting until you looked around and realized that your semester grade depended upon the ability and work ethic of each member of the team. You knew what you could accomplish, but what about the rest of the team?

One of the major disadvantages of partnerships is that the members do not always get to choose one another. Many times participants meet for the first time after the partnership is initiated and are unaware of the views held by others in the group. PreK–12 teachers may not have the opportunity to talk to their university partners until well after the overarching goals of the collaboration are decided. Ideally, all members of a partnership would be present at its inception and throughout its development and implementation. This is seldom the case.

Posturing occurs in a partnership as the personalities assert themselves. Leaders step forward and the team members decide which individuals they are most comfortable following. An interesting dynamic of partnerships is when multiple leaders within the partnership shift depending upon the action taking place. At one point, when working with parents or school board members, a superintendent in the partnership may take the lead; at another point, when seeking support of upper administration at a college or university, a dean or senior faculty member may step forward. Regardless of who is seen at any time during the partnership as the leader, others looking to that individual must trust that he or she has the best interest of the partnership at heart.

This trust, with its ensuing respect for and confidence in one another, is by far the most essential component of a successful partnership. Unfortunately, a relationship based on trust takes nurturing, and in many collaborative ventures there is insufficient time for trust to grow. When the Gates Foundation spearheaded a drive to establish early colleges across the United States, it provided 4-year $400,000 planning grants for universities and school districts willing to establish one. The planning support for early college initiatives that the Gates Foundation provided did more than allow for logistical organization, implementation, and planning; it gave the partners time to get to know one another well enough to trust in the talents and capacity each brought to the group. This essential component of the early college movement was probably one of its most effective.

CHALLENGES WITH MORALE AND COMMITMENT

Partnerships require give and take; not everyone will bring equally worthwhile ideas to the table or even equal enthusiasm for shared goals. There will be times when even the most supportive members of a partnership will find it difficult to give up, for the good of the group, an approach or idea in which they believe passionately. Often members resent the process required to partner effectively. Although necessary, keeping everyone informed, cutting through red tape, getting commitment from all parties, and making everyone feel they have equal voice can slow action and, at times, impede progress. Some good initiatives are left to squander and die. Those with the capacity to lead partnerships need the courage and patience to deal with this possibility. They must continually cajole, encourage, compliment, inform, rethink, consider, and adjust. These leadership skills will be necessary throughout the partnership.

When Tennessee launched its State Collaborative on Reforming Education (SCORE) in October of 2009, the shared goal was for Tennessee schools to be ranked number one in the Southeast within 5 years. Four key strategies were developed: (1) embracing high standards; (2) cultivating strong leaders; (3) the hiring and management of an excellent teaching staff; and (4) utilizing data to improve student learning.

The initiative received the approval of the Tennessee State Board of Education, the State Department, the governor, and school leaders throughout Tennessee. However, there were problems that needed to be addressed for the program to be a successful collaboration. These included sufficient funding for the cost of implementation, time necessary for implementation, the need for more school counselors and teachers, and an effective communication plan to address concerns of parents, members of the business community, and other stakeholders. The SCORE partners anticipated that it would take 3 to 5 years before any change SCORE made would be visible.

While this initial culture shift is occurring, SCORE anticipates having to inform interested parties that test scores may be lower than ever due to higher standards. This cannot be avoided but, in the interim, the partnership will need to weather the storm when upset students and their parents protest because test scores have dropped. For further information go to http://www.tennesseescore.org/.

Another disadvantage of a partnership is the knowledge that a change in the makeup of its members—individual or association—can lead to complete reorganization or dissolution. In an effort to help promising Native American students obtain baccalaureate degrees, South Dakota State University established a unique partnership called the 2+2+2 program. Targeted high school juniors and seniors on the Rosebud and Pine Bluff reservations were encouraged to cross the state and visit campus for events including plays, musical performances, library visits, and sporting events.

With transportation and housing provided for 2 years, these high school students were encouraged to visit campus as often as possible to familiarize themselves with the university. Two years of general education core courses taught on the reservation followed. The last 2 years found students living on campus and finishing the specialized coursework required for their major emphasis of study.

Connecting 2 years of high school, 2 years of basic education delivered on the reservation, and 2 years of study at the university allowed a number of Native Americans to complete a program of study and obtain a bachelor's degree. This partnership required the efforts of university administration, faculty, reservation high school teachers and administrators, parents, and tribal councils.

Many partnerships have to overcome unique handicaps. Distance was a major hurdle in the 2+2+2 collaboration in South Dakota. On opposite sides of a geographically large state, the partners had few opportunities to sit and work together. When members did meet, new faces were usually at the table, so there was the constant need for the partners to reestablish goals and rebuild trust within the group. Cultural differences also required understanding. Respect for one another was essential. Sustaining the partnership was always a concern, especially when changes occurred within the tribal council membership or administration at the university. For additional information regarding the 2+2+2 program go to www.sdstate.edu/. Too many shifts in leadership can cause frustration for any partnership as its members seek stability, respect, and trust in one another.

A common disadvantage of many of the partnerships attempted in higher education—or, if not a disadvantage, a deterrent to their formation—is the historical view held by many that schools and colleges of education are weaker than their sister schools and colleges of arts and sciences. Also, the elitist attitude held by some faculty makes collaborative partnerships between education and the arts and sciences difficult.

When this attitude pervades a department responsible for content in a teacher education program, it is usually reflected in the promotion and tenure process. Faculty of other colleges who wish to collaborate with education faculty are frequently advised against it. They are cautioned that their shared research and involvement in preK–12 education will not count toward tenure or promotion. Rather, they are expected to be involved in knowledge-based research—"real research"—not inferior action-based research in teaching. Thus, many faculty who would like to be involved in preK–12 education are reluctant. Instead, to ensure readiness for tenure and promotion, they remain focused on discipline research and avoid opportunities for shared research with education faculty.

RESPONSIBILITIES OF PARTNERS

Keeping Everyone Apprised

The old game "telephone" illustrates how information gets distorted. Someone in a circle whispers a sentence or phrase to the closest individual, and then that person whispers to the person next in the circle, and so on, until the last person tells what he or she heard. The message ends up nothing like the message whispered by the person who began and, of course, everyone laughs. News of a possible partnership can spread like wildfire and can become as confusing and distorted as the telephone messages.

Communication is necessary before, during, and after any partnership. In addition to keeping the constituencies who will be most affected by the collaboration informed, open meetings held for the greater public can deter opposition. These informational gatherings can provide a forum for individuals not closely involved in the partnership to have the opportunity to offer suggestions regarding its construction or purpose. Visiting with service clubs, the local chamber of commerce, and the parent-teacher association can help in spreading the word. From a partnership's inception throughout its existence, keeping everyone in the communication loop is essential. This is not always easy, but it is critical if the partnership wants the continued support of all stakeholders and interested parties. Newsletters, email, open meetings, regular updates, news media stories, and scheduled reports will assist in keeping everyone in the know.

Choosing the Right Players

The configuration and makeup of a partnership are critical. Once the purpose has been decided, membership selection should occur. Members play a key role in the speed with which a partnership proceeds and ultimately reaches its goal. Omitting any significant individual or institution from the partnership can be deadly. There are numerous preK–12 higher education partnerships that require participation of faculty in education and in the arts and sciences. Without the support of arts and sciences faculty, many partnerships are doomed before they begin.

Sometimes partner selection seems obvious because of existing common interests. Tennessee's voluntary preK program includes school systems, private child care providers, Head Start, community organizations, and local businesses. Through the collaborative efforts of a variety of organizations, including the public schools, Tennessee is able to deliver high-quality instruction for most of its at-risk 4-year olds. The collaborative grew out of the joint efforts of the Tennessee Association for the Education of Young Children and Tennessee Stand for Children. They joined forces and created the Tennessee Alliance for Early Education. The sole mission of this grassroots organization was to support the expansion of preK instruction throughout the state. For further information about voluntary preK in Tennessee, see www.tn.gov/education/prek/.

Seeking New Connections

Individuals who are privileged to have been members of successful partnership teams frequently search for other opportunities to collaborate. They view projects in a different way and the strength of groupthink becomes their source. Their heightened awareness of partnership possibilities has led to further partnerships as well as greater ease in the establishment of such partnerships; these experienced would-be partners are already familiar with the process and appreciate the outcome.

Several years ago a research and development business in Corpus Christi, Texas, was closing its doors. More than 90 PhD scientists and mathematicians were given the option to retire, relocate, quit, or be dismissed. Many of the individuals were reluctant to leave their homes, a number were close to retirement, and still others had children in the local schools and did not want to disrupt their education. They wanted to stay in south Texas even though most positions available in the area would mean huge pay cuts and lost benefits.

At the same time, local high schools were in desperate need of mathematics and science teachers. Texas A&M University–Corpus Christi's College of Education decided to respond to the needs of both groups by recruiting the scientists and mathematicians to become teachers and, then, training them without delay to take on their new roles.

Working quickly, key faculty and staff met and agreed to modify delivery of the MAC (master's and certification) program. This established program allowed individuals holding degrees in other disciplines to obtain a master's degree in education and teacher certification simultaneously. Having the MAC program already in place was a big help. Once it was agreed that compressed delivery of the MAC program was doable, the college visited with the research development firm and proposed the newly created MONARCH program—named to symbolize the metamorphosis envisioned for participants. Management was delighted to have another option for the displaced personnel and promised the college support if there was sufficient interest on the part of its workforce. Immediately, the college put together a recruitment team, including university admissions and records personnel, advisors, faculty in the program, and staff members, to go to the corporation. The research firm informed personnel of the recruitment visit, encouraged attendance, and provided meeting space and refreshments. More than 70 came; 59 expressed interest and filled out applications.

A former national Teacher of the Year, and top recruiter for the college, accepted the responsibility of getting everyone admitted and advised. But she continued to fret over what it was going to cost the individuals to retool. Conversations with the head of the Texas Workforce Commission, however, resulted in sufficient funding to pay the tuition for the displaced workers. The commissioner agreed to provide $290,000 for about 50 individuals to participate in the MONARCH program, receive their teaching certificate, and become mathematics and science teachers.

Because of the intensified delivery of the MONARCH program, members of the college's Strategies of Success (SOS) faculty were enlisted to mentor and assist these students with classroom management and pedagogy—even after completion of the program. SOS was staffed by part-time educators, usually retired, with years of classroom experience and expertise. Designed to provide mentoring and development assistance for teachers in their first 3 years of teaching, SOS enabled participating teachers to gain master's credit in this professional development program. Adding the MONARCH participants was easy. They had content expertise but many of them required the additional one-on-one assistance SOS provided.

The program was a success. More than 50 of the mathematicians and scientists, many holding PhDs, completed the program and accepted teaching positions, mostly as secondary mathematics or science teachers. Even more heartening is the fact that more than half of the individuals who participated in MONARCH are still teaching. This infusion of PhD biologists, physicists, chemists, and mathematicians into the local schools has improved instruction for students throughout the area.

Cheering the Troops

There are days when all of us become discouraged. An anticipated grant does not materialize, a partner becomes disgruntled and leaves the partnership, taking others with him or her, and a correspondence is misunderstood. Members of a partnership may find disappointments intensified because of the number of individuals who are affected. The leader of a partnership is its head cheerleader. As such, he or she must constantly provide encouragement for the members by celebrating their successes, getting the word out about their achievements, boosting their confidence, and supporting their goals.

Sustaining the Partnership

Sustaining a partnership can be difficult. If there has been outside funding and it has ended, finding sufficient resources to continue a collaborative effort is often difficult. Partners would be wise to address this eventual possibility early on in the collaboration to ensure that steps are taken to avoid disbanding a successful venture due to lack of funds.

An early college–high school in south Texas, supported initially by Gates Foundation funding, can continue indefinitely thanks to the initial financial agreement between the two major partners—the school district and the university. Although Gates funding got this program off the ground, the partners were always aware that the money would no longer be available after the initial 4 years of planning. Mindful of the need for long-term sustainability, the superintendent agreed to take a portion of the funding provided by the state for each child's education and use it to pay the tuition for the university classes her high school students were taking. In return, the university charged the early college students lower tuition.

Special fees were also adjusted on an individual basis so that early college students were assessed only those fees that corresponded to services they actually used. Once the students were enrolled in university classes they were included in the undergraduate count at the university. The semester hours they generated increased the formula funding the university received. In addition, the university was assured of enrolling 100 new students every year—all members of underrepresented groups that the university is charged to serve.

Using this funding model, everyone wins. Students (or their parents) save as much as 2 years of college tuition while completing college coursework. The school district benefits by not having to hire teachers for the courses students take at the university. The university saves by enrolling without recruiting expenses 100 new students of targeted populations each year.

Assessing Success

Partnerships must continually evaluate their effectiveness, adjust their goals or mission as needed, and assess the appropriateness of their membership. When fitting, the findings of the partnership should be shared with the public. An example might be the results of a math readiness collaboration in which fifth-grade girls were assigned math mentors as they entered third grade. Proven successful in raising girls' math scores and confidence, this good news story could raise awareness and a desire to repeat the initiative beyond the original collaboration.

Partnerships must be willing to adapt and change; when they are no longer effective, members should be encouraged to end collaborations gracefully. A successful partnership might end because the goals have been achieved or because other factors have interfered. Clark and Lacey note that the health of a partnership may be "seriously affected by (1) a cataclysmic leadership change, (2) recognition that a 'plateau' of change and achievement has been reached, or (3) decreasing viability due to less need, entry of other outside assisters, and/ or increasing divergence between strategic interests of the partners" (Clark & Lacey, 1997, p. 118).

CRITICAL COMPONENTS OF PARTNERSHIPS

A common mission is an essential component of a successful partnership. Without a common mission there is no reason to partner. Usually the mission is the result of a shared need or belief. It should also serve as a guide for the goals members seek to achieve. The expectations of individual members of the partnership may not reflect a common mission or the agreed-upon goals. If the partnership continues for a lengthy period, members may change their allegiance as well. The leaders of the collaborative will need to keep everyone apprised of the mission—especially if it changes over time.

Planning is also essential for a successful partnership. As an example, the collaborative establishment of early colleges across the United States would not have occurred so rapidly or effectively without the support of foundational partners Bill and Melinda Gates and Michael and Susan Dell. Jump-starting interested universities and school districts with 4-year $400,000 planning grants and foundation-funded national research, Bill Gates provided the financial impetus for an innovative approach to the delivery of secondary education. The 4-year grant funding allowed for the creation of partnerships and the time necessary for all parties to commit to those partnerships.

Making sure the right individuals or institutions are members of the partnership is critical for its success. Some individuals, such as classroom teachers, university faculty, and local community members, will be more involved; others, such as district and university administrators, foundation members, legislators, and business CEOs, will be less so. But all play important roles in whether or not a partnership succeeds. Initial selection of partners should be made carefully. Including a local legislator because of the clout he or she might carry at the state capital can be a double-edged sword, if the legislator uses the partnership as a political ploy.

Institutional support is imperative. Without the backing of the districts, universities, or businesses, the partnership will flounder. Changes in those persons representing the institutions can also have a negative or positive impact. If a district loses a supportive superintendent, or a university sees a change in leadership at the dean, provost, or presidential level, there can be a major shift in the support, or lack of support, afforded the partnership. Funding may be redirected, faculty may be reassigned, and resources may disappear. Making sure that the partnership has a written memorandum of understanding, agreed to and signed by all institutional partners, will not eliminate a negative impact of the entry of new nonsupportive members but can delay disruption and, potentially, give the partnership time to regroup and discuss possible options.

A plan for sustaining the partnership should be in place before its initiation. Some partnerships are intended to last for a limited time. Sufficient funding and resources are critical. If the partnership originated because of grant or foundational support, a strategy for new funding must be an integral part of any plan for continued success. If the initial funders pull out of the partnership, it should be able to continue effectively without them.

Assessment has to begin immediately and continue throughout for a partnership to be successful. The means for accomplishing this should be decided well before the actual initiation of the partnership project. Using an outside evaluation body can add credibility to the outcomes reported by the partnership. This service is often provided by a local university, regional service center, or commercial firm. Constant formal and informal evaluation is necessary to track goal completion and satisfaction of members of the team, among others.

CONCLUDING REMARKS

Partnerships are as varied as the individuals and institutions that comprise them. Those that are most common in educational settings tend to involve preK–12 schools and schools and colleges of education. Other partners often include community organizations, colleges of arts and sciences, community colleges, regional professional service providers, and state departments of education. There are advantages and disadvantages to forming collaborations. The leverage provided by consortia can be strong when supportive leadership is present. The critical components of a successful partnership are important. These include creating a common mission, making time for sufficient planning, selecting appropriate team members, obtaining institutional support, sustaining the partnership so that it may exist beyond its initial funding or support, and assessing the partnership from inception to end. Like the young musicians of the All City Children's String Orchestra, alone, an individual can voice his or her opinions and dream his or her dreams but may never have the opportunity to perform solo. Even if one does, he or she may not play the music loud enough or strong enough to be heard. Together, however, we can pool our resources and talents by forming partnerships with common purposes and goals. Together we can make ourselves heard. Together we can make beautiful music.

REFERENCES

Brandt, R. (2000). *Education in a new era*. Alexandria, VA: Association for Supervision and Curriculum Development.

Clark, T., & Lacey, R. (1997). *Learning by doing: Panasonic partnerships and systemic school reform*. Delray Beach, FL: St. Lucie Press.

Darling-Hammond, L. (1994). *Professional development schools: Schools for developing a profession*. New York: Teachers College Press.

Duncan, A. (2009, July 24). Education reform's moon shot. *The Washington Post*, p. A21.

Hopkins, D. (2008). Rethinking the structure of high schools in south Texas: An early college collaboration. In *The role of technology in tomorrow's schools* (pp. 103–110). Amherst, MA: Pearson Education.

Ravid, R., & Handler, M. (2001). *The many faces of a school- university collaboration*. Englewood, CO: Teacher Ideas Press.

Rubin, H. (2002). *Collaborative leadership: Developing effective partnerships in communities and schools*. Thousand Oaks, CA: Corwin Press.

Sergiovanni, T. J. (1994). *Building communities in schools*. San Francisco: Jossey-Bass.

Teitel, L. (2003). *Professional development schools: Starting, sustaining, and assessing partnerships that improve student learning*. Thousand Oaks, CA: Corwin Press.

Wagner, T. (2008). *The global achievement gap*. New York: Basic Books.

Van Roekel, D. (2009, October). *Preparing teachers for the world of tomorrow*. Paper presented at the Annual Meeting of the Evaluation Systems group of Pearson, Chicago, IL.

Types of Partnerships

David M. Byrd
D. John McIntyre

This chapter

- examines several types of effective partnerships,
- includes research on effective partnerships, and
- describes the governing structures of effective partnerships.

* * *

The Providence, Rhode Island, School Department and the University of Rhode Island (URI) partnered to develop the Providence Aspiring Principals Program to prepare educators from its schools to become effective school leaders. The goal was to develop leaders focused on improving instruction and student achievement.

The Southern Regional Education Board (SREB) analyzed the effort by the partners to design a principal-preparation program aligned to the district's vision of higher achievement for all of its students. Their analysis led to the development of a new educational leadership program, not simply a redesign of a traditional university-based program.

The project began as part of a 15-state initiative funded by a Wallace Foundation grant whose aim was "to put leadership at the core of systemic school reform by strengthening and diversifying a pool of potential leaders, improving the training of leaders through quality professional development, and creating conditions in which they can do their jobs better" (SREB, 2005, p. 1). A key component of the program was a common vision, which included belief in authentic field-based learning experiences and internships, and the development of indicators of program quality.

The SREB (2005) report stated that the creation of the Providence Aspiring Principals Program was an important strategy for ensuring that all of its schools had quality leadership. URI brought the contemporary research knowledge base, and the district provided the operational application base for the program design process. Working for a common purpose, these partners' mutual respect for one another allowed them to share insights about teaching, learning, and school leadership. In essence, the design teams have become a true learning community that is continuously discovering how to better prepare principals who can achieve the district's vision.

Because the university and the school district had cultural concerns, governance structures, financial policies, norms on academic freedom, and reward systems in place, it was necessary to ascertain which would be used as is and which needed adjustment to serve the partnership. University administrators and faculty had to consider new ways of thinking about content and structure as they partnered with Providence to design the Aspiring Principals Program. They had to make time for collective and comprehensive planning to engage in a course development process with the district. Instead of having complete ownership and responsibility for the program, they worked with the district to determine what would be taught and who would teach. Rather than faculty teaching solo at the university, they learned to co-teach with the district staff. This led to the creation of academic and clinical assignments that were designed to prepare participants with the ability to solve real-school problems. The university also worked with the district to recruit and select principal candidates (SREB, 2005).

School district personnel faced similar issues of having to work within the policies and conditions inherent in a different organizational culture. They developed and implemented a recruitment process that selected a limited number of the most promising candidates rather than waiting for volunteers to take the initiative to complete a program. They co-developed teaching materials and co-taught with university faculty. They also allocated and managed professional development resources in a different way. Instead of concentrating on professional conferences and workshops, they provided tuition assistance, substitutes to cover participants' release time for field experiences, and specifically designed training for mentor principals.

The report concluded that the district and its staff members were becoming more comfortable as university partners and developers of school leaders. The district received more assistance for making sound decisions about future appointments to the principal's position and had "access to a ready pool of better-prepared new leaders." (p. 6)

* * *

THE PARTNERSHIP CONTINUUM

School-university partnerships are not new. However, the depth and breadth of these partnerships vary depending upon a variety of conditions. Some partnerships may be designed for a short time period to accomplish a particular task such as the design of a new mathematics or reading curriculum or the implementation of a research project that examines student time-on-task in a particular grade level or school.

Perhaps the most common type of school-university partnership is the practice of schools hosting university students for early field experiences and student teaching (Lenski & Black, 2004). Book (1996) contends that this common partnership is generally directed by a university and lacks collaborative activities among K–12 teachers and university faculty.

The Holmes Group began in the mid-1980s as a consortium of 96 research universities with professional education programs. It formed in response to the elimination of schools of education by a number of prestigious universities and a general perception by policy makers and others that education schools were not meeting their responsibilities in preparing the next generation of teachers. The issue for the Holmes Group was how to make education schools matter in the profession. The Holmes Group began to build an agenda calling for a strengthening of connections with colleges of arts and sciences and building strong partnerships with school-based professionals to build a profession of teaching (see Holmes Partnership Goals, 1996). This initiative spurred many universities and schools to establish a new type of partnership—professional development schools (PDSs)—that are beneficial to both the university and preK–12 schools. In addition, professional development schools range in complexity from those that focus on the development of teacher candidates and experienced teachers to partnerships that also include a commitment to the community and preK–12 student services.

This chapter examines several different types of school-university partnerships and takes a look at the different types and expectations of agencies, including foundations and businesses, that may collaborate as partners.

DIFFERENT TYPES OF PARTNERSHIPS

Professional Development Schools

One of the earlier descriptions of partnerships that had continuous career development through a coordinated plan to meet the needs of teachers at "their own stage of professional development" was the teacher/teaching center (Collins, 1970, p. 544).

Teaching centers are often cited as the precursor to professional development schools and were formed to achieve many of the same goals—integration of teacher education with schools and universities, assumption of greater responsibility for preservice teacher education by public schools and for inservice development by the university, stable resource base through shared responsibility among partners for stablizing budgets, emergence of new roles for teacher educators in school improvement, and articulated sequenced transition from entry into the profession to advanced professional status (Collins, 1970).

The Holmes Group (1990) formerly initiated the concept of a professional development school to create an innovative partnership between institutions of higher education and preK–12 schools. In PDSs, university and school faculty and administrators work together to meet common goals that are more complex than the traditional cooperative arrangements for student teaching placements (Book, 1996).

Book (1996) states that the medical profession's teaching hospitals influenced the development of PDSs. Future doctors are placed in hospitals with licensed physicians. This allows doctor-trainees to work with real patients under the guidance of physicians and medical researchers, gaining hands-on experience.

This on-the-job training is one of the key features of the PDS model. The Holmes Group sought to develop school-university partnerships that would provide teachers and administrators with an opportunity to influence the development of their profession while, at the same time, providing university faculty with the opportunity to work in actual schools and classrooms to improve their practice.

In 1996, the Holmes Partnership, formerly the Holmes Group, developed six goals to assist in the development of PDSs. The goals focused on (1) professional preparation, (2) renewal, (3) equity and diversity, (4) scholarly inquiry, (5) faculty development, and (6) policy initiation.

In part, these goals led the National Council for the Accreditation of Teacher Education (NCATE) to develop its first set of national standards in 2001 (National Council for the Accreditation of Teacher Education, 2001). These standards were designed to support the development and assessment of PDSs as well as provide a critical framework for conducting research that focused on the outcomes of professional development schools. NCATE's five standards addressed (1) learning communities, (2) accountability and quality assurance, (3) collaboration, (4) diversity and equity, and (5) structures, resources, and roles.

In 2008, the National Association for Professional Development Schools adopted a set of essentials that they maintain must be present for a school-university relationship to be called a professional development school. These essential requirements are

1. A comprehensive mission that is broader in its outreach and scope than the mission of any partner and that furthers the education profession

and its responsibility to advance equity within schools and, by potential extension, the broader community;

2. A school-university culture committed to the preparation of future educators that embraces their active engagement in the school community;
3. Ongoing and reciprocal professional development for all participants guided by need;
4. A shared commitment to innovative and reflective practice by all participants;
5. Engagement in and public sharing of the results of deliberative investigations of practice by respective participants;
6. An articulation agreement developed by the respective participants delineating the roles and responsibilities of all involved;
7. A structure that allows all participants a forum for ongoing governance, reflection, and collaboration;
8. Work by college/university faculty and preK–12 faculty in formal roles across institutional settings; and
9. Dedicated and shared resources and formal rewards and recognition structures. (pp. 11–12)

These essentials support the importance of professionalizing the teaching profession through exemplary teacher preparation and professional development. Still strong, the PDS movement continues to focus on school renewal that is centered on student learning and teacher development (Boyle-Baise & McIntyre, 2008).

Community Schools

Blank, Melaville, and Shah (2003) describe a community school as both a place and a set of partnerships between the school and other community resources. Community schools have an integrated focus on academics, health and social services, and youth and community development/engagement leading to improved student learning, stronger families, and healthier communities. Schools become centers of the community and are open to everyone—all day, every day, evenings, and weekends. A typical community school uses a public school as the hub and brings together many partners to offer a range of support systems and opportunities to children, youth, families, and communities.

Blank, Melaville, and Shah (2003) report that a wide variety of activities can occur at a community school. Among these are adult education, arts education, before- and after-school programs, community-based learning, crisis intervention, cultural activities, dental services, family literacy, family nights, health care referral, job training programs, nutrition counseling, parent education, and substance abuse prevention.

In addition, the authors report that community school students show significant gains in academic achievement and in essential areas of nonacademic development; families of community school students show increased communication with teachers and the school; and parents demonstrate a greater sense of responsibility for their children's learning success. Community schools enjoy stronger parent-teacher relationships, increased teacher satisfaction, a more positive school environment, and greater community support. Community schools also promote better use of school buildings. Their neighborhoods enjoy increased security, heightened community pride, and better rapport among students and residents.

Community-Oriented Professional Development Schools

An interesting concept suggested by Boyle-Baise and McIntyre (2008) focuses on the creation of community-oriented PDSs that bridge the gap between PDSs and community schools. This partnership concentrates on teacher education within the school's community. Three key aspects of this partnership are service learning, emphasis on school reform, and inquiry. Although action research is an important component of many PDSs, inquiry in a community-oriented PDS specifically focuses on local history, addresses community issues, or uncovers lost history.

DIFFERENT PARTNERS, DIFFERENT WORKING ARRANGEMENTS

The movement toward partnerships and community engagement in public education has a long and varied history (Bainer, 1997; Kirschenbaum, 1999; Yendol-Hoppey, Jacobs, Gregory, & League, 2008). Schools have joined with a number of partners including community groups (Miller & Hafner, 2008), businesses (Hann, 2008; Mickelson, 1999), and institutions of higher education (Kirschenbaum, & Reagan, 2001).

School Districts and Higher Education

The Nature of Partnerships. Colleges and universities have been central players in forming partnerships with school districts. Partnerships are motivated by the desire to bring theory into practice, make a difference to their communities, and have a positive impact on schools. In addition, working in schools provides access to training sites for students and research sites for faculty (Kirschenbaum & Reagan, 2001).

Kirschenbaum and Reagan's (2001) case study of the University of Rochester's urban partnerships with the Rochester City Schools helps to expand our understanding of one type of partnership that exists between schools and colleges/universities and the extent of involvement that takes place.

The University of Rochester, an urban institution, has a typical range of academic divisions, including arts and sciences, graduate schools of education and business, a medical center and related schools of medicine and dentistry, a major art museum, and a school of music. Educational, medical, and cultural programs were offered through the Rochester partnership: 49% of the programs offered by the educational divisions, 30% by the medical divisions, and 21% by the cultural divisions of the university. Although there were significant differences in the frequency of programs, all branches of the university were engaged in a meaningful number of collaborations with the school district.

Almost half of the programs offered focused on curriculum enrichment. Examples included independent study projects in which high school students worked with the university's art museum staff, the medical school staff providing sexually transmitted disease education in middle school classrooms, and university arts and sciences faculty conducting weekly visits to work in elementary classrooms. Other types of collaborative efforts included efforts to promote health and social services programs in the schools, school-to-work programs with career days and job shadowing, and tutoring/mentoring.

Programs and services were equally directed toward elementary, middle, and high school students with the exception of school-to-work, which took place primarily at the high school level, and tutoring/mentoring, which took place primarily at the elementary school level.

Of the 57 programs offered, most were at least 5 years old, indicating that university-school collaborations can be long term and sustainable. Programs noted as having the highest levels of collaboration often had open and frequent communication, a shared perception of need, joint program development, the existence of a contract or written agreement, effective leadership at the school level, mutual respect, and faculty and staff support and involvement.

Factors Contributing to the Success of These Partnerships. Colleges and universities have increasingly recognized their stake in the success of public schools. Clearly, students who struggle in public school classrooms will either not have the opportunity to engage in higher education or will continue to struggle in university classrooms. Factors related to successful school-university partnerships include the following (Fuhrman & Streim, 2008):

- *Mutual respect.* The divide between academics at universities and practitioners in public schools can be wide and deep, with each believing that the other side does not understand how to improve schools. Joint study of issues and research that address such problems can maximize the exchange of ideas and solutions.
- *Sustained commitment.* Successful, sustained partnerships are built on honest relationships and equal levels of commitment to agreed-upon goals. Making any partnership succeed takes time. The partners

must learn one another's strengths and weaknesses, adapt to one another's cultures, and simply observe, over time, the programs they have implemented together to see what works and what needs improvement. Similarly, it takes time for fears, mistrust, and resistance to be overcome. At a minimum, a single cohort of students should have moved through a school before a partnership can be declared a success.

- *Quid pro quos.* There must be genuine, agreed-upon benefits for both partners. The university that sends its researchers into a public school merely to obtain data will generate resentment. Instead, universities must approach partnerships with the stated aim of improving student outcomes and then take responsibility for the results. They must also be willing to provide tangible benefits, such as professional-development opportunities for teachers, on-site specialists and interns to decrease student-to-teacher ratios, and access to campus resources. At the same time, the public school that looks merely for a handout will soon alienate its academic partner. Instead, the school must commit to a climate conducive to both research and change, with buy-in starting at the top and emanating from staff members, parents, and other stakeholders.
- *Engagement of all stakeholders.* If education is a product of all societal institutions, university partners must work to engage other institutions to make a university–public school partnership work. These other forces include community leaders and parents; city, school board, medical, and mental-health leaders; and teachers' union officials.

Fuhrman and Streim (2008) believe that partnerships require time, hard work, the commitment of resources (monetary and human), and the political will to succeed. They also believe that there are risks to engaging in partnerships. If public school students perform poorly, it can negatively reflect on the university. If the university pulls out of the partnership, the school loses capacity, and the university loses credibility. However, without partnerships, students will continue to fail.

Professional Development Partnerships. One of the most important roles partnerships play is in teachers' professional development. Sandholtz (2002) engaged in a case study to determine the types of professional development that teachers find most valuable. School-university partnership activities were found to be most valuable, while school-based activities not tied directly to the classrooms were found to be least valuable. Specifically, teachers perceived subject-specific conferences, which often provided time for reflection on actual teaching, as one of the most valuable learning experiences. They also appreciated teacher collegial interaction to examine their teaching and valued mentoring novice or student teachers.

Capitalizing on a Relationship with a University Faculty Member to Form a Successful Partnership

Cody Miller

Indian Creek Elementary School, San Antonio, TX

In the fall semester of 2007, I accepted the position as academic coordinator at Indian Creek Elementary in San Antonio, Texas. Having worked with me in another school-university partnership school, Misty Sailors from the University of Texas San Antonio immediately began discussions with us about forming a new collaboration at Indian Creek. The purposes of this collaboration were to provide preservice teachers with a site for high-quality early field experiences and improve the literacy education of students at Indian Creek Elementary through professional development of teachers. We worked together to plan the partnership and get the required approvals from our respective institutions.

Through this partnership, the university offered two courses at the elementary campus during the school day, one day per week. We designated a science lab for the use of the university students and their instructors and approached our teachers about hosting individual students in their classrooms for the semester, eventually including after-school tutoring. All teachers offered to host students, and we matched university students and cooperating teachers strategically to create a mutually beneficial relationship.

Our work together now includes a reading-program evaluation and collaborative professional development opportunities. Ongoing evaluation of the collaboration has included informal dialogue between the campus administration, university faculty, and teachers about areas of strength and needs in the program. The evaluation has also included the aforementioned reading program evaluation and two comfort surveys completed by the teachers to determine areas in which the faculty feels there is a need for professional development and improvement in their own instructional practices.

Our teachers have gained new ideas and insights about research-based comprehension instruction. Misty Sailors has been instrumental in helping our school set literacy priorities and goals that have driven our professional development offerings, even offering to present sessions on the elementary campus alongside our elementary faculty. Elementary and university faculty have presented collaboratively at national conferences.

(continued on next page)

(continued from previous page)

The greatest challenge that we have faced has been a lack of school district policies addressing the innovations and plans that have developed at our school. In some cases, plans have been scaled back due to misalignment between policy and ideas. For example, the university was interested in offering a site-based master's program in literacy. However, the school district had not developed the board policies needed to allow for such a program at a single campus. Despite setbacks, Indian Creek is a more effective school because of our collaboration with the university.

Teachers reported school and district inservice sessions as their worst professional development experiences because they felt that there was no direct or tangible benefit to students. Differences in the design of the activities were factors in teachers' perceptions of both best and worst professional development. Hands-on activities, opportunities to reflect and discuss topics with other teachers, or learning practices central to the content areas taught were perceived positively.

This study indicates that teachers, as adult learners, should be provided an environment in which they can expect to reflect, investigate, collaborate, and engage in authentic hands-on learning tasks. In short, partnerships have the potential to expand the range of effective professional development options available to teachers, and teachers have an expectation that they need to be actively involved for inservice to be effective.

In another case study, Bartholomew and Sandholtz (2009) examined how differing perspectives on common goals, on the part of a school district and university administrators and faculty, influenced decisions on how to implement school reform efforts. For example, district administrators and university educators held similar goals on issues of student performance on state testing. However, each group had a different perspective regarding the teachers' roles in reform efforts. District administrators determined the need to adopt a standards-based curriculum to improve student academic performance. They formed an articulated set of academic goals, standards, and assessments to ensure that students had a guaranteed and viable curriculum (Marzano, 2003). They found that teacher discretion decreased as the standards-based reform unfolded.

Conversely, university professors believed that the goal of the partnership was to develop a professional learning community with teachers to work together to enhance student performance on state testing. They viewed the teachers as professionals who should draw upon their expertise and knowledge base to make decisions about teaching and learning. They envisioned that teachers would have time to explore, reflect, collaborate, and engage in authentic learning tasks as active learners. Figure 2.1 delineates the different approaches used by district administrators and university faculty. This case study suggests that, while partners may share similar goals, they might not agree on professional development practices. Differing perspectives can confuse teachers and jeopardize any reform efforts (Bartholomew & Sandholtz, 2009).

Community Partnerships

A partnership that has recently emerged is the community partnership, not to be confused with community schools. Community partnerships bring together university, school, and community members, expanding the typical university-school partnership to involve community constituents.

FIGURE 2.1. Differing Views of the Teacher's Role In School Reform

District Administrators	*University Faculty*
1. Teachers as implementers Teachers were engaged in review of standards to ensure compliance with an agreed-upon curriculum. Administrators sought compliance more than input about directions for reform efforts.	*1. Teachers as learners* Teachers were envisioned as part of the professional learning community. Teachers drew upon their expertise and specialized knowledge to make decisions about teaching and learning.
2. Achieve teacher compliance Have teachers comply and buy in to approved curriculum standards. Fundamental decisions about how to develop standards, design tests, and organize all professional development around these tasks are made at the administrative level.	*2. Involve teachers as decision makers* Teachers were engaged in planning phase and given an opportunity to analyze priorities for schools relative to student achievement, curriculum, and instructional techniques. Teachers ensured projects were relevant to teachers' work.
3. Train teachers to deliver a standardized curriculum Using a "train the trainer" model, district administrators picked teachers and consultants to teach teachers how to write standards and tests items. Staff development is highly structured with defined outcomes.	*3. Emphasize instructional choices* Teacher expertise was recognized as an important factor in student learning. Teachers were engaged in sessions focused on examining instructional decisions and relationship of these decisions to student learning.
4. Align teaching and reduce ambiguity Align content standards, curriculum, instructional strategies, and testing practices. Teachers' role is to implement the established curriculum using approved strategies.	*4. Explore the complexity of teaching* Teachers' instructional choice was emphasized, with the belief that teaching is a complex task with an ever-shifting environment; formulaic solutions are not appropriate.

It is a widely held belief that the performance of children in schools is based in large part on the quality of their teachers (Darling-Hammond & Berry, 2006; Darling-Hammond, 2008). While teachers clearly matter, it is also important to keep in mind that the challenges their families face and the economic and social climate of their communities play important roles in how successful children are in school. Universities, with faculty members working across a range of fields and disciplines, have the breadth of expertise to help public schools address these issues. They also have the ability to access research on school reform.

A study of collaboration and leadership (Miller & Hafner, 2008) examined a community partnership. They found that community partnerships should be built on community-identified assets and needs; guided by strategically representative leadership; aware of and rooted in historical contexts; clear and realistic; and participatory. These recommendations call for changes in the way leaders are prepared to work with community groups and families to improve neighborhoods (Miller & Hafner, 2008).

Foundations and Business Partnerships

Support for educational reform and school improvement efforts, from both foundations and businesses, has been on the rise for the last 3 decades. As a result, business partnerships have become the most common type of partnership with up to 95% of schools having some form of business partnership activity (Brown, 1998; Hann, 2008; Hoff, 2002). Foundations and businesses share some goals and ambitions including concerns about workforce competitiveness, a desire to improve schools, and an interest in building goodwill in the community. The Foundation Center (Lawrence & Mukai, 2009) estimates that foundations donate more than $4.9 billion for education, with more than $1.5 billion going to K–12 education each year. The National Association of Partners in Education estimates that businesses contribute another 2.4 billion when commercial agreements (e.g., soft drink and vending contracts) are included (Ferguson, 2001).

Foundations. The Foundation Center is a nonprofit organization with a mission to provide public access to knowledge and information on philanthropy. The center supports those seeking information about how to secure grants and is also helpful to foundations, researchers, policy makers, reporters, and the public by providing a wealth of information through its print and online materials (http://foundationcenter.org/) about trends in foundation giving.

There are two principal types of foundations: private and public. A private foundation is a nongovernmental, nonprofit organization that has an endowment managed by its trustees and directors. Its goal is to aid charitable, educational, religious, and other activities serving the public good. A foundation makes grants available to other nonprofit organizations. The Foundation Center recognizes three different types of private foundations:

1. Independent or family foundations that receive endowments from individuals or families
2. Company-sponsored or corporate foundations receiving funds from their parent companies, although they are legally separate entities
3. Operating foundations running their own programs and services and typically not providing much grant support to outside organizations.

A public foundation sometimes referred to as a "grantmaking public charity" is a nongovernmental, nonprofit organization that receives funding from numerous sources and must continue to seek money from diverse sources in order to retain its public-charity status. As with a private foundation, its trustees and directors manage it. Its primary goal is to provide grants to benefit unrelated, nonprofit organizations or individuals. A public foundation is required to file with the IRS.

There are numerous types of public foundations. Community foundations seek support for themselves from the public but, as with private foundations, provide grants from the monies they raise. Their grants primarily support the needs of the geographic community or region in which they are located. Due to the broad public support they receive, the IRS does not consider them to be private foundations. Other public foundations serve a number of population groups and often have areas of specific interest, for example, education, health, and human services.

A number of new foundations have been established since the 1970s. Three factors have contributed to this growth: the loosening of tax laws; an increase in personal wealth; and an increasingly favorable attitude toward foundations among donors. However, the overall growth of new foundations has slowed since the turn of the century due to the stock market, the recession, and uneven economic recovery. Foundations are active across many fields, but education has consistently received generous support.

Business Partnerships. Partnerships between schools and businesses are common. Roslyn Mickelson (1999) provides a classification of corporate participation and their purposes: large philanthropic organizations, the work of corporate leaders, midlevel corporate personnel, and other personnel.

Large philanthropic organizations typically fund broad reform initiatives consistent with the framework of ideas and beliefs through which they interpret the world and their political ideals.

Corporate leaders, often through foundations linked to business, provide the resources and opportunities to establish and participate in national task forces. They also engage the media on issues related to workforce readiness and the performance of our nation's schools. In addition, corporate leaders also serve as members of local school boards and state advisory or policy panels.

Midlevel corporate personnel and other employees often engage in hands-on work regarding educational issues. This is often reform at the state or district levels. Other employees tutor or mentor students, or serve as guest speakers in local schools.

Business partnerships range from those with aspirations to reform education at the national level to those that have a local focus of helping children in after-school reading programs. When businesses engage with schools, businesspeople help to ensure an educated citizenry for their communities and are perceived as good corporate citizens. Recently, issues have emerged that have made business involvement subject to increased scrutiny. Corporate advocacy on education policy, privatization of public schools, and marketing toward younger children have resulted in the belief, or accusation, that some schools have become overly commercialized. However, most business-school partnerships are perceived as valuable additions to schools (Engeln, 2003; Hoff, 2002; Sanders, 2005).

EXPECTATIONS FOR DIFFERENT TYPES OF PARTNERSHIPS

Partnerships, in general, must address the issues of governance, resources, and roles if they are to successfully sustain themselves. Teitel (2003) refers to the structures, resources, and roles as the "building" that sits upon the partnership's "foundation." Continuing Teitel's metaphor, the "building" not only addresses the institutions that house the learning community or partnership, but also addresses the people involved in the collaboration and the resources available to them.

Governing Structures

Teitel (2003) describes four basic types of governance structures for connecting partners. The first type, *liaisons*, is the most basic. It involves appointing a person from each of the partners to provide daily person-to-person contacts as well as institutional linkages. This structure is exemplified with Southern Illinois University Carbondale's partnership with the Mt. Vernon Elementary District in the development of the Reflective Teaching Block (RTB) (McIntyre, Copenhaver, McIntyre, & Young, 2004). The RTB was developed by a site-based university faculty member who worked with teacher liaisons in each of the elementary buildings to deliver the program.

The second governance structure is the *steering committee*. It includes representatives from the various partners to deal with daily and long-term partnership issues. Warren, Witucke, and Redemer (2004) provide an example of this type of structure with their description of Illinois State University's partnership with the Wheeling Community Consolidated Elementary District #21. Their steering committee is composed of university and school district personnel who meet regularly to discuss such issues as mission, design, structure, cost, and preservice curriculum.

The third governance structure is the *multi-site coordinating council*. This type of governance structure is reserved typically for larger partnerships that include multiple sites. Ohio State University's policy board is an example (Johnston, 2000). This board is composed of representatives from one university and multiple school partners. Other examples of this type of governing structure are the Centers Council established through Texas A&M University–Commerce's PDS partnership (Walker, Zeek, Foote, & Naizer, 2008) and the Benedum Collaborative, a partnership between West Virginia University and local public schools (Steel & Hoffman, 1997).

Finally, the *transformative* model for governance applies to a partnership only when it is interested in a systemic initiative that would radically transform the existing institutional structures of the partners. An example of this structure is the Houston Consortium's consortium policy council as described by Houston, Hollis, Clay, Ligons, and Roff (1999). In this case, four universities, three school districts, and two educational agencies created a new interagency organization to prepare teachers to work in the Houston metropolitan area. Valli (1999) refers to this partnership as a "sea change in the way higher education and school districts typically relate" (p. 62).

Written Agreements

One outcome that often evolves from the more developed partnership governing structures is a written agreement that describes the mission, philosophy, and expectations of the partnership and, in some cases, the individual partners. Clark (1999) explains that there are advantages and disadvantages to having a formal, written agreement to guide a partnership. For example, during the early stages of some partnerships it is probably not a good idea to formulate a written agreement. Some formal agreements too soon can heighten mistrust rather than alleviate it. In addition, formal agreements at an early stage can create rigid expectations and conditions before the partnership has had the opportunity to experiment with a variety of approaches to determine the best course of operation.

On the other hand, there are advantages to developing written agreements. Clark (1999) states that having a written agreement can help alleviate the impact of leadership turnover, a problem that is not uncommon in any kind of partnership. It is also helpful when several partners are contributing financially to the partnership. The agreement can, and should, delineate the financial obligations and accounting procedures for the partnership. A formal agreement can outline the responsibilities and expectations of the various personnel involved in the work of the partnership as well.

Clark (1999) points out that any formal agreement is only words if it is not aligned to the partnership's philosophy or if the partners fail to apply the agreement to the daily operations of the partnership. He states that if an agreement is developed, it should contain the following major components (p. 112):

1. Preamble
    1.1. Statement of purpose and overarching goals
    1.2. General specification of responsibilities of partners
2. Main body of the agreement
    2.1. Specification of the partner to the agreement
    2.2. Detailing of specific goals
    2.3. Specification of responsibilities of partners
        2.3.1. Regarding accomplishment of the goals of the partnership
        2.3.2. Regarding governance of the partnership
        2.3.3. Regarding financing of the partnership
        2.3.4. Regarding research and evaluation to be conducted by or in relation to the partnership
    2.4. Term of the agreement
    2.5. Signatures of the parties to the agreement and date of signing

Examples of successful written agreements can be found on pages 113–188 of Richard W. Clark's book *Effective Professional Development Schools* and on the American Association of Colleges for Teacher Education website (AACTE; www.aacte.org/index.php?/Programs/Professional-Development-Schools/professional-development-school-sample-papartnership-agreements.html).

Roles and Responsibilities of Partners

Creating a partnership between a school, a university, and perhaps a community agency results in a new culture for school and university faculty to work together to meet common goals (Book, 1996). Prior relationships among those schools and universities can affect the success of the partnership (Clark, 1999; Teitel, 2003). It is clear that all partners must develop a strong belief in one another if the collaboration is to be successful. If any previous relationship between the partners has not been positive or has been at a very basic level, establishing trust may require patience, dedication, and time.

Even if the prior relationship between the partners has been positive, redefining roles and responsibilities requires a commitment to change. Clark (1999) asserts that the difference in cultures between the community, schools, and university is a barrier that must be overcome in order to create a new culture that can meet the partnership's goals. Even a shared mission of the university and the schools can be, and is often, perceived quite differently. Book (1996) explains that the reward structures for university faculty for promotion, tenure, and merit pay typically rely on publications, grants, and presentations to national conferences. In most cases, university rewards structures do not value the work involved in developing and maintaining a school partnership. In addition, the university mission is often viewed as remote from that of the local community and schools. On the other hand, classroom teachers view their mission as one of direct responsibility related to the success of their pupils and wonder how their participation in a school-university partnership can further that effort. In some schools, the work of teachers involved in a school-university partnership is devalued by their administration and colleague teachers who are not involved in the partnerships.

Simmons, Konecki, Crowell, and Gates-Duffield (1999) identified three metaphors that describe the roles and activities assumed by those working in successful partnerships. The first is a dream keeper. Dream keepers consistently try to focus on the principles, vision, and commitments that brought participants together in a collaborative effort. They state that dream keepers share certain common elements with coaches, ministers, advocates, CEOs, and therapists by attempting to build team spirit and a climate of shared hope.

The second role is that of a weaver. Weavers try to keep things moving smoothly and going forward as a group. Both school and university partners who serve in this role must come together as equals to address issues and promote partnership activities. Each must trust and respect the other to carry out this role effectively.

The third role is that of a shapeshifter. Shapeshifters must be able to change roles in order to effectively address issues and implement activities. For example, in a school-university partnership, a university professor may teach lessons in a third-grade classroom to demonstrate a certain instructional approach, to gain additional experience with elementary-age pupils, or to allow the classroom teacher to attend an event sponsored by the partnership. Likewise, a classroom teacher may conduct a workshop or teach a class for the university or serve as a building liaison for the preservice teachers placed in a particular building.

Funding

One of the most important factors for fostering the continuation of collaborative efforts is adequate funding to support the partnership's mission. University support is often limited, as is that available to preK–12 schools. Usually, neither is able to devote large sums to a partnership.

External funding is often given for start-up partnerships and specific activities within a partnership (Abdal-Haqq, 1998; Boudah & Knight, 1999; Teitel, 2003). However, as Darling-Hammond (1994) points out, supporting activities through an external grant can short-circuit a partnership because when the funds run out, partners are challenged to continue the efforts without the support of the grant. Lee Teitel in Chapter 3 provides ideas for reallocating time and resources to support partnerships without depending on external funding.

Assessment of Partnership Viability

Accountability is at the forefront of many of today's educational innovations and partnerships designed to improve preK–12 education. As demand for resources becomes more competitive, school-university partnerships must produce the evidence that they are improving the knowledge and skills of preservice teachers, experienced teachers, and preK–12 students (Abdal-Haqq, 1998; Teitel, 2003). This data-driven evidence must be shared with the community, school boards, media, and policy makers if school-university partnerships expect to receive the support they need to maintain innovative practices.

Although there remains a paucity of research and evaluation studies on the effectiveness of partnerships to meet their goals, a growing number of studies are supporting the assertion that school-university partnerships have great promise. For example, the Houston Consortium found that approximately 43% of preservice teachers believed they taught differently as a result of their participation in the partnership, made higher achievement scores on the state certification exam than a comparison group, and saw the achievement of preK–12 pupils on the state-mandated achievement test increase after their schools became part of the consortium (Houston, Hollis, Clay, Ligons, & Roff, 1999).

Castle, Rockwood, and Tortora (2008) conducted a longitudinal study on the impact of a professional development school on teaching practices and student learning over 5 years. They discovered that as teaching practices improved, student learning improved. Walker, Sorensen, Smaldino, and Downey (2008) assessed the effectiveness of a partnership with a university, community college, and public school district on preK–12 student achievement in reading and mathematics. Their data revealed higher achievement in mathematics and reading in three of four PDS schools.

Two studies (Brindley, Daniel, Rosselli, Campbell, & Vizcain, 2008; Neapolitan et al., 2008) revealed that teachers who completed their teacher preparation in a professional development school were significantly more likely to remain in the profession than teachers prepared in a traditional site. In addition, Snow-Gerono, Dana, and Nolan (2008) discovered that graduates from a professional development school's teacher preparation program appear to function as novice-teacher leaders who positively influence more experienced peers and who strive to positively transform the school culture.

Communication and Follow-Up

Partnerships need to communicate effectively within and across institutional boundaries (Robinson & Darling-Hammond, 1994). It is important that a partnership's mission, goals, and expectations and responsibilities for the various partnership roles be communicated to all constituents. It is only through effective communication that all partners can move toward a common goal and meet the partnership's mission.

Partnerships need to "market" their programs so that their activities are known beyond those within the partnership. In addition, partnerships should celebrate their successes so that others are aware of the contributions they are making in teacher development and pupil learning. See Chapter 3 for ideas on ways to celebrate partnership successes.

CONCLUDING REMARKS

Partnerships between schools, universities, foundations, and the business community are expanding daily. They vary in purpose, duration, and methodologies but often have similar universal goals for improving a school's level of functioning. School-university partnerships are among the most common type of partnerships. They have evolved from primarily informal arrangements for hosting practicum students to highly organized and inclusive professional development schools whose purpose is to promote research, impact policy, improve educator preparation, and support student learning.

Foundations and businesses continue to provide support for reform and school improvement efforts. Usually, both have similar goals to improve workforce competitiveness, improve education for children, and build goodwill within the community.

Community-based schools, another major partnership effort, integrate academics, health and social services, and community development to improve the lives of students and their families. Regardless of the type of partnership, certain features that increase the likelihood of partnership effectiveness include building a new culture based on shared goals, developing mutual respect and trust, securing program funding, and clearly outlining responsibilities and expectations.

Increasingly, accountability and the assessment of the effects of a partnership have become important measures of partnership effectiveness. Currently, research on the promise of partnerships across a range of outcomes includes increasing student achievement, teacher retention, and leadership development.

REFERENCES

Abdal-Haqq, I. (1998). *Professional development schools: Weighing the evidence.* Thousand Oaks, CA: Corwin Press.

Bainer, B. L. (1997). A comparison of four models of group efforts and their implications for establishing educational partnerships. *Journal of Research in Rural Education, 13*(3), 143–152.

Bartholomew, S. S., & Sandholtz, J. H. (2009). Competing views of teaching in a school–university partnership. *Teaching and Teacher Education, 25*(1), 155–165.

Blank, M. J., Melaville, A., & Shah, B. P. (2003). *Making the difference: Research and practice in community schools* .Washington, DC: Coalition for Community Schools.

Book, C. (1996). Professional development schools. In J. Sikula, T. J. Buttery, & E. Guyton (Eds.), *Handbook of research on teacher education* (2nd ed.) (pp. 194–210). New York: Macmillan.

Boudah, D. J., & Knight, S. L. (1999). Creating learning communities of research and practice. In D. M. Byrd & D. J. McIntyre (Eds.), *Research on professional development schools. Teacher education yearbook VII* (pp. 97–114). Thousand Oaks, CA: Corwin Press.

Boyle-Baise, M., & McIntyre, D. J. (2008). What kind of experience? Preparing teachers in PDS or community settings. In M. Cochran-Smith, S. Feiman-Nemser, D. J. McIntyre, & K. Demers (Eds.), *Handbook of research on teacher education: Enduring questions in changing contexts* (3rd ed.) (pp. 307–330). New York: Routledge/Taylor & Francis Group & The Association of Teacher Educators.

Brindley, R., Daniel, P. L., Rosselli, H., Campbell, C., & Vizcain, D. (2008). Eleven years and counting: The lasting impact of PDS experience on teaching careers. In I. Guadarrama, J. M. Ramsey, & J. L. Nath (Eds.), *University and school connections: Research studies in professional development schools* (pp. 393–409). Charlotte, NC: Information Age Publishing.

Brown, D. (1998). *Schools with heart: Voluntarism and public education.* Boulder, CO: Westview.

Castle, S., Rockwood, K. D., & Tortora, M. (2008). Tracking professional development and student learning in a professional development school partnership. *School-University Partnerships, 2*(1), 47–60.

Clark, R. W. (1999). *Effective professional development schools.* San Francisco: Jossey-Bass.

Collins, J. F. (1970). The teacher education center concept: A unifying approach to teacher education. *Educational Leadership, 27*(6), 544–547.

Darling-Hammond, L. (1994). *Professional development schools: Schools for a developing profession.* New York: Teachers College Press.

Darling-Hammond, L. (2008). A future worthy of teaching for America. *Phi Delta Kappan, 89*(10), 730–733.

Darling-Hammond, L., & Berry, B. (2006). Highly qualified teachers for all. *Educational Leadership, 64*(3), 14–20.

Engeln, J. T. (2003) Guiding school/business partnerships. *Education Digest, 68*(7), 36–40.

Ferguson, M. V. (2001). *Partnerships 2000: A decade of growth and change.* Alexandria, VA: National Association of Partners in Education. Retrieved May 10, 2010 from www.napehq.org/a.pdf

Fuhrman, S. H., & Streim, N. W. (2008, November 12) Universities and public schools: A partnership whose time has come. *Edweek, 28*(12), 30–31.

Hann, L. W. (2008). Profit and loss in school-business partnerships. *District Administration, 44*(5), 26–30.

Hoff, D. (2002). School-business partnerships: It's the schools' turn to raise the grade! *School Community Journal, 12*(2), 63–78. Retrieved April 5, 2009, from ERIC database, EJ659186.

Holmes Group. (1990). *Tomorrow's schools.* East Lansing, MI: Holmes Group.

Holmes Partnership Goals. (1996). Holmes Partnership. Retrieved March 13, 2009, from http://www.holmespartnership.org/ goals.html

Houston, W. R., Hollis, L. Y., Clay, D., Ligons, C. M., & Roff, L. (1999). Effectiveness of collaboration on urban teacher education programs and professional development schools. In D. M. Byrd & D. J. McIntyre (Eds.), *Research on professional development schools. Teacher education yearbook VII* (pp. 6–28). Thousand Oaks, CA: Corwin Press.

Johnston, M. (2000). Contexts, challenges and consequences: PDSs in the making. In M. Johnston, P. Brosnan, D. Cramer, & T. Dove (Eds.), *Collaborative reform and other improbable dreams* (pp. 1–17). Albany, NY: State University of New York Press.

Kirschenbaum, H. (1999). *From public relations to partnerships: A changing paradigm in school, family and community relations.* Washington, DC: Communitarian Network.

Kirschenbaum, H., & Reagan, C. (2001). University and urban school partnerships: An analysis of 57 collaborations between a university and a city school district. *Urban Education 2001, 36*(4), 479–504.

Lawrence, S., & Mukai, R. (2009). *Foundation growth and giving estimates: Current outlook 2009.* New York: Foundation Center.

Lenski, S. D., & Black, W. L. (2004). The power of partnerships: Introduction. In S. D. Lenski & W. L. Black (Eds.), *Transforming teacher education through partnerships.* (pp. 1–4). Lewiston, NY: Edwin Mellen Press.

Marzano, R. J. (2003). *What works in schools: Translating research into action.* Alexandria, VA: Association for Supervision and Curriculum Development.

McIntyre, D. J., Copenhaver, R. W., McIntyre, C., & Young, A. (2004). Southern Illinois University Carbondale—Mt. Vernon reflective teaching block. In S. D. Lenski & W. L. Black (Eds.), *Transforming teacher education through partnerships* (pp. 334–341). Lewiston, NY: Edwin Mellen Press.

Mickelson, R. A. (1999). International business machinations: A case study of corporate involvement in local educational reform. *Teachers College Record, 100*(3), 476–512.

Miller, P. M., & Hafner, M. M. (2008). Moving toward dialogical collaboration: A critical examination of a university-school-community partnership. *Educational Administration Quarterly, 44*(1), 66–110.

National Association for Professional Development Schools. (2008). What it means to be a professional development school. *School-University Partnerships, 2*(2), 10–16.

National Council for the Accreditation of Teacher Education. (2001). *Standards for professional development schools*. Washington, DC: Author.

Neapolitan, J., Hartzler-Miller, C., Kenreich, T., Wiltz, N., Schafer, K., Proffitt, T., et al. (2008). *School-University Partnerships, 2*(1), 61–72.

Robinson, S., & Darling-Hammond, L. (1994). Change for collaboration and collaboration for change: Transforming teaching through school-university partnerships. In L. Darling-Hammond (Ed.), *Professional development schools: Schools for developing a profession* (pp. 203–219). New York: Teachers College Press.

Sandholtz, J. H. (2002). Inservice training or professional development: Contrasting opportunities in a school/university partnership. *Teaching and Teacher Education, 18*, 815–830.

Sanders, M. G. (2005). *Building school-community partnerships: Collaboration for student success.* Thousand Oaks, CA: Corwin Press.

Simmons, J. M., Konecki, L. R., Crowell, R. A., & Gates-Duffield, P. (1999). Dream keepers, weavers, and shape shifters: Emerging roles of PDS university coordinators in educational reform. In D. M. Byrd & D. J. McIntyre (Eds.), *Research on professional development schools. Teacher education yearbook VII* (pp. 29–45). Thousand Oaks, CA: Corwin Press.

Snow-Gerono, J., Dana, N. F., & Nolan, J., (2008). Following up with professional development school graduates: An emergent theory of novice teacher leadership. *School-University Partnerships, 2*(2), 55–68.

Southern Regional Education Board (SREB). (2005). *A district-driven principal preparation program design: The Providence School Department and the University of Rhode Island partnership, Providence, Rhode Island.* Atlanta, GA: Author.

Steel, S., & Hoffman, N. E. (1997). The Benedum Collaborative: The story of an educational reform effort. In N. E. Huffman, W. M. Reed, & G. S. Rosenbluth (Eds.), *Lessons from restructuring experiences: Stories in professional development schools* (pp. 51–79). Albany, NY: State University of New York Press.

Teitel, L. (2003). *The professional development schools handbook: Starting, sustaining and assessing partnerships that improve student learning.* Thousand Oaks, CA: Corwin Press.

Valli, L. (1999). The transformative potential of collaborative partnerships: Reflections. In D. M. Byrd & D. J. McIntyre (Eds.), *Research on professional development schools. Teacher education yearbook VII* (pp. 61–67). Thousand Oaks, CA: Corwin Press.

Walker, C., Zeek, C. K., Foote, M. M., & Naizer, G. (2008). Re-creating teacher education through long-term partnerships. In I. Guadarrama, J. M. Ramsey, & J. L. Nath (Eds.), *University and school connections: Research studies in professional development schools* (pp. 203–220). Charlotte, NC: Information Age Publishing.

Walker, D. A., Sorensen, C. K., Smaldino, S. E., & Downey, P. (2008). A model for professional development school intervention: REAL findings. *School-University Partnerships, 2*(1), 6–26.

Warren, N. J., Witucke, C., & Redemer, J. (2004). School-university partnership: A shared journey. In S. D. Lenski & W. L. Black (Eds.), *Transforming teacher education through partnerships* (pp. 32–41). Lewiston, NY: Edwin Mellen Press.

Yendol-Hoppey, D., Jacobs, J., Gregory, & A., League, M. (2008). Inquiry as a tool for professional development school improvement: Four illustrations. *Action in Teacher Education, 30*(3), 23–38.

Part II

DEVELOPING, SUSTAINING, AND EVALUATING PARTNERSHIPS

This part of the book focuses on the nitty-gritty of developing, sustaining, and evaluating partnerships. Each chapter addresses one specific area of partnership work.

Chapter 3, written by Lee Teitel, describes the development of partnerships. This chapter begins with a discussion of the partnership continuum and the distinctions between transactional and transformative relationships. It uses this distinction to present specific ideas on how to find potential partners as a first step in starting, structuring, and sustaining strong partnerships. The chapter closes with specific ideas on how to deepen some partnerships to unlock their potential for mutual organizational learning.

Chapter 4, written by Diane Yendol-Hoppey, David Hoppey, and Ted Price, explains what it means to sustain a partnership. It presents in great detail a dozen challenges associated with sustaining collaboration across preK–12 and higher education settings and provides insights for collaborative leaders. It ends with nine lessons that collaborative leaders can use to strengthen their own partnership work.

Chapter 5, written by Jerry W. Willis, focuses on the evaluation of partnerships. The chapter begins with a description of the assessment process and how it should match the type of partnership developed. It then describes how to determine the type of data that should be collected based on the type of partnership formed. Five types of partnerships—technical, technical/support, conceptual, transformative, and emancipator—are used as a framework for determining the assessment process.

These three chapters offer concrete and research-based ideas for determining how to proceed in developing and evaluating the usefulness of partnerships for long-term success.

3

Developing Partnerships with Purpose

Lee Teitel

This chapter focuses on

- understanding the partnership continuum and the distinctions between transactional and transformative relationships;
- finding potential partners—other organizations with common purposes and mutual interdependence;
- starting, structuring, and sustaining strong partnerships; and
- deepening some partnerships to unlock their potential for mutual organizational learning.

* * *

John Carter and Mary Woodruff sat in the teachers' room at the Johnston High School drinking coffee and reflecting on the progress of their professional development school partnership. "In just 3 years we've involved almost half the teachers here," John, the school-based liaison for the partnership, said. "We've got teachers as mentors and coaches, as collaborative inquirers, with everybody doing a lot of learning and growing themselves."

"I'm even starting to see some changes at the college," said Mary, his college counterpart. "More of my colleagues are willing to place student teachers here, or in one of our other PDSs. Even the ones who were reluctant in the beginning are starting to come around; they see it is a better placement for student teachers. I've even gotten a couple of arts and science faculty involved and that's tough."

"Yeah," said John, "but do you remember that conference we went to a year and half ago on the whole professional development school model? They had that guy talking

about the four goals of PDS and how lots of partnerships mostly do two of them—the preservice teacher part and professional development for experienced teachers. The other two—improved learning for kids and inquiry—he said lots of places don't really do much of that—and he's right. Look at us. And he talked about how the partnership should really improve the school and transform the teacher education experience, so new teachers come out really prepared to teach in real schools, with real kids."

"I remember that, too," responded Mary. "You're right. In a way what we have is a better model for student teaching, with some professional development thrown in for the veteran teachers. We're not really making any major changes at either of our institutions, but everybody's happy with what we have done. And we are all so busy—going further would be tough. I remember at that conference, on the way home you and I plotted out how we could make this thing more than good, clustered student teaching. We were going to involve parents, community organizations. We were going to do a study of tracking in the school and how it adversely affects kids of color. We were going to form study groups. Do you remember?"

"Yeah . . . ," said John, dribbling off. "If only I could find my notes from then . . . Well, I gotta go to my class."

As they went their separate ways each wondered about the conversation. John realized how touchy Mary was whenever he or any of the teachers at Johnston made any comments about how the teacher education courses at the college needed to be more practical, more reality based. The college always seemed to resist really getting input into teaching or redesigning any of the college courses, even though John and several other teachers had volunteered to help. He wondered if he should bring it up again at the steering committee meeting next week.

Mary wondered about the attitudes of the mostly White teaching staff at Johnston toward students of color. The heavy tracking in the school and the poor achievement of many of the African American and Latino students seemed like unmentionable topics—she remembered the first time she brought them up as a concern at a PDS steering committee meeting—all the teachers looking down, discomfort obvious with the subjects. She wondered if she dared bring it up again, and if so, how? (Case vignette adapted from Teitel, 1996.)

* * *

John and Mary face a problem that is common to many partnerships. The relationship between their school and university has enormous power to help both institutions improve in fundamental ways—to actually get better at some of its core activities, like improving how the university prepares beginning teachers for the real, practical challenges they will face or how the school meets the educational needs of all students, especially its children of color. Yet, despite the fact that the partnership appears to be functioning well and is producing modest benefits in other areas, they are stuck—unable to take advantage of the deeper organizational learning that they each know is possible. Their partnership is succeeding in the "transactional" mode, clustering groups of student teachers, offering coordinated professional development to experienced faculty—things that just require minor adjustments in what each institution does. The deeper "transformative" possibilities—partnership benefits that would require changes much closer to the core of what each organization does—are in front of them but are much harder to realize.

Schools and universities are highly interdependent. Universities rely on preK–12 schools to prepare their incoming students; preK–12 schools count on universities to train their teachers and administrators. They have a broad common purpose of educating children and adults. Because of this interdependency and common purpose, they are extremely well suited to serve as transformative partners with one another. Who better than a school or school district could give feedback to a university on how to improve its teacher education program? Who better than a college or university could help improve the quality of learning students receive before they enter as freshmen? In fact, an early contributor to the concept of school-university partnerships, John Goodlad, refers to this as the opportunity for "simultaneous and mutual renewal" of both sets of institutions (Sirotnik & Goodlad, 1988, p. 3).

Yet, more often than not, school-university partnerships fail to take advantage of this potential for deep learning from and with each other. Learning how to realize this potential is the focus of this chapter: how to find, develop, and sustain transformative partnerships that help participating organizations get better at achieving their core purposes. The language and examples in the chapter come from the world of preK–16 school and university partnerships, but the ideas apply more broadly, to many others types of partnerships with purpose.

UNDERSTANDING THE PARTNERSHIP CONTINUUM

Little or No Connection ←→ Transactional ←→ Transformative

There are numerous typologies of partnerships (see Gajda, 2004, for instance) but for our purposes—keeping the focus on what matters for simultaneous renewal—I propose a simple continuum, ranging from little or no connection to transactional relationships to transformative ones (Teitel, 2008). The categories are neither linear nor monolithic. There is not a presumed incremental or inevitable march from left to right. Some partnerships never go beyond transactional and, perhaps, do not even aspire to it. Partnerships that operate in a transformative mode may also include transactional elements and they may also drop back over time being more transactional.

Little or No Connection

This is the condition that is characteristic of schools, universities, and other organizations that are interdependent but do not recognize or act on those interdependencies. The impacts of this disconnection can be powerful and pernicious. The combination of a shared but unrecognized joint purpose—the learning of preK–12 students—and the lack of institutional and personal connections to achieve that purpose can create more than just missed opportunities for mutual learning. It can contribute to blame and distrust, as each sector tries to improve itself independently and then, especially when accountability for outcomes ratchets up, can feel disappointment with its "partner."

In the absence of real partnerships, schools and universities deal with their interdependence by using a serial approach to partnership—"you work on them, then we'll work on them"—but this has serious problems. For example, when student teachers come to a school after years of university preparation, they are often greeted by a whole chorus of experienced teachers who say, "We don't know what they taught you over at the university but, welcome to the real world. We'll show you how it really works." University faculty members may often be (justifiably) concerned about how quickly approaches taught in teacher preparation institutions "wash off" in practice.

Some teacher education faculties—proud to see themselves on the cutting edge of educational theory—discuss how hard it is to find good placement sites. In extreme cases, they talk about how to "inoculate" their student teachers or graduates so they will retain the learning in the less-than-perfect environments in which they are placed.

Classroom teachers sometimes wonder when professors have last been, or if they have ever been, in a classroom, or why the incoming student teachers or recent graduates know some esoteric constructivist theories but do not know about basic things, like classroom management or how to show up for teaching on time and dressed professionally. Schools or districts, excited about the potential transformation of teaching through improvement strategies of their own—like the use of standards-based instruction—sometimes wonder why the student teachers or recent graduates of their neighboring universities come to them knowing little or nothing about the approach.

These disconnections have led not only to missed opportunities for learning, they have created barriers of distrust. Without opportunities to work together on their common purposes, individuals who travel in different worlds do not get to know one another. They tend to be suspicious of each other's motives or competence, making collaboration more difficult and mutual learning well-nigh impossible.

Transactional

Transactional approaches offer major improvements over the patterns of disconnection. They acknowledge a commonality of purpose and suggest that by making adaptations and adjustments in the way they work with one another, schools and universities can be more effective and efficient at reaching their individual and collective goals. These adjustments range from minor to more substantial but do not typically require any deep changes at the core of what each partner does, nor do they set up structures or create cultures where such changes are likely. Most professional development schools are, at least initially, transactional, as they figure out how to meet the four common targets of PDS: preK–12 student learning, preservice teacher preparation, professional development, and research for school improvement. These examples illustrate the common transactional patterns:

- A university professor gets a grant to try an innovative approach to teaching reading and obtains permission to implement it at the partner school. A subset of teachers volunteers to participate and it is put into place. After a few years, the funding runs out. Some of the teachers continue using the approach; others stop. Individual teachers and some students may have benefited, but there is no lasting impact or improved collaboration processes at either institution.
- Student teachers are clustered in the school (rather than placed in a variety of settings). The practicum course for student teachers is offered on site instead of at the university, and experienced teachers from the school come in as guest speakers. Perhaps a lead teacher or principal from the school becomes an adjunct professor, teaching a teacher education course on site or at the university. While these adjustments bring added convenience, and have the potential to form the basis of deeper collaboration, in a transactional setting practice at neither institution changes deeply.
- As part of the partnership, schools are willing to serve as sites for research projects conducted by university faculty. Research is conducted in the traditional way—more *on* the school than *with* it—and when it gets published in an academic journal, school personnel do not even know what the findings are.

Some of the adjustments in the transactional relationships may be more major than the ones listed here, but the defining difference is that the core of the work is not changed, even if the delivery and organization might be. Individuals involved in this get to know people from the other "side" (e.g., the university supervisor who now spends a day or more a week supervising student teachers becomes a visible presence in the school). They may see value in the transactions and even see a sense of common purpose but, generally, will not see any need for their organization or themselves to change.

Transformative

Simultaneous renewal necessitates a different, more transformative approach. The partners retain their identities but are willing to learn from and with each other about the core business they are in. Partners approach the four common purposes of PDS more collaboratively and with a greater willingness to explore deeper changes in practice.

In one partnership, when the school experienced a flattening of student performance in second- and third-grade math, the partners pulled together a "circle" on it—their mechanism for problem solving that, in this case, included grade level teachers, the school's math specialist, the principal, the PDS coordinator, two community representatives and, from the university, faculty members who taught math and math methods and the liaison to the school. After studying alternative approaches, they picked one to try for the next few years. All participants had input into the decision, which, once it was made, had ramifications for each. The math methods courses would be revamped to better support the adopted approach, so that the teacher candidates in the class, who did extensive tutoring of individuals and small groups of students at the school, would be prepared. The second- and third-grade teachers would be involved in learning the approach over the summer alongside the math and math methods faculty members. The PDS coordinator and principal would take the lead on tracking results, using formative assessments and student test data to sustain the ongoing inquiry into improving practice. The circle and its effects represent the tight linking of school and university in a culture of learning and renewal. The partnership has developed the practice of collaborating deeply on substantive issues in a spirit of mutuality and common purpose.

In transformative committed relationships, partners can take greater risks with one another in service of a common purpose and collaborative learning and renewal. The next example illustrates what can happen when one partner is willing to push another and talk about what is not usually discussed. Two thirds of the students in one of the elementary schools of an established partnership were English Language Learners (ELL), and the teachers, who felt they had developed effective approaches to working with ELL students were getting increasingly concerned about the lack of preparation of the student teachers coming from their partner university. Whereas prior to the PDS partnership, they might have kept silent (or maybe even shopped around for another university to place its students), here they spoke up. At a regularly scheduled partnership steering committee, the principal voiced the concerns of her faculty. The input was welcomed by the university PDS coordinator (who also served as assistant dean), who brought the relevant university faculty together to learn from the school personnel. Over the next few months, the courses were revamped and the field experiences revised to reflect the changes. The following year, pleased with the success in shifting the teaching of ELLs, the principal and teachers initiated a similar process around the teaching of special education. A comparable example (but with the pressure going the other way) can be found in partnerships in which university faculty, concerned by the numbers of African American boys they saw in special education classes in their partner schools, found a forum to discuss, analyze, and address the problem jointly.

These cases represent the kind of potential that John and Mary, in the opening vignette, yearn for. They both illustrate joint-organizational learning, through which individuals across the organizations know each other and work with each other well enough to deal with tough and potentially conflicting issues. They develop a sense of urgency, openness, and courage to go against the historical norms and have a common vision of shared outcomes. They can see the comparative advantages that each party brings and have developed enough trust and skills to manage the disequilibrium created by challenging each other and learning together. How do you find potential partners, build strong relationships, move some of those to deeper, more transformative ones, and sustain them over time?

FINDING POTENTIAL PARTNERS

The goal for this section is to help you identify partners who might help you to better meet your organization's purpose. I recommend a four-step process:

- Be clear in your purpose.
- Develop an inventory of current partners.
- Stretch the inventory to think broadly and outside the box about potential partners.
- Perform an initial assessment of where your relationships with current and potential partners fall on the "no connection—transactional—transformative" continuum.

Define Your Organization's Purpose

The first step in finding partners is to be clear about your own organization's purpose. This clarity will help you be strategic about searching for others with similar purposes or with whom you are interdependent. Start with a simple, clear, and jargon-free statement of your primary purpose.

Develop an Inventory of Current Partners

List the organizations your organization partners with currently—either formally or informally. Some schools may have just a handful of partners; others may be more like an urban high school I worked with that had a whopping 67 partners with some sort of formal connection. Examples might include

- arts in the school,
- tutoring partnerships with local volunteers and businesspeople,
- mentoring programs that link students with adults, and
- test-preparation support for students from volunteers and/or for-profit preparation programs.

Expand the Inventory of Potential Partners

Identify potential partnerships you may be overlooking by looking at the broad range of possible organizations that are interdependent with yours. It could be other schools in a district, other teacher or school leader preparation programs at other universities, parents, other youth-serving organizations in your community, or arts and sciences faculty at a university. See Figure 3.1 for some suggestions on using the "five interdependencies" to help find potential partners you may be overlooking.

Alternatively, take a close look at a deep challenge in your own organization, and then scan for organizational partners who can help. Pick one or two pressing, tough, seemingly intractable issues you face in your organization—things that seem to represent serious obstacles to achieving your purpose.

Take Stock of Where Your Current and Potential Partners Are

When you are done **with your inventory**, add the names of these potential partners to the list you already generated. You should have a hefty list of current and potential partners tied to your purpose, interdependency, and potential in helping to address the challenges you face. Use the grid from Figure 3.2 to make a quick assessment as to where these relationships are on the transformative continuum. Be thorough about potential partners, even if there is little connection now. Put an asterisk next to the partners with which the school already has some sort of relationship.

Identify which would be good candidates to move from no connection toward transactional and/or toward transformative. The goal is not to get all of your relationships to transformative—it is hard to imagine trying to do deep organizational learning from all of your partners—but rather to be thoughtful and selective about which partnerships can most help you and your partners improve how you work to achieve your purpose(s).

FIGURE 3.1. Ways to Expand the Inventory of Potential Partners

To systematically scan for possible partners, use the chart below identifying five kinds of interdependent relationships that your organization might have with others. Not all categories are mutually exclusive, so don't spend a great deal of time worrying if something is a type 1 or type 3 relationship; in some cases it may well be both. The point is to use the tool to stretch your thinking and identify a broad range of potential partners.

Relationship type	Examples for Johnston High School (JHS)
1. Serial/supply or value chain You rely on others to provide some service or add some value to something (or some people) that you then work with. You and your organization in turn supply others up the value chain.	• three feeder middle schools for JHS • the local state university and two private colleges, where 75% of the JHS graduates who go on to college typically go • the local state university, which provides about 2/3 of the JHS teachers
2. Parallel/peer Individuals, organizations, or subunits that have similar goals, technology, processes. You may see yourselves as collaborators or potential competitors.	• the four other high schools in the city • the six other designated professional development schools that State U had in the region
3. Silos Units or people with the same stated broader purpose but differentiated tasks. This might include subunits within an organization that are often seen as competing, e.g., teaching and learning, human resources, and professional development.	• within JHS itself, the different academic departments: social studies, science, math, and English • within the district, the human resources department (often not in sync with what they were trying to do in the PDS, making it hard to hire skilled teachers who trained in the PDS) • within the Johnston Youth Development program (although they worked with some Johnston youth, little to no contact or connection between the youth workers and the teachers, counselors, interns, or administrators of JHS)
4. Nested hierarchies These relationships have the same stated goals, but significant differences in power and authority (e.g., schools in relationship to districts, grade level teams within schools, teachers in relationship to principals, districts working with state agencies, teacher education programs within larger colleges or graduate schools or universities).	• within Johnston Unified School District (seeming lack of caring or understanding by school board and superintendent about the importance of the PDS work with the university on teacher preparation) reported similar lack of consistent support at the higher levels of her university
5. Combinations of above, or unconnected, unaligned, unaffiliated Some relationships are outside of the box: potential partnerships with people and organizations that don't know each other, or even think of themselves in the same universe (e.g., a teen health program at a hospital, a youth leadership program at a community center, and a school working together to create an HIV peer leadership program).	• John wasn't sure what to put here, but thought about a program for court-involved youth that was being run by the police department and division of social services. He wondered what connections he might be able to form.

FIGURE 3.2. Partnership Inventory and Assessment

Current or potential partner from inventory list	Little or no connection or recognition of common purpose and interdependence	←→ Transactional ←→ *In the interests of a common goal, each partner is willing to make adjustments in what it does (individually and organizationally).*	Transformative *Each partner expects to learn from the other (individually and organizationally) and from their work together in ways that can lead to deep change.*
Middle school feeder pattern schools			
State university teacher prep program			
State university Latino institute			
Johnston Youth Development Program			
Police dept. and division of social services			

Principal Speaks About
Developing and Sustaining a Strong PDS Partnership

Cynthia Slotkin

Jefferson Elementary School, New Rochelle, NY

In 7 years, Jefferson Elementary School in New Rochelle, New York, went from a failing school to a school of excellence. What sets Jefferson Elementary apart from other schools is a keen focus on analyzing data and cultivating thoughtful teacher leaders who have meaningful opportunities for professional development to improve student achievement. Jefferson Elementary, in partnership with Manhattanville College, is now in its third year as a professional development school (PDS). Collectively, we have created a highly professional learning environment for all students, their families, and the staff. Together, we have built a living, thinking organization.

(continued on next page)

(continued from previous page)

Using a systems approach, the PDS partnership offers opportunities for teachers to develop their instructional skills by working with an in-house liaison from the college who is on site 2½ days a week. The liaison has the time to get to know the teaching staff and is able to assist teachers by helping them reflect on their literacy practice through modeling and analysis of teaching strategies. By building leadership capacity within the teaching staff, the liaison and the principal share ideas to create a unified vision for increased student learning. Through the partnership, there is a forum for the principal to come together with other PDS partners to share expertise and learn more about advancing leadership.

The partnership between Jefferson Elementary and Manhattanville College is continuously evolving. At first, the priority was on meaningful student teaching assignments and learning how to develop trust between the liaison, the principal, and the staff within a college connection. It was important that the right match be made regarding the personalities and expertise of the principal and the liaison. Over time, through discussions and a celebration of mutual successes, professional development now includes in-house, field-work courses, mentoring for teachers with a focus on literacy, on-site graduate coursework, student teachers working in the after-school program, and hiring new teaching staff from Manhattanville College. By including student teachers in the fabric of the school, from fieldwork through internships, fledgling teachers become immersed in a positive and rigorous academic culture. Parents and students visit the college so that they become familiar with educational possibilities beyond high school. Through the partnership, Manhattanville College offers 50% tuition reimbursement to a deserving student with a 3.5 average who graduates from New Rochelle High School. As a result of the professional development school partnership between Manhattanville College and Jefferson Elementary School, there is a continual challenge to do better, to create, and to never settle for what is. The conversation is always about how we can better serve our students and the community.

STARTING, STRUCTURING, AND SUSTAINING STRONG PARTNERSHIPS

Although none of these processes is as linear as any writer might try to make it, here are some steps you might find helpful in setting up and sustaining a partnership:

- Get ready to partner; know how and with whom to proceed.
- Find and evaluate potential partners.

- Establish partnerships: set up structures, forge agreements, and find resources.
- Celebrate successes and keep track of progress toward your purpose.

Get Ready

The first step in building a strong foundation for a partnership is, perhaps counterintuitively, to look within. You have already given some thought to purpose—to being clear and public and jargon free about your purpose. That clarity and transparency form the motivation for, as well as the basis of, any partnership. A second introspective task is, before beginning a search for partners, to think about how good a partner your own school, university, or other organization would be. How open are you and your colleagues to outsiders? If change is on the agenda of a partnership, how "innovation ready" is your own organization? What is the internal culture among the adults like in regard to collegiality, experimentation, and high expectations?

Some organizations are more open than others, more comfortable sharing information on what is really going on inside, and more willing to listen to the voices and opinions of others. Organizations that are more open to outsiders will generally more readily form partnerships. To assess yours, generate some questions to ask yourself and your colleagues about how you respond to outsiders. For example, when faculty and staff transfer into your organization and have some different ideas about how to do things, do they run into a strong wall of "that's not the way we do it here" comments?

Another set of internal questions is about commitment and depth. How long of a commitment are you ready to make and for what? What is it that you want to get from the relationship? Is your partnership about transactional coordination or transformative change? It helps to think about this ahead of time, even though getting to a transformative partnership is almost always a developmental process and one that cannot always be fully predicted at the outset. I think it can be helpful if potential partners see and express mutual and simultaneous renewal as a goal, although I also know of places that paid their "partnership dues" and built enough trust on mostly transactional issues to take on deeper challenges.

After doing some internal work about your purpose and readiness to partner, go to the list you generated earlier to do some sorting and prioritizing. For this start-up section, focus on those potential partners where there is little or no connection, but where you see the possibilities for transactional and maybe even transformative relationships.

Think strategically about each relationship and the potential it has for helping your organization reach its purpose. Also think about reciprocity, since the strongest partnerships are mutual, through which both benefit at the transactional level and (for transformative relationships) both are learning from each other. Think also about the big picture—how you are managing your overall portfolio of partnerships? Are you able to see and foster some interconnectivity among your partners that can enhance their work and their impact on your purpose? At the same time, think about who is not at the table. Caught up in the excitement and the bona fide benefits that come out of professional development schools, partners sometimes fail to look at who is participating and who is not. Many PDSs, for example, are relationships between faculty and administrators from schools and from teacher education programs. The deepening of the relationships between these two sectors can bring about a great deal of positive energy and improvements for students and preservice and inservice educators (Murrell, 1998). But they can also limit, or even damage, the partnership by excluding others who could and should be engaged. Arts and science faculty members are often omitted, although they provide more of the instruction of (and, therefore, arguably have more influence on) preservice educators than teacher education faculty do. Parents and community members passionately interested in the education of their children and youth may be excluded—actually shut out as the school/teacher education relationships strengthen, possibly reducing the partnership's effectiveness in addressing diversity and equity issues. Furthermore, narrowly focused PDS partnerships may miss opportunities to connect with larger issues and forces in their communities. Business roundtables may have keen interests and ideas for teacher education and school improvement. PreK–16 councils or neighborhood revitalization tasks forces may provide opportunities to connect on larger and compatible sets of issues (Teitel, 2003).

Find and Evaluate Potential Partners

Once you have done the internal work regarding what you want and why, and have thought about which additional partners make sense to help you achieve your purpose, seek and develop relationships with potential partners. Take the list you generated and figure out how to meet those that have high potential. And although partnerships are between and among organizations, they are started and maintained by people. Initial contact can be made through professional organizations, introductions by third parties, individual (personal) networking, or even cold calls. Professional development school networks and preK–16 collaboratives (which exist in many states) can play roles as "matchmakers" for schools, universities, and others interested in partnering. You will find that often there is already some basic connection with the potential partners on your list, or a third party individual or organization that both of you connect with, who might make an introduction. Many partnerships grow out of individual connections—sometimes a neighbor or a friend can help make a connection to an organization on your list. You can send out requests for a partnership, as one enterprising group of teachers in a Massachusetts middle school did—sending letters of introduction and invitation to nearby universities until they got a response that led to a long-running collaboration. Other sources include local and regional conferences, state departments of education, existing larger PDS collaboratives that might be looking for new members, community groups, or faith-based organizations. Unions or teacher associations might be sources of contacts, or be interested themselves, as might public education funders or other organizations for school reform and improvement.

Once contact is made or a possible partner is identified, there is a whole set of questions that potential partners want to ask about one another, usually in the beginning stages, focusing on potential for compatibility, a common purpose, and trust. Some questions you might ask are listed below. They can be used informally and holistically, or you might use them in a more formal way, assigning points for each potential partner in each category and tallying the points. The questions listed are only suggestive—there will probably be others you wish to add (adapted from Teitel, 2003):

1. *Philosophy.* Does {potential partner} share matching or at least compatible approaches to teaching and learning with us?
2. *Proximity.* If it is relevant, are we close enough to {potential partner} for easy connections and travel?
3. *Historical relationship.* Has our experience with {potential partner} been positive, or at least neutral, or is there some organizational baggage that may get in the way?
4. *Interpersonal connections.* Are there people-to-people connections already in place with {potential partner} or will we have to start from the beginning?
5. *Supportive environment.* Does {potential partner} have clear support in its own organization to form a partnership, or might it be constrained by larger forces?

All these questions are designed to help prospective partners get to the first stage of partnership formation, what Ron Ferguson (1999) describes as the foundational step when "initiators find enough trust and interest among potential allies to justify proceeding" (p. 278). Ferguson's "interest" relates to what I have been calling common purpose, or sense of interdependency. And trust—that all-important building block for partnerships—can be defined as whether or not potential partners find that the other parties are competent, collegial, dependable, and have good motives (Ferguson, 1999; see also Covey, 2006). See sidebar vignette by Cynthia Slotkin.

Establish Partnerships: Set Up Structures, Forge Agreements, and Find Resources

Finding an organization that you trust and with whom you can see a common or interdependent purpose is the first step in partnership formation—necessary but not sufficient. Trust and common sense of purpose only get you so far without some sort of container in which the partnership can operate and develop. Once a foundation of trust is established, partners need to develop the agreements and structures to sort out issues of power, turf, and priorities; reach agreements on what they separately and together will be doing; and commit to and hold each other accountable for that work. (Ferguson, 1999; see also strong parallels to Lencioni's [2002] development of teams.) The details of which governance structure is best for you, how to write a partnership agreement, or where to secure resources for your partnership will vary by sector and situation. I suggest a few guiding principles:

- Set up governance structures that meet immediate needs, provide a container for development, and keep a long-term focus on broader goals and future possibilities.
- Forge partnership agreements that set up reciprocity and at least allow for future (and deeper) connection.
- Find resources through repurposing, exchanging, and creatively crossing boundaries in ways that capitalize on the comparative advantages of each party to the partnership.

Governance. I find it helpful to think of four sets of start-up tasks that partnership governance structures must address. Whatever governance structure you pick has to manage day-to-day tasks, build bridges between the partnering organizations, support mutual renewal, and assess and plan for the long term. Each is elaborated below. For details of the pros and cons of using the three basic governance structures of liaison arrangements, steering committees, and multi-site coordinating councils, see Teitel, 2003, or Teitel, 1998, from which the following is adapted.

- *Manage day-to-day tasks.* Governance bodies need to manage the immediate, short-term needs of the collaborative, including the securing and allocation of resources (people, time, and money) as institutional linkages.
- *Build bridges.* Because PDSs are formed between and among dissimilar organizations (schools, universities, and other partners), governance has to provide opportunities to air philosophical differences, sort out

the different goals and "turf" issues, and establish what activities are common and what are primarily the domain of one institution.

- *Support mutual renewal.* When PDS partnerships promote a simultaneous and mutual renewal agenda, their governance structures must go beyond merely linking two stable organizations; they must include roles for participants to play in each other's change processes, and must figure out ways for the new, joint governance to mesh with the preexisting structures of each organization even as the joint structure grows to take on increasingly important decision-making authority.
- *Assess and plan for the long term.* Governance bodies need to think long range in ways that facilitate the renewal process, assess progress, address the long-range needs and interests of each partner and of the collaborative, and secure stable revenue streams for the time and money needed.

In the start-up phase, while focused on meeting the day-to-day challenges of creating a partnership, this assessment is probably the last thing on your mind, or anyone else's. Yet it is important to think about this from the outset for several reasons. From a technical perspective, it is important to collect, from the beginning, baseline data for assessing your progress and impacts as a partnership. Second, long-range planning is essential for short-range day-to-day decisions— if you don't know where you are going as a partnership, it is hard to keep a focus and forward motion. Finally, it is critical as a philosophical stance. It helps you and your partners keep sight of why you got involved in the PDS in the first place. It allows you to use the organizing structure of the partnership from the beginning to provide opportunities to establish processes that keep bringing it back to its initial goals. Some partnerships, especially those in a multi-site network, have annual retreats that serve as assessments on the year gone by, reflection on progress toward goals, and long-range planning sessions—representing a good time to reconnect to purpose.

Partnership Agreements. There are advantages and disadvantages to having formal, written partnership agreements. If and when you decide to formalize a partnership agreement, you and your partners should take some time to think through what the document should look like, who should sign it, and so forth. Guiding principles include reciprocity—not just because it maximizes learning for both (or all) parties, but because it increases the sustainability if all parties are clearly benefiting. Furthermore, partnership agreements should have the flexibility to grow and to allow participating organizations to get into deeper and broader relationships. Below is a list of questions that may be used as a springboard to creating a partnership agreement. For additional sample partnership agreements for PDSs, see Teitel (1998).

- Do you want to have a statement of shared beliefs that underlies the agreement?
- Who should be the signatories and at what levels of the partnering organizations are they?
- What resources should be committed and by whom? Will there be any money changing hands (compensation for teachers, for example) or are the exchanges "in kind"?
- How will decisions about resources be made and, in general, what roles and organizing structures will be built in, or assumed by the agreement?
- Do you think the agreement should be open ended or have a fixed number of years for its duration and/or a point at which it is reviewed and possibly renewed?
- How explicit do you want to be about issues of mutual renewal and change?
- Do you want to build in any kind of assessment and, if so, what kind, prepared by whom, and for whose review?
- How should any new governance structures put into place in the agreement interact with existing structures in any of the participating organizations?

Resources. Partnerships take time. No matter how tightly purposed and focused, there are always collaboration costs—the most obvious being the time that key players need to put into developing trust, finding a common focus, and so on. Sometimes partners seek external funding to help defray these costs or incentivize the start-up. Indeed, external monies can help stimulate partnership opportunities, and collaborations that are well thought out can be attractive to funders. When funders are seeking deeper system change, they can respond favorably when two or more organizations, each of which holds a piece of the puzzle on a societal challenge, work together in a transformative or even a transactional way. At the same time, for deeper, long-term relationships, you will do well to try to repurpose internal resources. Build partnership and outward-focusing activities into job descriptions so partnership work is the core work of what people do. This can increase your sustainability. Finally, consider the ways in which, as your partnership deepens, you can increase trading as a resource strategy.

Some PDSs have made the exchange of services the backbone of their resource strategy. In an early work on PDSs, Case, Norlander, and Reagan (1993) describe how their PDS partnerships use existing resources for core activities and get external jointly written grants to augment their activities. Harris and Harris (1995) describe how several of the partnerships in the National Network for Educational Renewal addressed the challenge of finding time and money through creative exchanges. In one instance, the PDS used money the university would ordinarily pay to part-time student teacher supervisors to hire preservice teachers to work as half-time interns, thereby freeing capable cooperating teachers to supervise other preservice teachers. In another setting, cooperating teachers whose classes were being taught by capable preservice teachers replaced other teachers who were then able to attend professional development workshops and other development opportunities. Harris and Harris note that when dollar values were assigned to these activities, one PDS network (with 23 partner schools) had an operating cost of three quarters of a million dollars that was all exchanged in kind, with no money transferred at all. If this exchange idea is appealing to you, you may find Figure 3.3, adapted from Teitel (2003), useful for seeing what you are currently exchanging and purchasing and for determining ways to stretch to boundaries with your partners.

Overall, as you think about the resources—the people, time, and money— to fuel the work of your partnership, keep coming back to your underlying purpose and the value that your partnership is (presumably) adding to achieving it. The partnership should be helping you better reach your goals—even a transactional relationship should help you get to where you want to go in a cost-effective way.

Celebrate Successes, Reward Partnership Work, and Keep Track of Progress

Once launched, even successful partnerships need continued attention to sustain them. Partnerships need celebrations, acknowledgment, and rewards for joint work, as well as public and transparent tracking of progress toward joint goals.

FIGURE 3.3. Resource Exchange Template

Services, expertise, or other resources	Provided by school	Provided by school district	Purchased from outside collaborative	Provided by university	Provided by community or other partner

Celebrate Successes. Whether it is due to lack of time or some sense that it is too frivolous or self-indulgent, celebrating success is often a neglected aspect of PDSs and other partnerships. Celebration serves several purposes. It lets individuals know that the extra work they are doing as part of the partnership is valuable and valued (by their organization). It helps create a virtual cycle, where effort in collaborative ventures leads visibly to payoffs that matter. And it communicates to less involved individuals in the partnering organizations that this work matters. This is particularly important for newer members of your organization, who might not have been involved in the launch of the partnership and might not have as much understanding of why it is being pursued (Teitel, 2003).

There are both internal and external dimensions to this. Do you celebrate among the insiders—the folks doing the PDS work? Is evidence of it on the walls (at the university as well as the school), written up in internal newsletters, shared in celebration at various parties and public events? In addition, do stakeholders outside know of your work? Does a banner fly over the school proclaiming its PDS status and connection to the university? Do the schools and school district have a comparable place of visibility and celebration at the university or with any other partners? Are the joint accomplishments shared and celebrated at the central office of the district, or in the upper echelons of the university? Figure 3.4 provides a quick tool for helping you think systematically about celebrating your partnership's successes.

FIGURE 3.4. Celebrating Partnership Successes

Venue	What we are doing	What we could be doing	Who will follow this up
Internal Celebrations			
Visible evidence (walls, bulletin boards, etc.)			
Internal newsletter			
Parties, shows of appreciation			
Other			
Outside Stakeholders:			
At university			
At school district			
At other partner(s)			
For general public			
Other			

Reward Partnership Work. Celebrations will help you and your organization recognize the value of partnership work. It also makes sense to take a look at the hard work that partnership participants do—in many cases over and above their current jobs—and look at the ways in which your partnership and its partnering organizations value and reward the work. Below are three broad areas of possible reward (adapted from Teitel, 2003).

- *Recognition.* What kind of recognition and appreciation do participants get? Are there awards ceremonies; mentions in newsletters and publications of the partnering organizations; thank-yous from presidents, provosts, deans, superintendents, principals, nonprofit directors; and so on?
- *Feedback on impacts.* How are data collected and shared that show the impact the PDS is having (on students, on adults, on the community), so participants know that what they are doing matters and is effective?
- *Rewards (pay increases, promotion, tenure).* Does extra work in the PDS lead to extra pay, or other compensation (in time or other resources)? Does it count for promotion? Have you revamped your university's promotion and tenure guidelines (as several universities engaged in PDS now have) to give weight to PDS work? Are PDS participants able to do their PDS work as part of their job?

Track Progress Toward Partnership Goals. I have seen partners connect and jell with each other and even develop thriving partnerships that do, over time, lose sight of their deeper purpose and greatest potential. It is critical for partners to "keep their eye on the prize" and regularly reconnect with the sense of underlying purpose that brought them together.

I recommend regular and periodic retreats at which partners reassess the purposes that brought them together and take stock of their progress as a way of framing a deeper agenda. This is a way to both strengthen and reaffirm the commitment that even a transactional relationship takes and to investigate the possibilities of a more transformative arrangement that can lead to deeper learning and renewal.

DEEPENING PARTNERSHIPS
FOR MUTUAL ORGANIZATIONAL LEARNING

This section returns to one of the central ideas of this chapter—developing transformative partnerships. Whether you are working with a start-up partnership or deciding that it is worth trying to move an existing transactional relationship to a more transformative one, there are several guiding principles you may find helpful. This section assumes that there are structures and partnership agreements in place and that there is at least some relational trust in place, along with a willingness to see interdependencies and to learn how to tackle tough issues. Furthermore, in keeping with the recurrent theme in this chapter—that strong partnerships start with deep introspection and powerful groundwork within your own organization—the discussion assumes that your organization knows what it hopes to learn from and with your partner. With that groundwork done (building on the partnership formation ideas in the previous sections), you will want to (1) identify ways to surface content areas of mutual engagement to work on interdependently and (2) put into place processes that will help support the difficult work of mutual renewal.

Identify Potentially Transformative Content Areas

This can be done in several ways. For existing partnerships with some history and relationships with one another, a quick way is to simply ask participants for the tough issues that have arisen that nobody seems to want to discuss. Usually the internal members of a partnership know what their partnership needs to work on. They need to engage their colleagues in those tough issues and develop the will and skill to tackle them.

A second approach is to focus on an area for which one or both (all) partners feel stuck. For example, if potential partners are able to clearly acknowledge their struggles in doing so, they could lay the foundation for a transformative, learning partnership.

Another path is to have partnership members talk explicitly about the shared purpose and interdependencies. When John Carter looked more closely at one of the relationships with the Johnston Youth Development Program (JYDP), he saw they were underutilizing this program. The JYDP is about peer leadership and keeping kids out of gangs and in school and has an aggressive and active outreach to youth. They also have a different way of holding the kids in their programs accountable, with a much more relational approach than the fairly traditional and punishment-oriented discipline approach of JHS. John wondered if some of those ideas could be brought into the high school. He knew it might be tough to talk about this to his faculty colleagues, who suspected the JYDP of "coddling" gang members, but he was starting to see that they had the same goals he and his colleagues had—keeping kids in school, away from gangs and drugs, and learning citizenship.

Support the Difficult Work of Mutual Renewal

To do this work requires participants to see the big picture but address specifics, to recognize the deeper change issues that each organization might face, to be comfortable dealing with productive conflict, and to draw on strengths and commonalities to build trust for dealing with tough issues even while crossing over organizational boundaries. And, as in any of the partnership types discussed here, it requires a relentless reconnection and calibration about purpose.

CONCLUDING REMARKS

Partnerships are hard work, especially those that are truly transformative. For these partnerships to develop, a genuine recognition of common purpose and mutual interdependence, between the partners and with others outside their organizations, must occur among the members. Mutual support is critical; partners serve as allies in the change process at each other's institutions, recognizing that behind each of them, there are dozens of skeptical faculty and reluctant naysayers. Partners must keep the broad goals in mind, while working with each other and their colleagues on the details of the change. They must agree as to when a new approach will be used, as well as how they will react when there is pressure not to use it but, rather, to stay with the status quo. They must work together to assure changes in curriculum and pedagogy when necessary and must also approach how to prepare those persons teaching the curriculum and pedagogy. They must create contexts and containers for the messy painful details of change to be confronted honestly by participants at all partnering institutions. They must keep checking—publicly and transparently—on how they are all doing, moving toward their larger shared purpose.

And finally, the partners must trust each other enough to work together in a sustained and transformative way—to learn from and with one another, as individuals and organizational partners. They will need to have the vision and the skills discussed in this chapter, but they will also need courage: courage of conviction; courage of belief; and courage that their partnering matters. For me, this work is driven by the deep belief that without each other, we are inadequate to face the task of educating all children so they can thrive in our society. If we take seriously our commitment to children, we do not really have a choice. We cannot keep walking away from or not talking to people we don't like, or keep feeling self-satisfied by the partial gains made by our transactional partnerships. We must climb on. We must work and learn from each other and with each other. Our commitment to children leaves us no other choice.

REFERENCES

Case, C. W., Norlander, K. A., & Reagan, T. (1993). Cultural transformation in an urban professional development center: Policy implications for school-university collaboration. *Educational Policy, 7*(1), 40–60.

Covey, S. R. (2006). *The speed of trust.* New York: Free Press.

Ferguson, R. (1999). Conclusion: Social science research, urban problems, and community development alliances. In R. F. Ferguson & W. T. Dickens (Eds.), *Urban problems and community development* (pp. 569–610). New York: Brookings Institute.

Gajda, R. (2004). Utilizing collaboration theory to evaluate strategic alliances. *American Journal of Evaluation, 25*(1), 65.

Harris, C., & Harris, M. (1995). Launching and sustaining a partner school. In R. Osguthorpe (Ed.), *Partner schools: Centers for educational renewal* (pp. 127–165). San Francisco: Jossey-Bass.

Lencioni, P. (2002). *The five dysfunctions of a team: A leadership fable.* San Francisco: Jossey-Bass.

Murrell, P. (1998). *Like stone soup.* Washington, DC: American Association of Colleges for Teacher Education.

Sirotnik, K. A., & Goodlad, J. I. (Eds.). (1988). *School-university partnerships in action.* New York: Teachers College Press.

Teitel, L. (1996). Getting down to cases: Tackling the "undiscussable" issues of professional development school partnerships, *Contemporary Education, 67*(4), 200–205.

Teitel, L. (1998). *Governance: Developing professional development school governance structures.* Washington, DC: American Association for Colleges of Teacher Education Publications.

Teitel, L. (2003). *The professional development school handbook: Starting, sustaining, and assessing partnerships that improve student learning.* Thousand Oaks, CA: Corwin Press.

Teitel, L. (2008). School/university collaboration: The power of transformative partnerships. *Childhood Education, 85*(2), 75–80.

4

Sustaining Partnerships

Diane Yendol-Hoppey,
David Hoppey, and Ted Price

This chapter discusses

- what partnership means and ways to sustain a partnership,
- the meaning of a collaborative partnership, and
- barriers and facilitators to sustaining partnerships.

Sustaining collaborative partnerships requires a great deal of attention from those who broker partnership relationships. Brokering is a process of mediating between the organizations that comprise a partnership. As an illustration, let's eavesdrop on a conversation held after the American Education Research Association Professional Development School (PDS) Special Interest Group meeting for leaders of professional development schools. This group, which has been involved with partnership work for about a decade, has been getting together over the years to share dilemmas, identify similar threads of success, and offer advice and support.

* * *

The initial conversations began with personal updates that reflected the relationships that we had developed over the years, "How are your children?" "What did you do for your sabbatical?" "How was your trip to China?" and many others. Just as always, we found our conversations drift toward the dilemmas we were each experiencing as a part of our collaborative professional development school work. We began inquiring, "So what's new at work?"

This year, our dilemmas seemed different. Sensing a new frustration, Sonja began, "One would have thought that my state's belief in PDS would have been a good thing but it is not. I am not sure what to do because the state has now mandated PDS partnerships and this mandate has led to less effective PDS work. Everyone is a PDS now and that is beginning to mean nothing."

Terrance listened with great interest, nodding his head as Sonja spoke, and then he added, "There are definitely more PDSs every year but the accountability press has definitely shifted the nature of the work in our partnership. More and more schools are finding it hard to dedicate the time to PDS work. They are often unable to see how a PDS can help them navigate the accountability movement rather than compete with it."

John added, "Our work is now really complicated by the fact that the initial planning money that we had in the early years has dried up. Our partnership relied on these assets to pay participants for extra hours and extra duties. Those resources helped us create a shared partnership vision, blended roles, and a focus on both teacher education and school improvement. As the money disappears, I am seeing dedication disappear as well."

Diane nodded with interest as she heard the group collaboratively wrestling with these new dilemmas. She too voiced concern about the shifting nature of the key participants in the PDS over the last decade in the partnerships where she worked. Many teachers were retiring and leaders who weren't a part of generating the original vision were replacing many school leaders. Those who began the vision were not the same folks now trying to enact the vision.

Although the dilemmas emerged in different forms and often from different sources, these partnership leaders knew by the end of the evening that they were experiencing challenges associated with the sustainability of their work—the work that they had so passionately fought for, the work that required a great deal of relationship building, energy, and negotiation. Perhaps it was time for these collaborative leaders to think about strategies they could utilize to sustain their collaborative partnerships.

* * *

Over the course of the evening, as these collaborative leaders made their partnership dilemmas public to each other, the threads that wove their stories together began to emerge. Rather than adopting a "smoke and mirrors" approach in hope that these concerns would not be discovered by others, the "keepers of the partnership torch" did not fear that the emerging challenges would position them as poor leaders or hurt, compromise, or dismantle the partnership. Instead, by making challenges public they began to expose "the elephants in the room" and began sharing what they had learned about sustaining their partnership. These partnership leaders recognized that sustainability relies on partnership evolution rather than maintaining the original partnership.

DEFINITION OF TERMS

Sustainability and *partnership* are both terms that often lack conceptual clarity, and as a result, are worthy of defining here. Often people think of sustainability as maintaining the status quo over time. However, in reviewing the historical roots of the term, sustainability is really about both developing what matters *and* preserving what matters to the partnership. This does not represent "either-or" thinking but rather highlights the importance of "and-both" thinking. Sustained partnerships consider when it is advantageous to develop the partnership in new directions and when it is advantageous for the partnership to preserve aspects of its existing work.

We draw on Michael Fullan's (2005) definition of sustainability as the capacity of a partnership to engage in the complexities of continuous improvement consistent with deep values of human purpose. Similarly, Hargreaves and Fink (2003) describe sustainability as the act of "enabling people to adapt and prosper in their increasingly complex environment" while "building long-term capacity for improvement" (p. 694). Sustaining a partnership requires continuous shared learning focused on shared values among the stakeholders. Let's explore an example of this by eavesdropping on a governance committee discussion at a professional development school:

> I think we are recognizing that we can't remain static and operate exactly the same way as we have in the past. So many things have changed. We are over five times the size we were in the beginning. With the entry of new PDS leadership, new superintendents, new deans, and new department chairs, there is a lot of change. The question is how can we embrace the new ideas being brought to the partnership in a way that strengthens our work and moves it to the next level. You know, our dean is very interested in diversity and globalization. That is really a good thing for our program, the community, the college, our students. She is trying to provide an opportunity for all the stakeholders to have access to more diverse and global perspectives. On top of that, our new director is really trying to integrate more university faculty into the field and create more opportunities for university faculty and public school faculty to work side by side on shared interests, both global and local. She is trying to make sure that we are "walking the talk" of simultaneous renewal and inquiry

expected as a part of PDS accountability. Our sustainability is going to require embracing new ideas when they can enhance our work, while still protecting the foundational underpinnings of contextual and situated learning which is so important to the tenants of PDS work.

Diverse and sometimes loose applications of the term *partnership* also present conceptual complications for collaboration. Although many partnership typologies exist, we focus on collaborative partnerships, which can lead to transformative and generative activities as partners come together to work on shared goals. In defining *transformative* and *generative*, we borrow from the work of Mezirow (2000), who describes a learning process of "becoming critically aware of one's own tacit assumptions and expectations and those of others and assessing their relevance" (Mezirow, 2000, p. 4). In true collaborative partnerships, the partners collaboratively explore their assumptions, methods, and goals in a way that honors the expertise of all partners and produces new shared knowledge. The partners believe that their goals could not be achieved as efficiently or effectively by their individual organization. The result is a highly shared endeavor in which members eventually commit themselves as much to their common goal as to the interests of their own organization.

BARRIERS AND FACILITATORS TO SUSTAINING PARTNERSHIPS

Collaborative partnerships experience numerous challenges as they negotiate the natural ebbs and flows of organizational and environmental change. This section of the chapter addresses a dozen challenges associated with sustaining collaboration across preK–12 and higher education settings and provides insights for collaborative leaders. These challenges include (a) differing cultural profiles of school-university partners, (b) commitment of organizational leadership, (c) commitment of partnership leadership, (d) commitment of teachers and faculty, (e) commitment of stakeholders, (f) ability to move from congeniality to collegiality, (g) the degree of persistence, creativity, and patience that the partnership exhibits, (h) how the partners address mission contraction, mission creep, or mission misunderstandings, (i) the quality of community response, (j) the ability to collect partnership effectiveness data, (k) resource availability, and (l) communication between and among stakeholders. As facilitators of three different types of collaborative partnerships—professional development schools, school-university inclusion partnerships, and countywide partnerships designed to support at-risk students—we will share key concepts and practical examples of these partnership sustainability challenges culled from our own partnership experiences.

Differing Cultural Profiles of School-University Partners

Sustainability of a school-university partnership is complex since partnerships are composed of organizations with inherently different cultures. Additionally, these partners' organizational cultures don't remain static but rather shift over time.

Over 2 decades ago, James Leming wrote an article titled *The Two Cultures of Social Studies Education* in which he outlined the differences between public school and higher education faculty in their approach to curriculum as well as change. He discussed the gulf between the professoriate in higher education and the teachers within the public schools (Leming, 1989). Leming noted that a critical mass of faculty in higher education were rewarded for actively promoting major change in society and schools, whereas public school teachers were often encouraged to preserve traditional values and practices within their teaching context.

Universities have greater flexibility in hiring staff, often pay people on the basis of merit, reward individualism, change curricula, and face far less influence by labor unions. While higher education has its own economic and political challenges, public schools today face enormous accountability pressures that make time and resources increasingly precious. These organizational differences are important to understand when trying to sustain collaborative school-university partnerships. When school and university faculty have the opportunity to develop understanding of each other's cultures, we have a better chance of obtaining a successful, sustained partnership and improving teaching, learning, and services for all.

In order to further understand the importance of interorganization cultural knowledge in sustaining partnerships, let's examine the term *culture*. According to Schein (2004), culture refers to a pattern of shared assumptions that has shaped the organization. The process includes both external adaptation and internal integration. *External adaptation* refers to survival within the external environment. In public schools today, external adaptation emerges as schools struggle to survive within a context challenged by limited resources and high-stakes accountability. In today's universities, faculty are encouraged to respond to external demands such as entrepreneurial opportunities promoted by government, industry, and public services, as well as to compete individually for status. These external adaptations shape the nature of each organizational culture in different ways, often creating a cultural divide between partnering organizations.

Simultaneously, internal integration is occurring, which also helps define an organization's culture. *Internal integration* refers to the organization's focus on internal processes to ensure survival. Public schools strive to become more efficient, effective, and focused by targeting very specific accountability goals. On the other hand, universities strive to align resources to mission statements and long-range plans that seek to revitalize teaching, scholarship, and service.

Internal integration can also challenge sustainability as individual organizations shift internal processes to adjust to accountability demands.

Adaptation and integration by the partnership creates a distinctive culture composed of shared language, traditions, standards, values, mission, ways of thinking, meanings, roles, rewards, responsibilities, attitudes, and beliefs. Partners position themselves for success when they understand their partner's culture and are able to create a shared culture within their partnership.

Cultural differences create complexity as partners begin to conduct, adapt, and integrate shared work. Given that each organization brings a unique culture to the partnership, in sustaining our partnership we make a choice to (a) merge or blur cultural boundaries between organizations, (b) maintain organizational separation, or (c) create a new organization located somewhere in the middle. Figure 4.1 illustrates the way partners may choose to work together.

Figure 4.1. Three Ways Organizations May Choose to Work Together

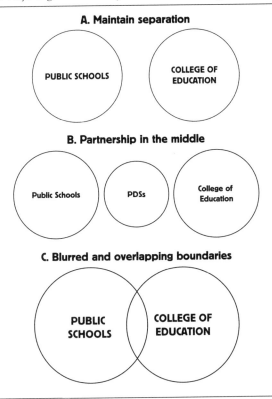

We suggest that merging and blurring cultural boundaries to create partnerships, although most difficult due to cultural differences between partners, is most likely to lead to *collaborative* partnership sustainability. Maintaining separation typically limits a partnership to "coordination," "communication," or "cooperative" functions. Creating an "organization in the middle" composed of participants from each organization, although attractive and able to be collaborative in nature, is risky with respect to sustainability. Unless that "organization in the middle" is composed of active participants from all levels within both organizations who can continually meet together to construct and maintain a shared vision and create funding streams that can maintain the middle organization, the organization in the middle will likely not sustain itself.

The State College Area School District/Pennsylvania State Professional Development School Partnership, composed of one school district with 11 professional development schools, illustrates the notion of merged and blurred boundaries. Within the partnership, the leadership of both organizations collaboratively identify two to three public school teachers who move out of their classrooms for a 2- to 3-year period and work with prospective teachers, practicing teachers, principals, and university course instructors. At the same time, university faculty members are released from their workload to work in schools on curriculum-based projects that the teachers see as promising for their schools and that lead to faculty research productivity. It is not unusual to see a science faculty member co-teaching in the public schools or a public school teacher co-teaching a methods course. Additionally, the university and schools have created methods course teams composed of school and university faculty who generate curriculum for prospective teachers as well as school and university faculty who serve together on curriculum committees to generate curriculum for public school students. By blurring boundaries to support a partnership, both partners gain insight and understanding of each organizational culture and use scarce resources wisely.

Another example that creates blurred roles for interorganizational cultural understanding can be drawn from the West Virginia University Benedum Collaborative's efforts. A mechanism was created to bring the university and public school faculty together to prepare high-quality teachers. Three adjustments were made that shifted the partnership from "the middle" to a more shared endeavor with overlapping roles. First, faculty workload was adjusted to promote engaged scholarship. This allowed faculty to engage in research while at the same time contributing to the mission of simultaneous renewal. Second, teachers joined university faculty to teach courses on campus and share the responsibility for supervising students. This allowed teachers to spend time blending their craft knowledge with the theoretical knowledge included in university courses and positioned the school-based teacher educators to help prospective teachers make connections between theory and practice. Finally, the meeting structure was changed. Instead of teachers and university faculty meeting separately about teacher education dilemmas, a space was created for them to meet together to plan for program improvement. This allowed the work to become "a part of" what the participants are doing rather than "an addition to." By having teachers and university faculty sitting side by side, they can make the important conceptual and practical links necessary to reach the partnership goals.

When partners can participate in each other's work spaces, that develops intercultural understanding and strengthens capacity. By providing opportunities to live in each other's organizational cultures, the partners develop new knowledge together that continually breathes life into the partnership and strengthens sustainability.

Commitment of Organizational Leaders

Partnerships involve many leaders. Leaders exist at the top of each organization, and embedded in the partnering organizations are leaders who are specifically responsible for maintaining the partnership work. One aspect that influences the sustainability of a partnership is each organization's leadership commitment to collaboration. Since collaboration is a process whereby organizations share common goals, imperative to sustainability is that leadership from all levels embrace a commitment to a shared mission. Leadership within each organization must be willing to embrace a shared mission and provide the resources and time needed for the shared work. This requires attending to shifting demands and resource allocation.

An example of various organizational leaders coming together to support a common goal is the Collaborative for Special Needs Children in Orange County, California. This collaborative was formed by leaders from the University of California, Orange County Department of Education, the 27 school districts in Orange County, and officials from the juvenile court system. The leadership united across multiple agencies to better serve children in need of special education services. They sought to find collaborative ways to provide services and control escalating costs. As a result of the organization's leadership actualizing this goal, the collaborative was expanded to include the probation department, the social services agency, and the Orange County Health Care Agency. This interagency collaboration strengthened sustainability by sharing scarce resources to achieve shared outcomes.

Commitment of Partnership Leaders

Leadership also exists within the partnership. According to Ansett (2005), the partnership leaders "do not necessarily lead from a position of public status or externally conferred authority. They are often hidden within organizations, in different guises and at various levels, and may not be immediately identifiable as leaders" (p. 38). These leaders serve as brokers or boundary spanners who rarely receive recognition or acknowledgment for their work, yet they are critical to achieving the partnership's goals.

This concept of partnership leadership *boundary spanning* is essential to the sustainability of a collaborative partnership. Boundary spanners are leaders within the partnership who identify and share information that facilitates the partnership mission. Let's take a look at boundary spanning in action by review-ing the collaboration of two different PDS networks. One approach to boundary spanning is to focus on the *activities* performed, since activities are the building blocks of a partnership. Our example draws on the work from the State College Area School District/Pennsylvania State University Partnership.

The partnership relies on shared work that leads to consensus building and shared knowledge that strengthens the expertise of all involved. Any decisions are the result of consensus, not votes, and the boundary-spanning opportuni-ties facilitate *frequent decision-making interaction* between key people across the partnership. For example, there are course teams. Public school teachers who are interested in certain methods courses agree to work with a university faculty member that is responsible for the course. During the year, the teachers and university faculty meet regularly to design and deliver a course to prospective teachers and develop lessons for classrooms that demonstrate research-based methods. University faculty co-teach with teachers in their classrooms so that faculty can see the reality of teachers' work. They also engage in teacher re-search together to build an understanding of effective teaching. Teachers and faculty who participate are rewarded in multiple ways (e.g., reduced workload, stipends, course credit, and professional development opportunities). The part-nership provides the opportunity for simultaneous renewal through shared work creating shared understandings of both the university and public school culture as well as the content of each other's work. Simultaneous renewal, an important outcome for sustainability, is based on the notion that improvement by one partner requires interaction with the other partner and that all stakehold-ers are responsible for such improvement. Simultaneous renewal is more likely when those leading the partnership encourage boundary-spanning activities.

Educational environments, characterized by uncertainty and rapid change, present partnerships with immediate constraints and opportunities that re-quire an opportunity for shared decision making to occur in a timely manner. The boundary-spanning activities reflected in the Pennsylvania State Univer-sity illustration appear to be essential to partnership sustainability in a rapidly changing educational world. The partnership leaders play an important role in assuring that these boundary-spanning roles exist and are supported.

Commitment of Teachers and Faculty

A variety of approaches can be taken to cultivate commitment from teachers and faculty. First, including stakeholders in decision making is essential. Public school teachers and university faculty are the people who affect and are affected by a school-university partnership's decisions. Cuban (2001) characterizes reforms that have the least potential for sustainability as those proposed by policy makers and officials who know little about the day-to-day practices of the workplaces they seek to change.

When the participants have an active role in designing the work, commitment typically remains high. For example, within the State College Area School District/Pennsylvania State University Professional Development Schools Partnership, those public school and university faculty who have a shared interest in the partnership goals suggest that the payoff for partnership participation is not monetary. Rather, a sense of camaraderie and renewal emerges from the collaborative work as teachers, public school administrators, and university faculty feel an increased sense of professionalism resulting from the developed partnership relationships. These relationships have been instrumental in helping all parties develop new knowledge about teaching and learning and meet organizational demands such as enhanced preK–12 student learning, improved teacher education, and increased research opportunities for university faculty. Partners who are truly committed to a shared mission that combines resources and roles, cultivates relationships, and achieves success on important individual and collective goals can be powerful and sustainable motivators. This approach to sustainability is much stronger than relying on tenuous resources as a partnership motivator.

Commitment of Stakeholders

The stakeholders' commitment to the partnership is also essential to sustainability. In school-university partnerships, stakeholders include teachers, public school students, their parents, university faculty and administrators, district administrators, and the state department of education. These parties have tremendous influence on the organization's leadership and the success of the partnership. Sustaining a partnership requires ensuring that the partnership is of high quality and benefits them. Stakeholder commitment can facilitate or inhibit a partnership's success. Let's eavesdrop on the voices of professional development school stakeholders in the Alachua County/University of Florida Professional Development School Partnership:

Our children benefit from having two teachers in the classroom.
—Parent

Because of our partnership, I find it much easier to hire excellent faculty even though we are a very rural school. —Principal

I appreciate the partnership because I have learned to work together to make schools and my teaching better. —University faculty member

Although the demands of learning to teach in a school-university partnership are much more intensive, I know that I am prepared to teach. —Intern

These stakeholders recognize and have made public the usefulness of the school-university partnership in meeting their individual needs. This recognition is a key to sustainability.

Ability to Move from Congeniality to Collegiality

One of the most difficult concepts that challenges partnership sustainability is the partnership's ability to move from a culture of *congeniality* to a culture of *collegiality*. Congeniality is a relationship that reflects a pleasant disposition that is friendly and sociable. Congeniality, although helpful, is not enough to create and sustain partnerships. Although important underpinnings to collaboration, positive personal relationships do not contribute significantly to simultaneous renewal.

Fullan (1992) describes another concept that moves beyond congeniality to what he calls *comfortable collegiality*. Comfortable collegiality promotes low levels of collaboration without asking tougher questions at work within the partnership. According to Fullan, comfortable collegiality does not challenge the status quo.

Sustainable collaborative partnerships require strong collegiality. This form of collegiality requires ongoing internal critiques of principles, practices, and assumptions. Dilemmas, failures, and uncertainties are not hidden but are embraced and celebrated. Collaborative partnerships move beyond congeniality to embrace collegiality. Collegiality requires creating a culture that allows partners to become united in a common purpose while respecting one another's abilities. True collegiality sustains partnerships.

An example of a strong collegial partnership is the work at Newberry Elementary School, a member of the Alachua County/University of Florida Professional Development School Partnership. Led by the principal and a university writing professor, the partners reviewed school level writing data to help with writing instruction. After identifying areas of weakness, the partners outlined how they would support one another's understanding of writing reform by sharing resources and expertise.

The university writing professor and her doctoral students began working with the faculty at Newberry Elementary on writing reform. Prospective teachers joined the writing reform effort as well to learn to teach and engage in school improvement. Although a bumpy road, the partners worked collegially by having deep conversations about the meaning of good writing instruction. Beliefs and assumptions were challenged. Hard questions were posed, producing many tensions as partners engaged in building and shifting understandings. However, by working through collegial tensions, a new orientation to writing instruction emerged and student writing gains, as measured on the state test, followed.

Persistence, Creativity, and Patience

Partnership sustainability is enhanced by boundary-spanning persistence, creativity, and patience. Ansett (2005) describes boundary spanning as complex and frustrating, but with time also rewarding. Since partnerships often breed conflict before resolution and growth, boundary spanners that facilitate sustainability demonstrate skills in negotiation and conflict resolution. Commitment to negotiating and resolving conflict is time intensive, exhausting, and a naturally occurring demand that challenges partnerships.

Creativity provides partnership members a chance to work around existing and emerging barriers to collaboration. For example, in sustained professional development school partnerships, stakeholders have creatively staffed teacher education courses by building course teams composed of both university and school-based teacher educators. This creative solution reduces expenses by using adjunct instructors to provide release to university faculty interested in collaborative research with partnership schools. Committed leaders are able to sustain partnerships by engaging in creative problem solving, such as unconventional course staffing. Creativity often requires patience, as leaders build comfort and confidence with partners, leadership, and other stakeholders in exploring outside-of-the-box ways to promote partnership activities.

Let's explore an illustration of persistence, creativity, and patience that occurred during Project INCLUDE, the partnership between the University of Florida's Department of Special Education and the Alachua County Public Schools. The partnership is dedicated to creating inclusive schools and combines the expertise of university and school-based faculty. The partnership provides support for teachers and administrators from partnership schools as they develop and implement inclusive reform. Initial success of the partnership was evident through the increased placement and academic achievement of students with disabilities. However, partnership schools initially did not have district leadership support during the pilot years. While top-level district leaders did not discourage schools from participating, they also did not fully endorse inclusive programming at the start. This left the schools to decide themselves if they wished to participate in inclusive reform. Thus, a lack of district leadership commitment to reform, an important challenge discussed earlier in this chapter, was evident early on in the partnership and limited the initial effectiveness of the project.

Creative and Cooperative Partnering to Develop and Sustain a Program for Students with Developmental Disabilities

Michael Mayton

West Virginia University, Morgantown, WV

The Independence Program at Tennessee Technological University has started its fourth year in Cookeville. It is designed for students with developmental disabilities who are from 18 to 22 years of age. The program is designed to increase competence in domestic, self-care, money management, and vocational skills within age-appropriate settings. The participants, all high school completers, named the program, chose the furnishings for, and set up the university apartment. They now run a personal shopping service for area residents, operate a business making and selling crafts, perform domestic tasks in the apartment, create monthly budgets, plan and cook meals, and work within community job placements. They also plan how to spend their profits to engage in the recreation and leisure activities of their choice, and they have access to university sporting events and facilities. In short, they are in pursuit of an increased quality of life suited to people their age.

Program initiation required cooperation among various university, school board, and high school personnel, but most integral to the partnering process was the teacher who designed specific program components and created the proposal presented to university personnel. Through the university's vice president of Extended Programs, school board personnel established critical contacts, including the provost, the dean of the College of Education, and the director of Residential Life. As a result of the presentation to university administrative personnel, the director of Residential Life was instructed to present a contract in which the school system would pay only the utilities for its use of a university apartment. In addition, a university faculty member in special education was appointed as liaison between the program and university. A state grant initially paid for all expenses, including the teacher's salary, but the school system has been taking on more of the cost to transition from soft money support.

Application of a range of curricular assessments has shown significant increases in participant skill sets, and research conducted by university graduate students has shown significant increases across relevant quality-of-life indicators. Social validity data from participants and their family members continue to be overwhelmingly positive about the perceived benefits of the program. In addition, practicum students in university special education programs benefit through their work with program participants, and all university students have benefited in that the makeup of their campus population is now closer to being like that of the "world at large."

However, in spite of the lack of district-level commitment, strong principal and teacher creativity, persistence, and patience emerged from within the schools. Supported by ongoing coaching and mentoring, the partnership schools began successfully implementing school-based inclusion programs. Paramount to the schools' successful implementation were teacher leaders and principals who became the "vision keepers" that kept inclusive education alive. In most cases, strong teacher leaders and visionary principals creatively worked together to build inclusive classrooms.

Although not planned, the lack of consistent commitment from district leadership up front actually encouraged principal and teacher leader persistence and creativity. As success stories were shared, other schools began to demonstrate interest and as a result district leadership became increasingly supportive. Additionally, as vocal parent advocacy groups began to raise questions about the need for the inclusion partnership at other schools, the district began to explore how to systematically provide inclusive special education services. In the end, creativity, persistence, and patience paid off. A district-based inclusion plan, driven by this partnership, generated sustainable reform for inclusive education throughout the district.

Mission Contraction, Mission Creep, or Mission Misunderstandings

As partnerships grow in size and maturity, the mission often shifts. At times this is healthy and at other times these activities can limit the partnership's effectiveness and even its sustainability. *Mission contraction* occurs when a partnership is not fully attending to enacting its goals in totality. *Mission creep* refers to expanding the partnership beyond its original goals. At times, partnerships engage in mission creep as they recognize that the initial goals are not enough to actualize the power of the collaboration. Finally, *mission misunderstanding* can also emerge as partnerships grow over time without clear attention to maintaining a shared understanding of partnership goals. Each of these can be threats to sustainability.

An example of avoiding mission creep or mission misunderstanding occurred in the Collaborative for Special Needs Children in Orange County, California. Collaboration based on maintaining a shared mission was promoted during regularly scheduled interagency meetings even when different points of view, backgrounds, experiences, and goals existed. Case studies were used to create discussion and consensus building about their mission allowing attendees to walk away maintaining the mission and using their shared expertise to provide services.

Community Response

A community's response to the partnership can also influence a partnership's sustainability. For example, the State College Area School District/Pennsylvania

State University Professional Development School Partnership was uniquely designed as a co-taught, year-long internship. To better support the needs of public school students, the partners placed a preservice teacher with each mentor teacher for a year-long, co-teaching experience. This was a decision designed to support both prospective teacher and student learning. The co-teaching approach created important support from community members since they recognized that placing two teachers in a classroom for the entire school year improved both student and prospective teacher learning. This strengthened the partnership and eventually the community response pressured the partnership to create a district–wide partnership program.

Another example of positive community response occurred when parents provided the pressure needed to change how inclusion operated within one Florida school district. The impetus for special education reform in Alachua County, Florida, actually emerged as a small group of parents rallied a community's commitment to inclusive practices. Inclusive school plans that targeted student placement, school practices, student achievement, and teacher professional development became the norm because of community pressure. Eventually, the district involved the community in developing a shared vision for inclusion and created of a 5-year strategic plan. Other key partners in developing the district initiative were, not only the University of Florida and key parent advocates, but also other community-based collaborative service providers, such as the Florida Inclusion Network, the Florida Diagnostic and Learning Resources System, and the Center for Autism and Related Disabilities. Community response to the collaboration was instrumental in sustaining the partnership's effectiveness to provide inclusive education.

Supportive Data

Related to the community response of sustaining collaborative partnerships is the ongoing challenge of providing supportive data that demonstrate that the partnership's mission is being realized. Within our current accountability context, demonstrating improved outcomes is central to partnership sustainability. Partnerships strengthen their credibility as they share empirical data to demonstrate the partnership's effectiveness. For instance, the State College Area School District/ Pennsylvania State University Professional Development School Partnership collected teacher, administrator, prospective teacher, and public school student data to identify the benefits of the partnership. Additionally, the district reviewed data that identified the PDS partnership as a vehicle for providing a pool of exceptional candidates for district teaching positions. As a result of collecting this data, the partnership was able to make the case for the resources needed to create additional blended roles as the network began to expand district wide. The additional blended roles created more opportunities for additional teachers to come out of their classrooms and serve as a bridge between university and schools, which strengthened the partnership. Additionally, by expanding the partnership to all district schools, teachers had access to partnership professional development resources, and the university secured additional increased PDS student placements.

The Alachua County Inclusion Initiative also provides a powerful example of how a partnership uses data to sustain an initiative. This partnership strengthened its sustainability by demonstrating improved student achievement as measured by high-stakes accountability measures. The Inclusion Initiative data included both qualitative and quantitative measures. Over the first 3 years of the initiative, the proverbial achievement gap began to close as standardized test results for students with disabilities included in general education classrooms dramatically improved for participating schools. As a result of sharing this data, the partnership spread to other Alachua County Schools. Students at risk for failure, including students from low socioeconomic households, students from various minority groups, and students with disabilities across the district, clearly benefited from this sustained school-university partnership.

Beyond test scores, equally important to the success of the inclusion initiative was how students viewed and responded to being part of an inclusive school. For example, at Newberry Elementary School the partnership provided data that indicated that students reported enhanced acceptance of students with autism and more significant disabilities as members of their classroom community. In the end, meeting the challenges associated with including students in the general education classrooms, not only resulted in increased behavioral and academic gains for students at Newberry, but also resulted in increased acceptance of students with special needs.

Resource Availability

Resources, both fiscal and human, are important to partnerships. Just like other organizations, partnerships need to have dependable resources that allow the partners to plan strategically over time. Today, public schools and universities face lean times as fiscal resources are being reduced and students demand increased levels of support and services. The question has become "How do we do more with less?" Conventional wisdom would suggest that during these economic tough times one ought to hang on to the resources one has. However, evidence suggests that by collaborating and sharing program responsibilities, services can be improved and more services can be provided. By sharing resources, partnerships work smarter.

Within the Alachua County/University of Florida Professional Development School network, rather than exchanging dollars, the partnership sustains itself by sharing tasks and human resources. An example of sharing human resources to realize partnership goals, the Newberry Elementary principal, Lacy Redd, taught a seminar related to planning for instruction and using data-based instructional decision making to the cohort of 18 prospective teachers at her school. In return, the university faculty member who specialized in writing instruction led teacher professional development at Newberry Elementary. At another partnership school, a fourth grade teacher taught the language arts methods course to a cohort of 24 prospective teachers engaged in a field experience at his school. Simultaneously, the university professor taught writing workshops to the fourth graders. This exchange provided the university professor an opportunity to study how high-stakes accountability was impacting student writing instruction and allowed the fourth-grade teacher to offer prospective teachers a bridge between theory and practice. In this way, the partnership capitalized on differentiated knowledge by adjusting roles and responsibilities to meet the demands of the activity.

Foundation support can both facilitate and complicate sustainability. In some partnerships, foundations have provided planning dollars. These planning dollars are helpful in creating programs as long as the planned program does not rely on these external funds to sustain itself. The State College Area School District/Pennsylvania State University Professional Development School Partnership benefited by bringing teachers and faculty together using initial foundation support.

Relationships began before external funding even existed. However, within the first few years, the partnership received a substantial grant from the Lucent Foundation to support the development of theory to practice course teams and the integration of technology into these courses. Rather than using this funding to pay participants for their work, the funding was used to generate new knowledge and relationships that would support sustainability through the creation of boundary spanning roles.

This distinction between "paying for the work" and "providing time and resources to do the work" is important when seeking sustainability. In this example, the relationship and new knowledge that underpin the collaboration are sustainable even when the funding ends. We encourage those who use foundation support to build partnerships for which sustainability plans exist that creatively integrate recurrent funds to support the partnership.

As indicated, sustaining partnerships requires thinking differently about resources and resource allocation. By shifting how we use our existing resources, we move away from a paradigm of protecting, "holding on to," and maintaining a paradigm of partnering to use scarce resources more efficiently. Instead of only thinking about holding on, partnerships have to think about letting go and integrating. Instead of competing for the few dollars available, partnerships share resources as a way to sustain, integrate, and expand opportunities and programs. Resource availability, an essential element of sustaining partnerships, requires partnerships to garner, allocate, and often share fiscal and human resources in creative ways.

Communication and Public Relations

Edens, Shirley, and Toner (2001) suggest, "Partnerships should work diligently at fostering deep conversation—productive conversations about issues, conflicts, and differences that culminate in mutually satisfying resolutions. Hearing is not enough. The voices should be heeded" (p. 31). These productive conversations are the essence of the simultaneous renewal and productivity that underpin sustained partnerships and collaboration. As a result, sustaining partnerships requires creating and maintaining communication vehicles that reach all partners and stakeholders. Additionally, an environment must be created that allows for problems to be posed as well as conflict and differences to be explored, negotiated, and resolved. Creating the trust needed for these real conversations is not easy.

The size of the partnership also has a great deal of influence on the communication vehicles needed to sustain collaboration. Both formal and informal lines of communication help to sustain a partnership. At the Benedum Collaborative, a formal, complex governance structure was developed to facilitate communication across the partnership composed of five counties and 31 schools. While this is critical to the overall work of the collaborative, the complex governance structure can slow communication, creating miscommunication across the layers of the collaborative. In particular, as program changes are being proposed and developed, communication problems arise.

Let's explore the complications associated with communicating within the collaborative. With a large network that affects the lives and work of public school superintendents, principals, and teachers as well as deans, department chairs, faculty, and students at the university, it is not possible or feasible for every person to have a voice in every decision. To help address this dilemma, the partnership's executive committee increased the meeting frequency. This executive committee consists of the collaborative leaders as well as representatives from university faculty, teachers, and administrators. Representatives to the executive committee are elected from the various groups that meet across the network throughout the year to discuss ideas related to leadership, teacher education, and professional development. When the partnership communicates effectively, this collaboration strengthens student learning and teacher education.

Communication is also strengthened across the Benedum Collaborative partnership as school-based teams meet regularly at their sites to develop goals and to target professional development needs. These teams typically include principals, site-based teacher education and professional development coordinators, university liaisons, and mentor teachers. Therefore, in a collaborative of this magnitude, communication flows not only down from the executive committee to the various partners but also up the network from any number of school-based groups.

Beyond creating communication vehicles that promote open and honest conversation between partners, positive public relations also helps sustain partnerships. Finding ways to share partnership success stories is critical to sustainability. An example of public relations at its best also can be seen in the Alachua County Inclusion Initiative. The partnership created opportunities for students with disabilities to share their stories with peers, faculty, parents, and the community. A powerful public relations example occurred when a high school student with significant challenges assumed a self-advocacy role for inclusion. This student provided lectures to her peers and was also an invited presenter during campus seminars to share her experiences as a student with disabilities. A critical event in the partnership evolution occurred when she had the opportunity to share her experiences and perspective on inclusion with the faculty at her former elementary school. This elementary school historically had not been an inclusive school. As a result of these public relations efforts, the Alachua County Schools became more motivated and eventually successful in including students with disabilities.

This same partnership also illustrates the importance of sharing your success stories to broader audiences. The inclusion initiative has shared its success story at national conferences and in educational publications using student achievement results. The partnership also created a video focused on how local schools provided inclusive services. This award-winning video titled *The Inclusive Classroom: The Very Best Opportunity for Children* highlighted the partners' work and was used to show the possibilities and hope of inclusive education in the district and across the state of Florida.

PROBLEM-SOLVING STRATEGIES FOR SUSTAINING PARTNERSHIPS

Weathering the storm is key to strengthening a partnership and refers to the process of working collaboratively through challenges during a difficult period without harming the partnership. We have found that repackaging, damage control, and ongoing vitalization are valuable problem-solving or problem-avoiding tools.

Repackaging

Repackaging can help partnerships respond to internal and external organizational changes and/or shifting priorities of the partnership. Repackaging refers to the process of identifying the partnership's positive aspects and putting these into an attractive form. In repackaging, the partners remake the partnership to be more desirable, typically by making the partnership more efficient and aligned to new and innovative goals.

Repackaging can be a powerful way to generate new commitment and resources for a partnership's work. The University of Florida and the Duval County Public Schools elementary apprenticeship program demonstrated how repackaging strengthened the original partnership commitment and added much-needed resources. Originally begun as a partnership between the School of Teaching and Learning and the Duval County Board of Education associated with the U.S. Department of Education Transition to Teaching Program, the partnership developed a relationship with the Lastinger Center. The Lastinger Center is a foundation-supported outreach office of the University of Florida. The Lastinger Center had concurrently been working on developing cohort-based teacher leadership programs in urban contexts throughout the state of Florida to enhance school improvement in challenging contexts.

As the Lastinger Center deepened its work, the partners in the elementary apprenticeship recognized overlapping resources being dedicated to the schools by the Lastinger Center and the apprenticeship program. At times the two partnerships even competed with each other since they operated without a systematic connection between the partnerships. Given the diminishing fiscal resources, the partnerships decided to repackage their individual work and form a collective mission. This repackaging effort led to the Lastinger Center and the elementary apprenticeship program combining their teacher leadership for school-improvement work and their inquiry-oriented professional development. By repackaging, the resources were aligned to improve teaching and learning within struggling urban schools and provide quality new hires for those schools that were prepared for the challenges of urban education.

Damage Control

Damage control was historically used by navies for the emergency control of situations that could hazard the sinking of a ship. We use the concept of damage control in partnerships to describe the actions needed to respond to problems that could jeopardize or sink collaborative work. Some suggestions for engaging in damage control include addressing the questions in a straightforward and honest way, being up front with important information, reaching out to your key constituents so that they hear news from you rather than from someone else, providing a consistent and clear message, and explaining how the partnership will review and improve practices that might be used to avoid problems in the future.

As the Alachua County/University of Florida Professional Development School partnership moved to create a culture of collegiality around writing reform, conflict occurred between the university faculty and the public school teachers. One of us, as the partnership director, shared:

> We knew that we were going to experience tension as we began to explore theory-to-practice disconnects between the writing philosophy used by the university teacher educators and the writing pedagogy embraced by many of the school teachers. However, given that the goal of a professional development school is to engage in ongoing simultaneous renewal that strengthens shared and individual knowledge, we knew that the dissonance created by exploring diverse viewpoints was essential to improving writing instruction for prospective teachers as well as public school students. There was definitely a curriculum conflict that frustrated the teachers, prospective teachers, and university faculty. As a result, the principal, the university field advisor, and the director of the partnership had to meet with teachers and the university faculty member to mend hurt feelings and frustration. By providing an opportunity for the frustrated participants to air their concerns and by negotiating solutions for future writing curriculum work, the partnership leaders reduced the dissonance initially created and allowed the partnership to move forward. (Diane Yendol-Hoppey, personal communication)

Ongoing Vitalization

Although damage control and repackaging are necessary sustainability tools, both are reactive rather than proactive as organizational problem-solving strategies. A much more proactive sustainability tool is the process of paying attention to ongoing vitalization and renewal of the partnership. By being proactive, partnerships can prevent some conflict.

Hargreaves and Fink (2003) describe sustainability as the act of "enabling people to adapt and prosper in their increasingly complex environment" while "building long-term capacity for improvement" (p. 694). Tyack and Cuban (1995) remind us that to sustain our partnerships we must engage in ongoing evaluation and reconsideration of the partnership, as the contexts are continuously changing. This ongoing evaluation is coupled with negotiation focused on how we can achieve these goals together in changing contexts with changing roles. Collaborative leaders help the partnership to sustain itself by navigating and pushing the partnership forward by providing ongoing attention to the partnership's health.

CONCLUDING REMARKS

Given that collaborative partnerships are complex, tricky to navigate, and difficult to sustain, this chapter provides examples that collaborative partnership leaders use to sustain partnership work. Nine lessons emerge for those interested in strengthening partnerships (see Figure 4.2).

We believe that the most important lesson is the power of continual shared learning. Over a decade ago, Tyack and Cuban (1995) explained that sustainability relies on "gradual and incremental tinkering with the system" (p. 5). In this same text, they identified three common reasons that help us understand why partnerships may fail to sustain themselves, including (1) fidelity to the original model, (2) achievement of predetermined goals without the evolution of new goals, and (3) the goal of longevity in and of itself. Keeping these characteristics of failing partnerships in mind, sustainability results as both partners commit to a shared goal and create mutually beneficial outcomes needed to solve the complex issues facing schools today. The sustainability of a partnership will be highly influenced by the degree of pressure and support each formal and informal organizational and partnership leader provides for meeting partnership goals, as well as by the value and commitment that the partnership participants demonstrate for actualizing those goals and maintaining the partnership's health.

FIGURE 4.2. Lessons Learned about Sustaining Collaborative Partnerships

1. Sustaining a collaborative partnership is a shared endeavor that requires a shared mission and continuous shared learning that creates simultaneous renewal.
2. The cultural differences between organizations in the partnership challenge partnership sustainability. Collaborative structures and boundary-spanning roles that blur organizational boundaries can help soften organizational cultural differences.
3. Partnership sustainability requires a broad degree of commitment.
4. Collaborative partnerships require collegiality to sustain their work.
5. Sustaining a collaborative partnership requires persistence, creativity, and patience.
6. Partnership sustainability is strengthened by positive community response and attention to public relations.
7. Sustaining a collaborative partnership is facilitated by supportive data.
8. Sustaining a collaborative partnership requires effectively sharing human and fiscal resources.
9. Repackaging, damage control, and ongoing vitalization are problem-solving or problem-avoiding strategies for sustaining partnerships.

REFERENCES

Ansett, S. (2005). Boundary spanner: The gatekeeper of innovation in partnerships. *Accountability Forum 6,* 36–44.

Cuban, L. (2001). *How can I fix it: An educator's road map.* New York: Teachers College Press.

Edens, K. M., Shirley, J., & Toner, T. (2001). Sustaining a professional development school partnership: Hearing the voices, heeding the voices. *Action in Teacher Education, (23)3,* 27–32.

Fullan, M. (1992). *Successful school improvement: The implementation perspective and beyond.* London: Open University Press.

Fullan, M. (2005). *Leadership and sustainability: System thinkers in action.* Thousand Oaks, CA: Corwin Press.

Hargreaves, A., & Fink, D. (2003). Sustaining leadership. *Phi Delta Kappan, 84*(9), 693–700.

Leming, J. S. (1989). The two cultures of social studies education. *Social Education, 53*(6), 404–408.

Mezirow, J. (2000). *Learning as transformation: Critical perspectives on a theory in progress.* San Francisco: Jossey-Bass.

Schein, E. (2004). *Organizational culture and leadership.* San Francisco: Jossey-Bass.

Tyack, D., & Cuban, L. (1995). *Tinkering toward utopia.* Cambridge, MA: Harvard University Press.

5

Making Evaluation Useful: Improving Partnerships Through Ongoing Collaborative Assessment

Jerry W. Willis

This chapter describes

- the assessment process and how it should match the type of partnership: technical, technical/support, conceptual, transformative, emancipatory;
- how the foundational assumptions of your partnership shape what you decide to measure; and
- transformative and emancipatory partnerships' need for data at several points in the process.

* * *

One of the best known and most widely discussed school-university partnerships began in 1989 and ended roughly 20 years later in 2008. It was the Boston University-Chelsea School District (BU-CSD) partnership. In 1988, the district was a failed system by almost any standard—from high levels of corruption and problematic leadership to low achievement levels and dismal graduation rates. Only a depressing 20% of students who graduated from high school even had a *desire* to go to a college. Predictably, the Chelsea district served a population of poor and immigrant families and had neither the leadership nor the resident expertise to solve its problems. It was within that context that John Brennan, the mayor of Chelsea, a suburb of Boston, approached Boston University (BU). John Silber, the controversial president of BU, was ready to champion a partnership and the result was the only instance thus far of a university that completely took over a school district. The goal of the partnership was to "provide the highest quality of education and educational opportunity for the children of Chelsea and to make Chelsea's public schools a national model of urban education" (Paletta, Candal, & Vidoni, 2009, p. 470).

The partnership also selected 17 objectives, including an improvement of test scores, a decrease in the dropout rate, and an increase in the number of students attending 4-year colleges. The initial partnership was for 10 years, but it was extended twice. The foundation of the partnership was that the school district "ceded its authority to a management team of BU personnel. This team would appoint and oversee the school superintendent and take any action necessary to fulfill the partnership goals, so long as such actions complied with state and local law" (Paletta, Candal, & Vidoni, 2009, p. 472). The district board required regular reports from the BU leadership team and also had veto power over decisions, but clashes between the board and the BU leadership team were not common.

BU created a partnership that included many agencies and groups in the reform effort, and while the BU team was clearly the core leadership and decision-making group, it distributed the leadership responsibilities across school-based, community-based, and government units and agencies so that it was not a "top down" or authoritarian model of leadership. Two forms of management emerged—*political* management and *operational* management. Political management set policy and helped keep disparate groups and organizations involved and invested in reforming the school district. Operational management was responsible for seeing to it that new innovations, such as programs to increase attendance, enhance learning opportunities for parents, and support teen parents, were successfully implemented.

Assessment of the BU-CSD partnership was multifaceted but the focus was on outcomes. Primary measures were achievement test scores and graduation rates. Student achievement, particularly in the elementary schools, did increase significantly during the partnership. However, despite the clear goals of enhancing achievement and increasing graduation rates, and the implementation of many different innovations, "raising test scores and graduation rates at the high school level in Chelsea . . . proved quite difficult" (Paletta, Candal, & Vidoni, 2009, p. 478). Assessment also looked at possible reasons for the relative failure of the partnership to achieve objectives at the high school level. One was high mobility rates (32% of students enter or leave the district each year), which meant that a large number of students who took achievement tests were in the district for short periods of time. Further, Paletta, Candal, and Vidoni (2009) suggested that because Chelsea is a depressed area, students who leave often do so because of family upward mobility while those who enter the area are more likely downwardly mobile.

While outcome data had been the primary focus of assessment, since the partnership was funded in 1989, annual interviews with Chelsea teachers and administrators have been used to gather data on possible causes of any improvements as well as to gather information about the perceived status of the district and its students. The interviews suggested that improvements were at least in part due to four factors:

1. *A shift in the expressed and practiced organizational philosophy.* Initially, the district's expectations for students were very low, and there was a widespread feeling that Chelsea was a district that had been forgotten by the state and by local leaders. The management team initiated by BU gradually installed administrators at all levels of the district who were "devoted to inculcating the idea that every child can learn" (Paletta, Candal, & Vidoni, 2009, p. 481). This was backed up by new professional development opportunities for teachers by BU professors to support higher expectations.

2. *The widespread use of a participatory but guided decision-making process.* Although BU was given almost dictatorial power over the district, it used that power to push for broader rather than narrower participation in decision making. This aspect of the program did not, initially, go well. "After a few initial stumbles whereby BU was negatively perceived as a white knight on a horse coming in to save a poor, struggling community, key players in the partnership made a conscious effort to include all stakeholders in decision-making processes, especially those related to implementation of curricula and standards, in an effort to improve student achievement" (Paletta, Candal, & Vidoni, 2009, p. 481).

3. *Vast improvements in teacher preparation and teacher support.* As noted above, BU initiated a number of teacher preparation and teacher support programs, all aimed at helping the district and teachers to reach the stated objectives of the partnership.

4. *Effective mobilization of financial resources for capital and environmental improvements.* When the partnership began in 1988, many of the district's school buildings were in such sad states of repair they were near condemnation. However, the leadership team was able to both manage available funds and secure additional funds that allowed existing buildings to be rehabilitated. New, showcase buildings were constructed, and funds for needed teacher resources were increased.

Another issue when evaluating this partnership is that the goal was not to create a stable relationship that would continue indefinitely. Instead, the goal was to build "sustainability of the system once the partnership [came] to an end" (Paletta, Candal, & Vidoni, 2009, p. 482). One issue with regard to sustainability involved the participation of the Hispanic community, including parents, in the partnership. Chelsea's substantial Hispanic community was one of the critical stakeholder groups that did not always consider itself an active and respected member of the partnership. There were many disagreements, some of them intense and acrimonious, about everything from bilingual education to the choice of who would become the principal of a local school. Boston University sometimes made decisions that were not supported by the Hispanic community and as a result the university was characterized by some as an enemy rather than ally. This negative view of Boston University was not helped by the lack of Hispanic members on the elected local board of education (called the school committee). Fortunately, an agreement between the federal government and the Chelsea city government changed the election process to allow for consistent Hispanic representation on the school committee. Paletta, Candal, and Vidoni (2009) concluded that the partnership succeeded in calming the waters between the White and Hispanic populations, the principal stakeholders of the district. Although critics question whether Chelsea is today the model for excellence in urban education that all parties hoped for at the inception of the partnership, the relative gains that have been made in Chelsea over the past 18 years are undeniable. In this sense, Chelsea may be called a model for the turnaround of a district.

WHY ARE PARTNERSHIPS HARD TO EVALUATE?

While the BU-Chelsea partnership represents a broad, comprehensive effort, many partnerships are more focused. An example might be a partnership in which relatively narrow goals are to be accomplished through a summer program partnership focused on the needs of at-risk students. Despite substantial differences between broadly and narrowly focused school-university partnerships, they have a number of elements in common that have important implications for any effort to evaluate or assess a partnership. The first is that many partnerships cannot be evaluated using the traditional research methods most of us were taught in graduate school. Nor can most be evaluated by comparing experimental and control groups on three or four quantitative variables that everyone agrees will show whether the partnership "worked" or not. Such variables rarely, if ever, exist, and in the real world of applied research, those who evaluate partnerships are likely to be frustrated and unhappy if they search for these mythical holy grails. What we should be looking for are multiple sources of data, both qualitative and quantitative, that give us hints, insights, and suggestions about how a partnership is performing. In trying to draw some conclusions about the BU-Chelsea partnership, the authors of the report that was summarized above relied heavily on relatively flexible interviews with a wide range of stakeholders. They also used available empirical data such as attendance numbers and achievement-test scores. However, despite the amount of time and effort invested in gathering information about this relatively well-known partnership, there is nothing definitive about the study. There are still groups who disagree strongly on whether the partnership worked or not, whether it was a good idea or not, or whether it was done in the best way possible. Definitive conclusions on such questions are simply not available nor are they likely to be.

School-university partnerships come in many different formats and serve many different purposes (Callahan & Martin, 2007). Those many differences are one reason the assessment methods used by partnerships are also quite varied. The form, purpose, and foundational assumptions of a partnership are a significant influence on the choice of assessment methods. There is no single method for assessing partnerships that we can all master and then use in confidence because it is *the* method that both scholars and practitioners have deemed superior to all others. This, of course, complicates the process of developing an assessment plan for partnerships, and it also opens the door for significant differences of opinion about how a particular partnership should be assessed.

A TYPOLOGY BASED ON PURPOSE

There have been a number of attempts to provide some conceptual scaffolding that can be helpful when making decisions about partnership assessment and program evaluation. Figure 5.1 presents a typology that incorporates other frameworks (e.g., Greene, 2000) and is based on the partnership's purpose, the roles of participants, and the methods used to accomplish the purpose. The five general partnership purposes are technical, technical/support, conceptual, transformative, and emancipatory.

Technical Partnerships and Technical/Support Partnerships

In many technical and technical/support partnerships, most of the major decisions about the partnership are decided beforehand or upon initiation. Teachers are typically on the receiving end of technical training about how to teach in a particular way. The methods used in that training are determined by the trainers, often university faculty, and the success of the partnership is generally determined by how well the teachers implement the new methods being taught.

FIGURE 5.1. A Typology of Partnerships Based on Purpose, Methods, Focus, and Roles

Primary purpose	Methods	Level of focus	Roles
Technical	consulting, professional development, one-shot workshop	change in technical practice	experts (often faculty) train teachers in techniques/methods
Technical/ support	consulting, professional development, training and ongoing support	change in technical practice	experts train teachers and a support system assists teachers during implementation
Conceptual	consulting, professional development, action research, participation in dialogues and discussion groups	change in guiding principles will lead to changes in practice	teacher participation in dialogues, action research, discussion groups, etc. faculty often plan and lead partnership activities
Transformative	dialogue and exploration with a focus on the guiding principles and models of practice, participatory action research, narrative inquiry, reflective journaling and reflective practice	changes in worldview leads to changes in guiding principles leads to changes in practice	dialogue and exploration with a focus on the guiding principles and models of practice leadership and planning work is often shared among all participants
Emancipatory	reflection, analysis of local context, participatory action research, journaling, dialogical collaboration, collective action, leadership with "emancipatory intent"	active exploration of worldviews leads to changes in worldview (raising critical consciousness), which leads to changes in guiding principles, which leads to changes in practice	leaders from outside or inside focus on creating conditions that raise critical consciousness and then progress toward actions designed to reduce oppression, enhance democratic participation and social equity

Technical partnerships focus on how-to training. The prototypical method used in technical partnerships is the notoriously ineffective "one-shot workshop." However, one advantage of this approach is that it is clean and clear. The focus is on training teachers to use a set of techniques or methods in their classrooms, and the consulting, workshops, or other methods used in the partnership are designed to accomplish that purpose directly. However, accumulated research and professional-practice wisdom over the past few decades have confirmed that one-shot workshops as well as the use of short-term outside consultants, are, at best, weak ways of bringing about change in schools. As that became obvious, another model emerged that emphasized both initial training and ongoing support for teachers. This more extensive and long-term model of partnerships would, it was argued, both prepare teachers to teach differently and provide support for them during the critical early stages of implementation when problems and frustrations are virtually guaranteed. That is, they begin with decisions already made about what is to be done and how teachers, and the school system, are to be prepared to implement the change. Regardless of the innovation being introduced, however, there is a wide gap of knowledge and expertise between being vaguely aware of a teaching method like problem-based learning or anchored instruction and being able to use them successfully in the classroom. Thus, the training and support tends to be about how-to rather than why, or when or if. When such partnerships are evaluated the focus is often on whether the teachers have mastered the technical aspects of using the new instructional innovations and are successfully using them in their teaching. This can be assessed through evaluations of teachers' mastery of the training content and comparing their teaching performance to a benchmark or standard for correct use of the innovation.

Evaluation in Technical and Technical/Support Partnerships

Evaluation for both technical and technical/support partnerships tends to rely on objective, empirical measures of knowledge and skills needed to teach in a certain way; in other words, how well teachers have mastered and can perform the technical components of an innovation. Technical and technical/support partnerships appear to be some of the easiest to plan and implement because they are based on relatively clear-cut and fixed assumptions about what is important. That impression may be accurate when these partnerships focus narrowly on a small set of goals and objectives as well as a relatively simple innovation and a simple training program. Partnerships like that do exist but they are not representative. Many technical and technical/support partnerships tend to have diverse, multiple goals, support complex and often multiple innovations, and provide several types of training and support. Such partnerships are not so easy to evaluate using traditional methods. Evaluation of such partnerships often involves the use of qualitative methods as well.

Case Study as a Partnership-Evaluation Method. One of the most popular methods for evaluating a partnership is the case study. One reason for that is the broad and diverse meaning of the term. At times it seems that anything can be called a case study and that any type of data can be used in a case study. When thinking about case study methodology as a framework for evaluating a partnership, my suggestion is that the case study be considered a comprehensive approach to thoughtfully analyzing the entire partnership process and outcome—from how it was initiated and how it operated to the impact it had relative to the purposes for which it was established. Case studies are not puff pieces extolling the virtue of a partnership while ignoring the hidden and not so hidden problems, barriers, and difficulties. Instead, they provide readers with in-depth information on a partnership, how it worked, where it failed (and why), and where it succeeded (and why).

An example of this type of case study research is an evaluation of the Principals Leadership Academy of Nashville (PLAN), a partnership between Vanderbilt University, area school districts, and community organizations (Goldring & Sims, 2005). The authors relied on data from interviews with major stakeholders, but their case study includes detailed information on everything from how the partnership was initiated to the ways participants linked their formal participation to changes in professional practice. PLAN began with a request by school districts for the university to provide quality professional development for their school principals and vice principals to help them with the challenges of helping all children learn in a climate of accountability and competition. The partnership group created a program and invited selected education leaders, nominated by their superintendent, to participate. Each cohort group attended evening meetings once a week during the school year and attended an intensive, 2-week summer session. They also participated in coaching activities, shadowing, and peer-learning sessions during their participation. When Goldring and Sims evaluated PLAN they interviewed 14 stakeholders including participants, community organization leaders, and administrators such as the dean of education and the director of a participating foundation. Goldring and Sims were themselves intensively involved in PLAN and, thus, used their own experiences in doing the evaluation. They used the qualitative data analysis package, NUD*IST, to code the interviews after they were transcribed. After that they looked for themes, ideas, and concepts in the data. They then compared their emerging themes and conclusions to what they found in the existing literature on partnerships and to the perceptions of respected principals in the school district who read and critiqued the authors' interpretations and conclusions. The result of this analysis constitutes the details of the case study they report. Some of the case study simply provides information on what happened. For example, "the top-level leaders—in this case, the dean, the director of schools, and the president of the Nashville Public Education Foundation—were the original founders of PLAN" (p. 231). Other aspects involve an assessment of various aspects of PLAN. For example, a principal is quoted as saying, "All three of our organization's top leaders have been incredibly supportive. I mean there's been very little that we have asked for, discussed, or dreamed about that they have not made a reality. They have been absolutely essential to PLAN" (p. 232). When a partnership is relatively complex and you are interested in a comprehensive look at the partnership, rather than only one or two components, case study methods should be considered. And, because case study methods are so flexible, they are suited to the assessment of all forms of partnerships, including those that have been operating for many years. For additional information on how to conduct case studies, see Robert Yin's (2009) *Case Study Methods: Design and Methods* and Hancock and Algozzine's (2006) *Doing Case Study Research.*

Formal Program Evaluation Methodology. Partnerships are an example of programs, and the vast literature on program evaluation is a useful source of guidance when deciding how to evaluate your partnership. However, these resources can also be a source of frustration because they are so vast and so diverse. Program evaluation methods tend to involve a selection of the same methods used for other research purposes. With that in mind, I suggest two very good, and free, resources for program evaluation. The *W. K. Kellogg Foundation Evaluation Handbook* (www.wkkf.org/Pubs/Tools/Evaluation/Pub770. pdf) is available online and contains some of the most practical advice available on how to structure and conduct a program evaluation. Another free book on program evaluation that is available online is the National Science Foundation's *The 2002 User Friendly Handbook for Project Evaluation* (www. nsf.gov/pubs/2002/nsf02057/nsf02057.pdf). Both these guides offer advice on how to do program evaluations using both quantitative and qualitative data.

Figure 5.2 is a summary of the commonly used evaluation methods and procedures for the five types of partnerships.

Conceptual Partnerships

While technical and technical/support partnerships remain popular, they are based on the assumption that when a solution or innovation is selected, it can be successfully implemented by a partnership that focuses heavily on training teachers to implement it correctly. This approach is based on a technical-rational definition of professional practice (Willis, 2007), which has been heavily criticized by a number of opponents including Donald Schön (2003). In essence, the approach is based on the idea that making good professional practice decisions in the classroom is a matter of identifying the critical characteristics of the situation, selecting the best approach to that situation based on the available research, and then implementing the approach. Many educators and theorists (Schön, 2003) have argued that teaching, or any other profession for that matter, is not a well-structured technical-rational process that is relatively simple. Instead, they assert it is a fuzzy, ill-structured, reflective process (Spiro, Feltovich, Jacobson, & Coulson, 1995) in which the teacher must make many thoughtful decisions about what to do in a situation that calls for a careful consideration of the specific context in which the decision will be applied. Even then, the decision may not work well. The teacher must then reflectively analyze why and add that information to his or her store of background and contextual knowledge that can be used in the future.

FIGURE 5.2. Assessment Methods Matched to Type of Partnership

Type of partnership	Assessment focus	Assessment methods	Assessment sequence
Technical	• teacher mastery of technique and method • teacher implementation of technique and method in classroom • may also include outcome measures of impact of innovation on student performance	• objective assessment of performance of new methods in training context • observation and critical evaluation of classroom performance using rubrics, observation instruments or other objective measures • objective assessment of impact of new techniques on students (e.g., achievement tests)	• objective assessment of each component of the training and implementation process • often done by "external" evaluator
Technical/ support	• all of the above plus understanding of general principles of new technique	• direct/indirect measures of specific knowledge/performance • case study methods • program evaluation methods	
Conceptual	• understanding of general principles, guidelines, and concepts of an innovation • ability of teacher to flexibly adapt the innovation to local needs	• teacher reflections during exploration and implementation of an innovation • action research studies • observations, field notes, and group discussions of successes, problems, and needed revisions • case study methods	• work usually proceeds in stages that include an exploration or reconnaissance stage followed by iterative cycles of implementation, evaluation, revision, and then implementation • each stage documented and assessed
Transformative	• process of dialogue and discussion often a focus of assessment along with the structural organization of the partnership (Is it democratic? Inclusive? Participatory? Open?) • Who leads? Why? Whose input is valued? • How are decisions made?	• methods for assessing conceptual partnerships also used to assess transformative partnerships • participatory action research • narrative inquiry	• group dialogue and discussion help participants develop shared understanding that leads to plans for action; leadership shared • action reviewed and assessed by the group, revisions made, new round of implementation and evaluation begins • professional expertise valued and used in assessment
Emancipatory	• raised consciousness and the development as well as implementation of action plans to help the oppressed overthrow oppression and make education more democratic and equitable	• emancipatory partnerships use a wide range of qualitative and quantitative research methods • difference in the interpretation of results, which tends to be ideologically based on one or more critical theories	• three recursive phases typical: 1. attempts to raise consciousness and help participants throw off "false consciousness" (i.e., beliefs that keep them oppressed) 2. new and enlightened understanding leads to plans for action 3. plans for action are implemented and evaluated; process may then begin again

Conceptual partnerships represent an important step away from a technical training focus. Conceptual partnerships are typically based on the general idea that there are no prepackaged answers to many of the issues and questions that arise in professional practice. That is because (a) the context of the decision has a major influence on whether something works or not and (b) our base of how-to knowledge is not well established and "proven." It is, in fact, often contradictory and unsuccessful. For an innovation to be successfully applied in the classroom, a teacher must understand the underlying concepts, theoretical foundations, and guiding principles of the innovation. Certainly the technical aspects of using the innovation are important, but it is the concepts and guiding principles of the innovation that will help a teacher make good decisions. That is because the teacher must be flexible in making decisions rather than applying a lockstep and unchangeable pattern that is simply replicated or parroted in the classroom. Advocates of conceptual partnerships assert that this should be the focus.

The work of John Bransford and his group at Vanderbilt (CTGV, 1990, 1993) focuses on conceptual partnerships and emphasizes the core concepts of pedagogies such as anchored instruction. Most conceptual partnerships include some technical training, but what distinguishes them is that a major goal is to help teachers understand the innovative pedagogy or curriculum—what it is, the foundational assumptions it is based upon, and the conceptual links between idea and professional practice.

Evaluation of Conceptual Partnerships

Planning the evaluation of a conceptual partnership is difficult because the focus is not on easily measureable or observable behaviors that can be prespecified in detail. Instead of learning the technical skills of managing an innovative pedagogy like problem-based learning and then using those skills to closely guide behavior in the classroom, teachers must wrestle with the underlying concepts and ideas of problem-based learning. The primary goal is a cognitive change, an understanding of the ideas and beliefs that underpin and guide practice. And, while there are some technical components of problem-based learning that might be assessed directly, most conceptual partnerships do not have a universal and automatically correct solution to each dilemma or decision point a teacher faces in the classroom. Making good decisions is a process that includes considering the uniqueness of the local context. What appears to outsiders to be the same "situation" in two different classrooms may actually be quite different to experienced and reflective teachers, and they may quite "correctly" make different decisions because of their different local and tacit knowledge.

Reflective Journaling for Partnership Evaluation. Conceptual partnerships are often assessed through qualitative methods because those methods provide more insight into the way participants are thinking. Reflective journals, for example, are popular. Participants keep journals while they are exploring and learning about an innovation, and they continue to journal while they implement the innovation. Reflective journals provide a way of understanding how a teacher is thinking about both his or her practice and the innovation. Conceptual partnerships do not necessarily use teacher journals to discover whether teachers are "thinking right" or "doing right"; the journals provide, instead, a way to better understand participants' perceptions, thinking processes, and understanding of both the context and professional practices under study.

Action Research as an Evaluation Method. Another common framework for evaluating conceptual partnerships is action research, a methodology that was developed by Kurt Lewin (1946). Action research represented, for Lewin, a way of making a real difference in what happened to people in schools, in neighborhoods, and in society. There are two basic purposes for action research. One involves selecting and/or implementing an action that is evaluated to see if it solves a problem. The other is the careful study of a particular context or setting such as an inner-city school or a high poverty, minority neighborhood to understand it better and thus develop better ways of dealing with problems. Figure 5.2 on page 106 summarizes the general model of action research proposed by Lewin.

Transformative Partnerships

Transformative school-university partnerships are what Butler, Lauscher, Jarvis-Selinger, & Beckingham (2004) refer to as *collaborative models* of professional development that "emphasize the importance of nurturing learning communities within which teachers try new ideas, reflect on outcomes, and construct knowledge about teaching and learning in the context of authentic activity" (p. 436). These authors discuss approaches such as collaborative inquiry and learning communities, as well as concepts such as situated learning, legitimate peripheral participation, and self-regulated learning. It is an expression of a constructivist/interpretive approach to partnerships based on the idea of shared expertise and responsibility. Such approaches attempt to reduce the dominance of "academic knowledge" in the marketplace of professional practice and to assess the value of, and search for, forms of knowledge and understanding that emerge from practice.

In transformative partnerships university faculty are more colleagues, learners and "co-constructors of knowledge" in the partnership than they are experts and authorities. Such partnerships do not begin with preselected solutions that will be taught to teachers. Instead, they begin with "joint inquiry" and the heart of that is "teachers' collaborative problem-solving in pursuit of common goals. Groups of teachers and/or researchers work together locally, within schools, or peripherally, for example, in meetings separate from immediate practice, to develop new ways of teaching. Individually or collectively, teachers try out new ideas in classrooms and monitor the success of their efforts. They come together to review their instruction, talk about outcomes, and critically reflect on their teaching" (Butler et al., 2004, p. 437).

Butler and her colleagues (2004) refer to this process as communities of practice (COP), but there is little, if anything, in the description of their work that conflicts with other models such as participatory action research (PAR) and the idea of learning organizations as advocated by Senge (2006). Other authors (Berger, Boles, & Troen, 2005) describe examples of transformative partnerships based on different theories and models, such as "teacher research." They argue that the tendency toward the use of universal standards is in opposition to their concept of transformative, teacher-research approaches to partnerships because universal standards devalue and ignore differences from one local context to another and, thus, also devalue the local knowledge teachers can construct and use to guide their decision making. Berger et al. describe the clash between the ideologies of universal standards versus efforts to create local knowledge as being on a "collision course." They thus propose a model of transformative partnership in which "teacher research could be a mover or shaper of the [school] culture itself" (p. 94). Transformative partnerships represent a significant break in the continuum of partnership types. Technical, technical/support, and conceptual partnerships all tend to begin the partnership with a solution and then organize partnership work around activities that (a) prepare teachers to implement the solution already selected and (b) support the implementation process. Transformative partnerships begin with a set of values such as co-constructing meaning in context and collaborative inquiry. Often, neither the problem to be addressed nor the solution to that problem or issue is known at the beginning. Both emerge through dialogue and discussion and are then used to guide efforts to enhance student learning. Transformative partnerships are as open, democratic, flexible, and unpredictable as technical partnerships are closed, fixed, authoritative, and predictable. And, of course, the way you assess a transformative partnership is quite different. You cannot state hypotheses before the partnership begins because often neither the goal nor the solution has been identified. And you cannot plan in advance the type of data you will collect because you do not know where the partnership will take the group. Thus, papers on transformative partnerships are often written in narrative style. The methods of narrative inquiry are used to gather data on the process, and results of a transformative partnership, and the resulting paper, tell the story of that partnership along with reflections and analysis. Narrative inquiry is, however, only one of the possible approaches to assessment.

Evaluation in Transformative Partnerships

Transformative partnerships clearly view the process of change and renewal as much more complex, and difficult, than technical or even conceptual partnerships. The "supply lines" of transformative partnerships are longer because they assume that complex and deeply held beliefs and perspectives must change in dramatic ways if the worldviews of both organizations and individuals are to change. They believe changes in worldviews are important because they lead to changes in guiding principles, which lead to changes in practice.

In addition to the traditional "code and search for themes" model used in many qualitative research studies, there are actually a number of other alternatives for partnership evaluation from which to choose, but they all diverge considerably from the research and evaluation models that are commonly used to assess the performance of technical, technical/support, and conceptual partnerships. They tend, for example, to involve participants in the evaluation process—from planning to interpretation of the results. They also tend to begin with questions rather than solutions and to value a wide range of data rather than privileging objective, empirical data over all other types. Four assessment methods for evaluating transformative partnerships are briefly described.

Participatory Action Research (PAR). One form of action research that is compatible with the guiding principles of technical and conceptual partnerships has already been discussed. There are many other forms of action research, and while there is something to be said for each of them, I think Lewin's original vision of action research remains the critical core of its meaning. Lewin developed action research as a method for addressing problems in the real world. Although there are many models and procedures for doing action research, the method is, at its core, relatively simple, with only four guiding principles:

1. Action research addresses issues of practice in the real world and is conducted in the context in which those issues arise.
2. Action research blurs and blends the roles of researcher, practitioner, and concerned citizen by including these and other groups as decision makers in the research process. Those who will implement changes, and those who will benefit or suffer from them, often have a significant voice in the process.

3. Action research occurs in a spiral or iterative process that proceeds through a series of steps that include planning, action, and evaluation—followed by another cycle, and then another. The assumption is that each cycle of action research will help participants understand the issues better, which should allow the team to develop better solutions to the problems they face.
4. Action research integrates research and practice so that it is difficult to untangle or separate these two aspects from each other. Action research *is* practice, and it *is* research.

Many of the activities in the action research cycle happen at the same time. You may, for example, be concurrently implementing *and* evaluating an action or intervention. Often, changes are made in the action while it is being implemented and evaluated. Thus, action research is more fluid and nonlinear than often implied.

Participatory action research, because it places such a high emphasis on collaborative participation across the stakeholder groups, is well suited to the assessment of transformative partnerships. There are a number of excellent resources on how to implement PAR methods. One especially useful book on PAR, *Participatory Action Research for Educational Leadership* (James, Milenkiewicz, & Buckman, 2008), was written for school leaders, but it is a valuable resource for anyone involved in a school-university partnership. The book includes many examples of PAR in educational settings. Alice Mcintyre's (2007) short book, *Participatory Action Research,* is also a very useful overview. There are also a number of examples of PAR to evaluate partnerships.

Eisner's Connoisseurship Model. Elliot Eisner's background is in the arts and in art education but his influence has expanded well beyond those boundaries. As a professor in the School of Education at Stanford University for many years, he has developed and advocated a profoundly holistic and open model of research that is now called the connoisseurship model of research (Eisner, 1997). Although Eisner's approach is interpretive and constructivist at its foundation, the methods he proposes are very similar to the way literacy criticism, or film and theatre reviewing, or wine selection and grading are conducted. In essence, an expert, such as a wine connoisseur, uses his or her background knowledge, experience, and expertise to evaluate a new vintage, play, or production. The result is a nuanced and sophisticated assessment that most of us could not do because we lack the connoisseur's talents and skills. But we can understand and appreciate the critique the connoisseur shares with us.

Eisner's connoisseurship model of research is more complex than my brief introduction shows, but it is fully explored in *The Enlightened Eye: Qualitative Inquiry and the Enhancement of Educational Practice* (Eisner, 1997). Research based on a connoisseurship model typically expects the connoisseurs to take on the complete process, including writing their critique and review.

Narrative Inquiry and Storytelling. Narrative inquiry is sometimes referred to as storytelling because the goal is not to abstract out of data a set of objective statements about how the world is but, instead, to "tell the story" of a particular context and set of experiences. As American education has developed more respect for constructivist and interpretivist paradigms of research that emphasize the constructed rather than discovered nature of meaning and knowing, there has been a corresponding movement away from research as a search for universal truths and increased respect for scholarship that helps us develop a sophisticated and contextualized understanding of human experiences. Clandinin and Connelly, two of the most influential and sophisticated practitioners of narrative inquiry in education today, propose three roles for narrative inquiry (Clandinin, 2007; Clandinin & Connelly, 2000):

1. It provides an alternative epistemological framework for thinking about scholarship.
2. It is a method for doing research in professional practice fields like education.
3. It is a method of scholarly discourse.

All three roles need to be considered when evaluating narrative inquiry as a framework for doing partnership evaluations. Narrative inquiry asks you to think carefully about the nature of what you want to accomplish, about the methods you will use to accomplish your purposes, and about how you will communicate to others the understanding you develop. The entire process of conducting narrative inquiry is quite different from the models of research taught in the past in many introductory educational research courses.

One interesting example of the use of narrative inquiry or storytelling is a paper by Richard Clark (1999) on school-university partnerships and professional development schools. Clark's paper is based on his analysis of two such partnerships, one in El Paso, Texas, and one in Tucson, Arizona. The paper is more the story of how these partnerships began and operated than anything else. Thus, his paper uses narrative to tell the story of the two partnerships, which is the third role of narrative discussed by Clandinin and Connelly (2000). Clark applies a connoisseur's skill to the telling of those partnership stories. He weaves his insights, comments, and reflections into the narrative, using experience gained "from observing hundreds of such partnerships around the country and from a comprehensive review of the literature" (p. 167). His insights are interesting and to the point:

> Partnerships succeed only when participants have the same clear understanding of
> the collaboration's purpose and functions. This is best achieved by extended con-

versations among the participants, not by formal agreements drafted by a few and passively accepted by others.

On occasions when the function for the university participants in a partnership is to play the role of expert evaluator, it may be wiser to call the arrangement a consultancy than to establish in the minds of participants the expectation of mutualism commonly associated with a partnership. (p. 168)

While Clark does not present empirical data for any of the points he makes, his status as a connoisseur of partnerships serves as a foundation for his advice and interpretations. Within Eisner's connoisseurship model of research, this is a valid and worthy foundation that warrants our attention. As an interpretivist, Eisner does not expect a connoisseur to always have the one right answer. Just as different reviewers of a play or movie may have different insights and different assessments, so too will different connoisseurs of partnerships. However, since interpretivists do not expect empirical research to lead us to the one right answer either, that is not a great loss. Clark's use of narrative as a means of scholarly discourse is an example of how different forms of qualitative inquiry can be integrated into one study. Clark's paper illustrates the use of a connoisseurship model as well as narrative inquiry to evaluate partnerships.

Cooperative Inquiry. One additional model that seems particularly suited to the evaluation of transformative partnerships is called cooperative inquiry. John Heron (1995), one of the creators of this approach views it as

[a] form of participative, person-centered inquiry which does research with people, not on them or about them. It breaks down the old paradigm separation between the role of researcher and subject. In its most complete form, the inquirers engage fully in both roles, moving in cycling fashion between phases of reflection as co-researchers and of action as co-subjects. (p. 19)

While cooperative inquiry has much in common with participatory action research, it is more personal and more intensive than many forms of action research. Peter Reason, who teaches at the University of Bath, is another developer of cooperative inquiry. Both editions of his *Sage Handbook of Action Research: Participative Inquiry and Practice* (Reason & Bradbury, 2007) have been excellent resources for anyone considering the use of more participatory methods to assess partnerships and professional practice.

Emancipatory Partnerships

Emancipatory partnerships seek to empower groups that have been suppressed or dominated. A classic paper by Liston and Zeichner (1987) defines as an important goal of teacher education "efforts to bring about more emancipatory educational practices in our public schools" that should "help to create a more democratic and just society" (p. 117). The authors maintain that "in the classroom the teacher is first and foremost an educator and only tangentially (if at all) a political activist. Teachers, as citizens and workers, can and should engage in political action outside the classroom . . . but teachers, as educators, must struggle to help students find their own voice and develop their own identities" (p. 122).

Liston and Zeichner propose five strategies for helping teachers develop their own understanding of teaching, learning, and schools: (1) action research, (2) ethnographic studies, (3) journal writing, (4) curriculum analysis and development, and (5) supervision with the goal of emancipating teachers. These strategies support teachers as they reflect on their view of their world. Their vision for radicalizing teacher education involves becoming much more active in the political and policy-making arena and moving out of the university enclave and into schools to support efforts to make American schools more democratic, open, and equitable.

Other, more radical, perspectives urge a more active and aggressive approach to forcing change. School-university partnerships based on such a foundation generally have as a goal more revolutionary changes that happen quickly and result in reformations in the foundational assumptions of education as well as in the way education is controlled and the way it is practiced.

Evaluation of Emancipatory Partnerships

There are few reports of emancipatory partnerships in the literature and even fewer papers on the evaluation of such partnerships. However, a recent paper by Miller and Hafner (2008) can almost serve as a prototype for evaluations of emancipatory partnerships. The focus of their analysis is on why many partnerships fail. They found that "the most pervasive dilemma, however, is that partnerships have inequitable distributions of power" (p. 69), and they noted that in school-university partnerships "the university is almost always in control" (p. 70).

Miller and Hafner based their research on Paolo Freire's (1970) concept of dialogical collaboration as a lens through which to view a particular university-school-community partnership. Freire's idea of dialogue and collaboration is based on the assumption that there are four foundations that must be present if such collaborations/partnerships are successful—humility, faith, hope, and critical thinking. Miller and Hafner accepted Freire's assertion that these four characteristics are essential to successful dialogical collaboration and that a partnership can be assessed by thinking of it as an instance of dialogical collaboration.

COMMUNICATING RESULTS: PR? SCIENCE? OR STORYTELLING?

A final issue to be discussed is how you communicate the results of an evaluation. That, I think, depends on the audience. There are internal audiences such as the participants in a partnership, local and regional audiences such as the public, local policy makers, and the "double i"—the interested and influential. At the national level, there are professionals who want to know about your partnership because they are thinking about doing something similar, and there are also policy makers, lawmakers, and other scholars who have their own, sometimes quite idiosyncratic, reasons for studying your evaluation.

Communicating to these different groups will not be successful if you create one report and make it available to all of them. The paper read by other professionals interested in your project is not what you want to hand out to local reporters as a press release. Similarly, the paper you write to influence policy makers who influence whether funds will be allocated to support partnerships is not the same paper you write for professionals who want the benefit of your experience with, and evaluation of, a partnership.

Begin thinking about how you communicate the results of your evaluation by identifying the audiences you want to reach. Then, develop major and minor goals for your communication with each audience. Once your goals are clear, decide what format and style of communication would be most likely to both reach your intended audience and be effective. In some cases the result will not be a document at all. A 2-minute video about the program might be the best way to reach parents when it is shown at parent meetings, on the local access channel (with notes sent home to parents alerting them to when it will air), and made available on the school or district website for downloading and viewing (again with notification made to parents about availability). On the other hand, that same 2-minute video might be considered more a "public relations piece" than an evaluation report by policy makers or professionals. Different types of documents are needed to reach them. (However, the video might be used in a conference presentation to illustrate the type of communications made to parents.)

The point is that communicating the results of your partnership evaluation is not a singular activity. It does not begin and end with a conference presentation and an article submitted to a scholarly or professional journal. There are many audiences and many reasons for communicating. Successful communication with many groups requires careful consideration of both the content of the communication and the medium used. What is appropriate and effective will vary considerably from one group, and one purpose, to another.

CONCLUDING REMARKS

Although it might be easier to think of the evaluation process as being different from, and quite separate from, organizing and leading a partnership, such an approach will generally lead to less useful information. Decisions about far too many aspects of the evaluation process depend on the type of partnership being evaluated, the stage and progress of the partnership, and the underlying theoretical and conceptual foundations for the partnership. Some evaluation decisions can be made before the partnership begins, and some can be made quite early in the life of the partnership. Others are made in the middle of the action, so to speak, when the partnership is operating and questions as well as opportunities develop in unpredictable but interesting ways.

Given such a pattern, I recommend that when it comes to deciding how to evaluate a partnership, the participants and stakeholders also serve as the decision makers. However, like Thomas Jefferson's ideas about the ideal citizens for a democracy, there are caveats. Jefferson thought a democracy would work best if the citizenry is educated, because education prepares people to make thoughtful and informed decisions. That is just as true when it comes to making decisions about how to evaluate a school-university partnership. The group making the decisions should be knowledgeable about the options available, the fit of those options with the goals and procedures of their partnership, and the strengths as well as the weaknesses of different evaluation methods. And, because these issues are intimately intertwined with the details and context of your particular partnership, these decisions are not necessarily made well by an external expert who knows evaluation well but not your particular context or partnership. For better or worse, you and the partnership participants are the ones who should be deciding the why, how, who, and when of the partnership assessment (see sidebar vignette by Stephen Wilhite).

Developing and Evaluating a University-Based Elementary Charter School

Stephen C. Wilhite

School of Human Service Professions, Widener University, Chester, PA

To provide an educational alternative for the children of Chester, Pennsylvania, Widener University, in collaboration with families in the community, launched the Widener Partnership Charter School in Fall 2006 under the leadership of Widener's School of Human Service Professions. With an enrollment of 300 students in grades K through 5, the school is designed to address the many obstacles that plague charter schools in underresourced urban areas. To support the charter school's focus on partnering with parents, Widener education

(continued on next page)

(continued from previous page)

faculty provide consultation and undergraduate and graduate education students provide instructional support in the implementation of the curriculum that emphasizes writing and technology in support of instruction and the intensive use of art, music, drama, foreign language, and physical education to promote overall healthy development of students. Interdisciplinary resource teams of graduate students and faculty from clinical psychology, education, social work, and physical therapy provide a comprehensive range of intervention and prevention services to students and families with the aim of addressing emotional, behavioral, and familial issues that could negatively impact academic success.

In order for this collaboration to happen, support was needed from the highest levels of the university administration and from the faculty of the School of Human Service Professions. The collaboration is being sustained because the charter school has become the most visible symbol of the university's strategic commitment to partnering with the Chester community and because of the numerous opportunities it affords Widener faculty and students for interdisciplinary experiential learning and research. Supplemental funding from state and federal sources has also contributed to the sustainability of the collaboration by providing funding to support professional development of teachers and administrators at the charter school. The effectiveness of the collaboration is being measured through a range of educational outcomes for children in the school, with initial results from state-mandated assessments showing that children in the school are scoring significantly higher than children in all other schools in the district. Other outcome measures include assessments of social and emotional development of the students; surveys of charter school parents regarding the school's accomplishment of its stated mission; assessments of the impact of charter school placements on the learning outcomes of university students; and documentation of the influence of charter school involvement on the scholarship agendas of university faculty. Despite the procurement of supplemental external funding for the charter school, a number of university offices have assumed responsibilities to support the operations of the school, and the amount of funding provided to offset the costs of services provided have not been sufficient to permit the hiring of university personnel whose primary or sole responsibility is to provide services for the charter school. Nevertheless, preliminary assessments suggest strongly that the positive impact of the collaboration in the community and within the university far outweighs the negative impact on the administrative infrastructure of the university.

REFERENCES

Berger, J. G., Boles, K. C., & Troen, V. (2005). Teacher research and school change: Paradoxes, problems, and possibilities. *Teaching and Teacher Education, 21,* 93–105.

Butler, D., Lauscher, H., Jarvis-Selinger, S., & Beckingham, B. (2004). Collaboration and self-regulation in teachers' professional development. *Teaching and Teacher Education, 20,* 435–455.

Callahan, J., & Martin, D. (2007). The spectrum of school-university partnerships: A typology of organizational learning systems. *Teaching and Teacher Education, 23,* 136–145.

Clandinin, D., & Connelly, F. (2000). *Narrative inquiry: Experience and story in qualitative research.* San Francisco: Wiley.

Clandinin, D. (Ed.). (2007). *Handbook of narrative inquiry.* Thousand Oaks, CA: Sage.

Clark, R. (1999). School-university partnerships and professional development schools. *Peabody Journal of Education, 74*(3/4), 164–177.

CTGV. (1990). Anchored instruction and its relationship to situated cognition. *Educational Researcher, 19*(6), 2–10.

Eisner, E. (1997). *The enlightened eye: Qualitative inquiry and the enhancement of educational practice* (2nd ed.). Englewood Cliffs, NJ: Prentice Hall.

Freire, P. (1970). *Pedagogy of the oppressed.* New York: Herder & Herder.

Goldring, E., & Sims, P. (2005). Modeling creative and courageous school leadership through district-community-university partnerships. *Educational Policy, 19*(1), 223–249.

Greene, J. (2000). *Understanding social programs through evaluation.* In N. Denzin & Y. Lincoln (Eds.), *Handbook of qualitative research* (pp. 981–999). Thousand Oaks, CA: Sage.

Hancock, D.R., & Algozzine, R. (2006). *Doing case study research: A practical guide for beginning researchers.* New York: Teachers College Press.

Heron, J. (1995). *Co-operative inquiry: Research into the human condition.* Thousand Oaks, CA: Sage.

James, E., Milenkiewicz, M., & Buckman, A. (2008). *Participatory action research for educational leadership.* Thousand Oaks, CA: Sage.

Lewin, K. (1946). Action research and minority problems. *Journal of Social Issues, 2*(4), 34–46.

Liston, D., & Zeichner, K. (1987). Critical pedagogy and teacher education. *Journal of Education, 169*(3), 117–137.

Mcintyre, A. (2007). *Participatory action research.* Thousand Oaks, CA: Sage.

Miller, P., & Hafner, M. (2008). Moving toward dialogical collaboration: A critical examination of a university-school-community partnership. *Educational Administration Quarterly, 44*(1), 66–110.

National Science Foundation. (2002). *The 2002 User-Friendly Project Guide.* Retrieved August 18, 2010, from www.nsf.gov/pubs/2002/nsf02057/nsf02057.pdf

Paletta, A., Candal, C. S., & Vidoni, D. (2009). Networking for the turnaround of a school district: The Boston University Chelsea partnership. *Education and Urban Society, 41*(4), 469–488.

Reason, P., & Bradbury, H. (Eds.). (2007). *Sage handbook of action research: Participative inquiry and practice* (2nd ed.). London: Sage.

Schön, D. (2003). From technical rationality to reflection-in-action. In P. Jarvis (Ed.), *Adult and continuing education: Major themes in education* (pp. 258–298). New York: Routledge.

Senge, P. (2006). *The fifth discipline: The art and practice of the learning organization* (Updated ed.). New York: Currency/Doubleday/Random House.

Spiro, R., Feltovich, P., Jacobson, M., & Coulson, R. (1995). *Cognitive flexibility, constructivism, and hypertext: Random access instruction for advanced knowledge acquisition in ill-structured domains.* Retrieved February 10, 2009, from http://ksei.bnu.edu.cn:82/old/elr/zhuanti/rzandxx/rzandxx012.pdf

Willis, J. (2007). *Foundations of qualitative research.* Thousand Oaks, CA: Sage.

W. K. Kellogg Foundation. *Evaluation Handbook.* Retrieved August 19, 2010, from www.wkkf.org/knowledge-center/resources/2010/W-K-Kellogg-Foundation-Evaluation-Handbook.aspx

Yin, R. (2009). Case study methods: Design and methods. Thousand Oaks, CA: Sage.

Part III

COLLABORATIVE LEADERSHIP

This final part of the book focuses on the people responsible for developing, sustaining, and evaluating partnerships. It addresses collaborative leadership from the perspective of both preK–12 and higher education.

Chapter 6, written by Shelley B. Wepner, addresses the question What is collaborative leadership? This chapter defines and describes collaborative leadership before examining essential characteristics and strategies needed for collaborative leadership. A discussion of one's psychological mindset for collaboration also is presented. Examples of how school district and higher education collaborative leaders develop partnerships are used to highlight the criticality of certain skills and strategies.

Chapter 7, written by Jeffrey Glanz, addresses the question: How do collaborative leaders cross boundaries? With a particular focus on the principal, this chapter delves into the many reasons that collaborative leaders reach out to other institutions to improve their schools. A model of school-community collaborative leadership is presented as a backdrop for describing best practices for partnering with community institutions to contribute to students' achievement. Research, theory, and real-life examples are incorporated into the discussion to demonstrate how a school leader can evolve into a collaborative leader.

Chapter 8, written by Shelley B. Wepner, uses the ideas from previous chapters to address why and how collaborative leaders forge ahead with partnerships. Different types of partnership examples are described to highlight reasons for their success. This chapter closes with specific guidelines for becoming a collaborative leader.

Together, these three chapters use myriad examples from firsthand experiences and reported case studies to present different pathways that collaborative leaders can take when they adopt and use the specific skills and strategies that are described.

6

Defining Collaborative Leadership

Shelley B. Wepner

This chapter

- describes collaborative leadership for both preK–12 and higher education leaders;
- delves into the essential characteristics, strategies, and psychological mindset needed for collaborative leadership; and
- provides examples of ways in which both school district and higher education collaborative leaders use their skills and strategies to develop partnerships.

* * *

In response to an elementary principal's request to have teacher education candidates placed in her school for an entire year, the K–12 curriculum coordinator approached a School of Education's (SOE) director of field experiences to inquire about such a possibility. As the curriculum coordinator explained, the school district had been put on warning by the state because of its low standardized test scores and was searching for ways to provide additional assistance to the children. The elementary principal thought that if there were teacher candidates interested in eventually teaching full time in an urban school district, they could get experience in her school, be interviewed for any possible job openings in the district and, most importantly, provide free assistance to her children. The SOE's director of field experiences was excited by the idea and communicated with her dean, who also was intrigued. The SOE director also checked with the department chairperson of the elementary education program so that there would be support and involvement from faculty for changing the way in which field experiences typically were done at the college. In the meantime, the K–12 curriculum coordinator sought permission from his assistant superintendent and superintendent to pursue the idea so that, when the time came, a partnership agreement would be signed and the appropriate resources would be allocated.

Once the K–12 administrators and the higher education administrators indicated support, they came together as a group. The SOE dean invited the four K–12 administrators—the elementary education principal, the K–12 curriculum coordinator, the assistant superintendent, and the superintendent—to meet with the field experiences director, the department chairperson, and a faculty member who would be in charge of overseeing the program in the school.

The elementary principal explained that she wanted continuity for her students. Teacher education candidates who had been placed in her building in the past for field experiences would come 2 days each week for a semester, and then never return. Her children would get attached to these teacher candidates, and then get disappointed by the teacher candidates' disappearance. She wanted the teacher candidates to do both their field experience and student teaching semesters in the same classroom in her building so that they would spend the entire year with her students. She also wanted someone from the district to interview the teacher candidates before they were placed in her school to be as certain as possible that they were sincerely interested in urban teaching. In return, she would guarantee these teacher candidates would have an interview for any job openings in the district, and she would conduct individual, mock interviews to prepare them for such interviews. She also would meet periodically with them as a group to help them acclimate to her school.

Such an arrangement meant that the college had to establish a special program for a small group of teacher candidates, alter scheduling patterns, change a faculty member's teaching load to work with the students throughout the year, develop a different structure for the seminar course, and conduct special interviews with these teacher candidates to determine their potential success in the school.

Once the administrative group understood and agreed to the program, they brainstormed ways to make it a showcase for both the school district and the college. Teacher candidates would have an additional technology requirement. They would receive a portable computer for this requirement through an internal grant. They also would be required to conduct three case studies. Cooperating teachers would be required to take a newly created one-credit mentoring course to help them work effectively with the teacher candidates assigned to their classrooms. Cooperating teachers also would participate every other month in the seminar course so that they were part of the discussions related to their own classrooms.

After 6 months of planning, the project began, and continues today 15 years later. This special "urban placement" program for teacher candidates has enabled the college to work closely with a district and has enabled an urban district to get additional help *for their elementary students at very little cost. The program is now in three elementary schools in the district.*

Six (75%) of the original administrative group has left the college or the school district. The only two left are the elementary principal and the key faculty member. While they have been critical to the program's successful implementation, they know that they did not have the wherewithal to develop a project of this magnitude.

* * *

Why could this project transcend significant administrative changes? What does this project have to do with collaborative leadership? Responses to these two questions introduce this chapter's focus on collaborative leadership in both preK–12 and higher education settings.

In response to the first question, "Why could this project transcend significant administrative changes?" no one person was solely responsible for this project. It was a collaborative effort between two different institutions with those involved having different roles and responsibilities needed for the partnership. Although the principal had the original idea, the curriculum coordinator initiated the partnership. Any of the other school district administrators who had had a conversation with the principal could have initiated the program. Alternatively, someone from the college could have initiated it to help promote urban education.

The original administrative group created a structure that could be fully integrated by both institutions. The resources that were required were manageable, and the changes made were sensible and doable. The administrative and teaching staff from both institutions were appropriately prepared and recognized for assuming their respective responsibilities. By the time members of the original administrative group began to leave, the project was succeeding well enough to be incorporated into each institution's annual goals and objectives.

In response to the second question, "What does this project have to do with collaborative leadership?" different leaders were willing to reach beyond their own institutional walls to explore and experiment with new ideas with other people who were committed to student achievement and teacher preparation. They also were willing to work with others to make changes to their systems to improve opportunities for their respective students. Even though their level of time and commitment to the project varied because of their own roles and responsibilities, they nevertheless contributed in some way to the partnership.

At the school-district level, the curriculum coordinator served as a collaborative leader for the project and was critical for beginning the conversation between the two administrative teams and overseeing the project at the district level. He worked closely with the field experience director, assumed new responsibilities and, most importantly, reached beyond his own district to initiate something new and different. He negotiated regularly with his administrative team and the university's team to garner support and acquire needed resources. The principal (with the original idea) served as a collaborative partner for the project. She worked closely with her teachers so that they were prepared to work with teacher candidates for an entire year. At the college level, the field experiences director served as a collaborative leader for the project by working closely with the curriculum coordinator to design and implement the project across institutions and with the faculty and her supervisor to implement the project. She too assumed new responsibilities. The faculty member from the administrative team served as a collaborative partner. He worked closely with his department to make the necessary programmatic changes and serve as the faculty liaison and field supervisor to the school.

The curriculum coordinator and field experience director also needed the support and involvement of their respective supervisors as collaborative partners; otherwise, the partnership could not have been launched. The top-level administrators needed to come together to identify why the partnership would be beneficial for their own institutions and how they could work together to create something that was exciting, yet not prohibitively expensive, and demonstrate to their supervisors the value of making such changes within their own systems. Their collaborative work enabled the curriculum coordinator and field experience director to develop the partnership protocol and involve those who would bring life to the project.

In essence, there is no such thing as one collaborative leader for a partnership. There are at least two, and possibly more, collaborative leaders who come together for the purpose of creating something bigger than what already exists. There also are collaborative partners, who while not as proactive, play a participatory role in the collaboration (Rubin, 2002). For someone to succeed as a collaborative leader, there are certain characteristics and strategies that are essential for success.

DEFINITION OF COLLABORATIVE LEADERSHIP

Collaborative leadership is the ability to reach out to others to create teams that do not mimic the leader but rather provide different and equally important strengths for the organization (Reeves, 2006). Collaborative leadership is about taking risks to convince others of the merits of pursuing something new, appreciating varying points of view, and demonstrating acceptance and respect for others involved in the pursuit of new ideas. Collaborative leaders work cooperatively and collegially with others on a task or initiative over time to achieve mutually agreed upon goals for innovative educational and professional development programs (Gross, 1988; Ravid & Handler, 2001). Collaborative leaders use communication and trust to build a climate that enables others to have a shared vision and work together for a common purpose. Critical to collaborative leadership is the ability to build and sustain the interest and involvement of each collaborative partner (Rubin, 2002), which usually requires sensitivity to and an awareness of interpersonal, institutional, and interinstitutional politics. A leader who is able to inspire commitment and action, lead as a peer problem solver, build broad-based involvement, and sustain hope and participation exhibits collaborative leadership skills (Turning Point, 1997). Collaborative leadership can exist within an organization, across organizations (school districts, colleges, businesses, and community organizations), or as any combination of these.

MOVING TOWARD COLLABORATIVE LEADERSHIP

An effective educational leader strives to strike a balance between attending to day-to-day managerial tasks and being a visionary leader; having time to be reflective and having time to be a visible leader; grappling with data and assessment strategies and addressing issues around teacher collaboration or building relationships with students; and attending to detail and logic, values and emotions. Given that a lack of time is a chronic issue for most leaders (Gmelch, Wolverton, & Wolverton, 1999), how leaders use time to approach their jobs and make decisions reveals their leadership orientation. For example, a leader who begins faculty meetings with information about students' test scores and spends such meetings presenting information about general operational procedures is oriented differently from a leader who uses faculty meetings to have teachers work together on innovative projects for the school. Similarly, a leader who spends at least half the day meeting with people is different from a leader who is cloistered in an office with emails and memos. Any and all of these approaches are useful, yet they reveal what is most important to leaders.

School district leadership practices are calling for a shift in focus from a single individual to a team of individuals as leaders (Marzano, 2003) who make decisions about programs, students, and projects. This collaborative work requires leaders to have yet another set of competencies. Even university leaders, who have been immersed in such collaborative work, still need to help their faculty and staff collaborate more, better, and differently. Particularly challenging for both school district and university collaborative leadership is the task of motivating faculty to collaborate beyond their own institutions.

School District Collaborative Leadership

Teachers need to understand *why* they are collaborating; in other words, they need to have an overall goal and know that their efforts will make a difference

(Kise & Russell, 2008). When teachers trust the process, they are willing to share ideas, take suggestions for improvement, and deal with conflict productively. The formation of collaborative professional learning communities within a building helps teachers work together. Teacher teams collaborate on the development of field trips and other events, action plans for struggling students, rules for homework and grading, rules for behavior and consequences, lesson planning, and common assessments (Leonard & Leonard, 2001).

Once teachers have experience with collaborative professional learning communities within their own buildings, they can apply many of the same skills and strategies to interinstitutional collaboration, especially if they do not have to contend with scheduling and workload obstacles, have the right people on their teams, and have guidance during the process.

Principals, as the building leaders, are primarily responsible for facilitating teacher collaboration within and across their schools. As studies have indicated (Fullan, 1985; Leithwood, 1992; Sergiovanni, 1994), the principal is a key player in promoting any type of school change and reform, especially communities characterized by collaboration. Some ways that help to build such a climate include the provision of time within the school day or compensation outside the school day for teachers to work together; effective communication so that teachers trust that such collaborative work is valued by the administration and community; and the inclusion of teachers in the decision-making process so that their leadership skills are developed.

Higher Education Collaborative Leadership

At the university level, the challenge is often getting faculty to develop collaborative teams with those outside their "hallowed halls" who can help them stay current with the realities of preK–12 classrooms. University faculty are experienced with collaborative work because they participate in committees that make recommendations about the curriculum; faculty hiring; reappointment, tenure, and promotion; student admissions; and resource needs. Seasoned faculty know what it means to share ideas, take suggestions for improvement, and deal with conflict productively.

Education deans or their counterparts, seasoned with faculty collaboration, know that they must share leadership through consultation and collaboration to succeed. Although they are successful in working with faculty on intra-institutional programs and policies, they might not be as skilled in exciting their faculty about inter-institutional initiatives. In addition to providing incentives (e.g., release time or stipends), they need to convince faculty of the benefits of working in partnership schools. Education deans need to identify ways to place a premium on such work in reappointment, tenure, and promotion guidelines; showcase such work within their own schools and across their universities; and reward faculty generously for their efforts in preK–12 schools.

Making Connections as Collaborative Leaders

A person's ability to lead others means that others are willing to listen, follow, and subscribe to one's requests and direction. Others see this leader as a role model who exemplifies what others strive to become. As Hank Rubin explains (2002), collaborative leaders possess the ability to manage people and institutions and to build bridges between the two. Collaborative leaders help others connect their personal needs with a shared public purpose and identify ways to work with others to accomplish something bigger and better than any one individual. Collaborative leaders truly understand how to balance individual personalities with bottom-line institutional interests, so that those involved in a collaborative effort believe that the additional work is worthwhile.

EIGHT ESSENTIAL CHARACTERISTICS OF COLLABORATIVE LEADERS

This section discusses eight common characteristics of collaborative leaders. Examples are given to demonstrate how collaborative leaders incorporate these characteristics into their partnership activity (Wepner, Hopkins, Damico, & Johnson, 2008). Figure 6.1 provides a definition for each characteristic.

FIGURE 6.1. Eight Essential Characteristics of Collaborative Leaders

1. *Knowledge*: information that is a result of actual and vicarious experiences
2. *Vision*: big picture ideas and dreams of what can be for an institution, given what is feasible in relation to the institution's history and current situation
3. *Interpersonal skills*: ability to relate to others through communication, shared understanding, and interaction
4. *Entrepreneurial skills*: ability to develop an institution's vision by taking personal, political, and financial risks
5. *Negotiation skills*: ability to confer with others to arrive at an agreement on goals and plans
6. *Managerial skills*: ability to direct all or part of an organization through the deployment and supervision of human, financial, material, and intellectual resources
7. *Work ethic*: belief in the moral virtues of hard work and diligence
8. *Confidence*: self-assurance about his or her ability to serve effectively

Knowledge

Knowledge refers to information and understanding derived from vicarious and actual experiences. It is something learned—the result of our process of inquiry (Dewey, 1938).

As educational leaders, we need to be knowledgeable about all that is within our aegis: the programs (curriculum, instruction, and assessment), the people (faculty, students, other administrators, parents, and community members), special initiatives, and organizational components (mission, goals, and action plans; administrative orientations; finances; and policies and procedures). Experience within the profession and in specific leadership roles contributes to our knowledge. Most of us, whether in preK–12 or higher education leadership positions, come to such positions after teaching in specific areas (elementary education or secondary mathematics) and serving in leadership roles (department chairperson, assistant superintendent, or assistant dean).

Our ability to serve as collaborative leaders requires that we (a) have in-depth knowledge of the components of our organizations that are possibly attractive and useful to potential partners; (b) know how prospective partners can contribute to our organizations and benefit from our organization's unique qualities; and (c) understand how to form and sustain partnerships so that our efforts are not in vain.

One of my best memories is of a middle school principal who used her vast knowledge of middle school education to develop a transformative relationship with a local university. In addition to her own experiences as a middle school teacher and administrator, she had risen to be president of her statewide middle school association. When she began discussions about forming a professional development school (PDS) with the education dean of a local university, she expressed her desire to use the PDS partnership as a mechanism for enticing elementary and secondary education students and faculty to come to her school. She volunteered to make presentations in education courses and conducted tours of her school. Within a year of forming a PDS partnership, 25% of her teachers and students were working with the university students and faculty, which was unprecedented. She used her knowledge to expose university faculty and students to the benefits of middle school education, which ultimately generated a new level of excitement in her school.

Vision

A vision is an idea, a vivid mental image, or dream of what can be. To be a visionary leader means that one believes in one's dreams *and* inspires others to move toward having those same shared dreams. Such a leader has the big picture of the institution; what currently exists and what can exist in the short term and long term. This leader has created a forward-looking, yet realistic, trajectory for the institution that takes into account its organizational components, programs, and people.

In higher education, if an education dean leads a school or college of education that requires faculty to teach seven to eight courses a year, that institution is primarily a teaching institution. This education dean cannot expect faculty to get multimillion-dollar grants or publish a book each year in their discipline because they do not have the same amount of time to write as those faculty who teach two to three courses a year. While this education dean can work to increase scholarly engagement and external grant funding, and can collaborate with other university administrators to reduce the teaching load requirements, he or she needs to have a vision that is consistent with the institution's teaching focus.

Similarly, if a high school principal works in an impoverished high school with issues of low achievement, high absenteeism, and high mobility, that principal cannot expect a 95% acceptance rate to top-notch universities without instituting major long-term changes. While this principal can transform the school to focus on academic achievement and increase the number of students who attend college, he or she cannot expect the school to have the same college acceptance profile as affluent private schools. Although difficult to accept at times, leaders need to have their big-picture agenda rooted in the reality of their situations.

Visions are realized when a leader identifies possibilities for taking an institution to its next level and enticing others to serve as catalysts for making changes. Partnerships between institutions arise when the leaders believe in the same vision for one or both institutions. In preK–12 and higher education, these shared visions usually focus on preK–12 student achievement, faculty development, and teacher preparation. As previous chapters in this book demonstrate, examples of preK–12/higher education partnerships abound in elementary, middle/junior high, and high schools across content areas in urban, suburban, and rural districts. Classroom teachers, special education teachers, and different types of specialists and administrators work with higher education faculty and administrators from all disciplines to improve pedagogical practice, enhance students' instructional experiences, conduct action research, and better prepare future teachers and leaders. Partnerships can have a specific focus or multiple purposes.

Development of a Shared Vision. I use my own work at Manhattanville College, Purchase, New York, to provide an example of the evolutionary process of a shared vision. Manhattanville College is surrounded by suburban school districts and small cities, many of which have seen the achievement gap grow because of an influx of Hispanic students. An alumna of the college offered a small-grant opportunity to those who developed innovative ideas for the college. We eventually received funding for the Changing Suburbs Institute® (CSI), designed to provide program development and professional development to schools, teachers, and administrators in nine school districts that have had the largest influx of Hispanic students.

We tested our idea at a breakfast with the school district superintendents and influential members of the Hispanic community. While the Hispanic community group was enthusiastic, the school district superintendents were somewhat skeptical because they had seen so many initiatives fizzle out in their districts, and thought of this as just another underfunded, underdeveloped project by a group of ivy-tower types. Somewhat discouraged, yet still determined, we moved forward with our plan to host an all-day educational forum that included keynote addresses and provided an opportunity for college, school district, and community representatives to meet in teams to identify and suggest ideas for addressing challenges specific to the Hispanic population. Although costly and under-subscribed, the forum proved to be helpful because we learned that, for our vision to be a shared vision with school districts and the community, we needed to create specific pathways for professional development and include the parent community.

In revisiting our vision for CSI, we have been able to develop and implement a three-pronged approach. First, we established professional development schools in our CSI districts to promote professional and program development. Each PDS has a faculty liaison who spends 2 days a week in the school collaborating with teachers and supervising student teachers. Second, we established a Parent Leadership Institute. Parents from the CSI districts come to the college for an annual day-long conference, all delivered in Spanish, to learn how to help themselves and others work effectively with the schools. Some of the PDSs also conduct their own parent workshops, also in Spanish. Third, we instituted an annual conference to showcase those serving as leaders for CSI and highlight projects that have taken place through CSI.

The Role of Leaders in Developing A Vision. A successful collaborative venture or partnership requires the contributions of multiple persons and the integration of multiple perspectives. It also needs a leader who can communicate the visionary message that compels others to believe in and act on an idea. The opening vignette and the CSI example indicate that the initial idea or vision for change does not necessarily have to begin with the collaborative leader, but has to be heartily adopted and internalized by such a leader so that it becomes that person's vision for change.

Partnerships with institutions require that leaders work together and represent their institution's perspective in developing a vision. Collaborative leaders need to involve their own institutional representatives as collaborative partners in pursuing the vision. Collaborative partners can be administrators, faculty, and staff who participate in one or more ways with the partnership. Different leadership configurations can exist, depending on the number of institutions involved in the partnership and the type of leadership structures that exist within institutions. Figure 6.2 provides examples of different partnership configurations.

For a vision to be realized, collaborative leaders need to have intrainstitutional and interinstitutional influence. They need to convince their own supervisors—board of education or board of trustees, a superintendent or a college president, or a principal or a dean—that their vision makes sense for their institution. They need to convince those they supervise—their administrators, faculty, and staff—that the additional time, work, and resources expended will be worthwhile. They also need to convince their newly acquired and/or long-term partners of the penetrating benefits of such a vision, so that their partners can persuade their own constituencies to be supportive and involved.

Collaborative leaders need to believe in their idea, know how to sell their idea, and believe in the people to whom they are selling the idea. They need to have the data to be persuasive and they need to collect such data continuously, so that they are able to reinforce their followers' decisions to support the vision. The quality and types of interpersonal relationships inside and outside the institution are critical to realizing a vision.

FIGURE 6.2. Examples of Different Leadership Configurations

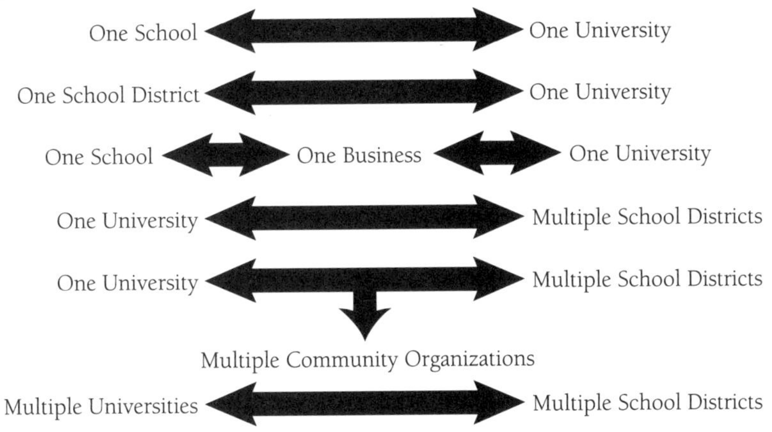

Interpersonal Skills

Interpersonal skills refer to our ability to communicate and interact with others in order to achieve certain effects or results. Communication, the process by which we assign and convey meaning to create shared understanding, promotes collaboration because of our orientation to process, listen to, and observe others.

Interpersonal skills are critical to the success of a collaborator. We can be knowledgeable and visionary as educational leaders, yet unsuccessful at developing partnerships because of an inability to reach out and communicate with others. Skillful communication promotes collaboration because it helps to build consensus with individuals and groups involved in partnerships. Consensus connects the partners' self-interests to the collaboration's purpose (Rubin, 2002).

Interpersonal skills influence both intra-institutional and inter-institutional collaboration. Slater (2005) found that those principals who had healthy interpersonal relationships were the most likely to promote collaborative work. They were communicative and supportive. They listened to their staff and were open to suggestions from their staff for solving problems and making decisions. They became role models for others' collaborative work and showed how relationships were building blocks to collaboration.

Barbara White, principal of Lakeview Elementary School in Ridley Park, Pennsylvania, exemplifies the way building leaders use positive interpersonal skills to engage in highly successful school-college partnerships. Barbara thinks of her teaching staff as an extended family. She works individually with her teachers to reinforce what they do well and encourages them to move to the next level of their professional growth. Her teachers feel secure enough to experiment with new instructional approaches that involve team teaching, technology infusion, and arts integration. Her teachers also trust her judgment about decisions that she makes for the school because they know she will do anything for them and their students.

Barbara's positive relationship with her teachers made it easy for her to form a PDS when approached by her local university. Her teachers quickly embraced the idea of receiving teacher candidates on a regular basis and working with university faculty to experiment with new projects. Teachers' enthusiasm for working with the university mirrored Barbara's positive stance. As a result, everyone benefited, with some of her teachers participating in programs with their students, which they never could have done without the assistance of university faculty and students.

Diana Quatroche from Indiana State University describes a situation at her university where a grant-funded program for the development of teacher candidates in the local schools was stagnant until a leader with positive interpersonal skills was put in charge. This new grant director, who also was an associate dean for the college of education, reengaged both the school district and the college faculty by communicating that she was there to support what they wanted to do for the program. She held open meetings to promote participation, supported faculty efforts to research different ways to implement the grant, and allowed the program's activities to emerge from the faculty. Eventually, she had faculty volunteers who were willing to participate in the schools as coaches for teachers and field supervisors for teacher candidates.

While these two examples portray leaders who used their interpersonal skills to create positive outcomes, they did not necessarily experience consistently smooth transitions as they developed their partnerships and cultivated new professional relationships. There was tension and anxiety at times because of the demands from the partnership, the personalities of some involved, and the conflicting demands on their time. Both knew from their experiences as administrators that they needed to maintain high-quality relationships with key persons within their organizations as they cultivated their relationships with those outside their institutions, so that their key persons could help sustain momentum.

Entrepreneurial Skills

Entrepreneurial skills allow a leader to realize one's vision by organizing and assuming the risk of an initiative. A leader can be knowledgeable and visionary, and know how to get along with people, yet still not successful because of a lack of entrepreneurial skills. To be entrepreneurial means that we are willing to take personal, political, and financial risks to develop what often is, at best, an amorphous idea that has potential. We are willing to reach out to potential partners, request time and resources from our own supervisors, solicit help from our colleagues, and set aside other demands to focus on a possibility. We are able to create and methodically pursue a plan that allows for the development of the partnership vision. As entrepreneurs, we need to be patient, persistent, and creative. We need to accept that our partners and constituents need time to absorb, accept, and support new ways of doing business. We need to persist in the face of adversity because, as with any new venture, there are up and down days. We also need to be creative in how we "choreograph" our enterprise (Arends, Reinhard, & Sivage, 1981) so that we select and guide the right mix of human and material capital to develop a system that works.

Eileen Santiago, principal of the Edison Community School in Port Chester, New York, uses her entrepreneurial skills to develop her vision of a school that brings the community into her building daily. She runs before- and after-school programs for both the students and parents, whether it is one-on-one tutoring, adult education programs, bilingual courses, or homework guidance programs. She has a medical and dental clinic for new immigrants, and does whatever she can to help her primarily Hispanic population thrive in her school community. Eileen transformed her school over a 10-year period by identifying and pursuing different types of partners and funding sources who could help her realize her vision. One such partnership involved the formation of a PDS with Manhattanville College so that she could get professional development assistance for her teachers and additional help for her students (see sidebar vignette by JoAnne Ferrara and Eileen Santiago).

Eileen took small and big risks as she worked with her teaching staff and supervisors to convince them to support her many different ideas for changing the focus of her school. She brought together and choreographed the many resources inside and outside her organization to create a new concept for her district. Although it was not always easy, she worked daily at figuring out new and different ways of attracting potential partners to contribute their resources. Today, her school is a showcase for the concept of a community school, with others clamoring to replicate what she has been able to accomplish.

Negotiation Skills

Negotiation skills help us to confer with others to arrive at an agreement of some matter. Most of us have negotiated the best possible prices for our homes and automobiles. We learned from experience that an original price listed was not necessarily the bottom-line price acceptable to a seller. We used information from our realtors, other buyers, family and friends, and consumer guides to help us negotiate back and forth until all parties agreed on a price. Similar types of negotiation skills are required for creating partnerships. Collaborative leaders are able to negotiate with every group that is directly or peripherally involved with a partnership until there is agreement on goals and plans. Collaborative leaders use information from their own faculty and administrative teams, their potential partners, other colleagues, and their own research and environmental scans to determine what and how to negotiate for the best possible outcome.

Particularly important to negotiate are key players' roles and responsibilities to keep them appropriately involved, aware of and respectful of boundaries, and honest about their level of participation and contributions to the partnership.

Collaborative leaders also are vigilant about negotiating their own roles and responsibilities so that they do not get buried in detail, yet do not relinquish so much power that they cannot continue to drive the partnership's direction.

Changes in programs breed conflict and disagreement (Arends, Reinhard, & Sivage, 1981). Partnerships are especially susceptible because of the inevitable mix of people and perspectives. Collaborative leaders' ability to negotiate can determine the fate of partnerships, because if conflicts are not resolved, people might not continue.

Working Together to Create a Shared Vision for a PDS

JoAnne Ferrara and Eileen Santiago

Manhattanville College, Purchase, NY,
and Port Chester School District, Port Chester, NY

The Manhattanville College/Edison Professional Development School Partnership (PDS) began in the fall of 2002. Prior to its official designation as a PDS, JoAnne, as the teacher educator from the college, had spent a year at the school supervising student teachers. During that time, JoAnne had ongoing discussions with Eileen, the elementary school's principal, about a shared vision of teaching, professional development, and teacher preparation. It soon became apparent to both that a more formal agreement was needed to support the work they envisioned doing at the school. Eileen saw this as an opportunity to bring resources from the college to the classroom. JoAnne wanted to work with a receptive principal and staff who valued innovation in professional development and demonstrated a high level of commitment to the profession. Both were critical for providing leadership to the PDS initiative and convincing the superintendent, the board of education, and the dean of the school of education of its merit.

The PDS started with a small amount of seed money allocated from the college and the district that allowed for retreats, substitute coverage for visitations, planning, and all program initiatives. We formed a school-based leadership team to oversee the budget and make recommendations for program initiatives. This leadership team, which meets monthly, uses data collected each year to determine future program initiatives.

Our formal and informal data for evaluating the partnership includes action research projects, student achievement scores, teacher retention statistics, teacher hiring statistics, surveys of participating adults (student teachers, field placement students, and classroom teachers) and children, and staff participation in professional development activities. The data collected thus far indicate that the partnership is working. The positive outcomes to date include easier hiring and retention of qualified candidates, better prepared teachers (new and veteran), improved school climate (characterized by trust and collaboration), and direct support for student learning (of student teachers and tutors), and research and publishing by both professors and teachers.

Even with the chronic challenges of time constraints and limited funding, this partnership continues to be mutually beneficial for the school and the college. It has been sustained by a common vision and philosophy of teacher education and by a shared definition of "what good schools look like and do for children."

Managerial Skills

Managerial skills enable us to direct all or part of our organization by deploying and supervising human, financial, material, and intellectual resources. Collaborative leaders are effective and efficient managers of their own organizations so that they have the time to build and sustain new partnerships (Rubin, 2002). The same level of managerial skills used to operate our organization needs to be extended to the partnership organization so that the costs do not exceed the partnership benefits.

Good managers take charge of their daily challenges. They manage people and plans so that people do what they are supposed to do to follow through with plans. Effective managers are not necessarily the persons who interact directly with all that is needed for an institution. They do not have to be the ones who work with, for example, assessment and scheduling databases and student evaluations. They know how to work judiciously with faculty and managerial teams so that specific tasks and plans can be accomplished. Knowing what, how, and to whom to delegate enables a leader to be available to pursue innovative initiatives such as partnerships.

Leaders' managerial skills need to be applied to partnerships, albeit a bit more cautiously, to accommodate one or more partners. Partners need to learn from each other which responsibilities are shared and which are assumed individually. They need to include as much as possible in written partnership agreements so that both shared and individual responsibilities are clearly articulated and formally accepted. (See Chapters 2 and 3 for more information about formal agreements.) Leaders should oversee partnership personnel, projects, resources, and paperwork as effectively and efficiently as they do for their own organizations.

Work Ethic

Work ethic refers to our belief in the moral virtues of hard work and diligence. It is our interpretation and treatment of our professional roles and responsibilities. Those with a strong work ethic expend a great deal of time and effort on work-related tasks to enhance the organization's growth, development, and vitality. A leader's work ethic has a significant influence on the morale of an organization because he or she serves as a powerful role model for those who work for the organization. When leaders work hard to help a partnership succeed, they communicate that they believe in the partnership's worth.

Leaders who share the load and do what they promise to do for the partnership build credibility and acquire supporters because they are demonstrating that they are sincerely committed to its success. On the other hand, leaders who cannot be reached, do not respond to emails or return phone calls, and do not do what they commit to doing, communicate that they do not really care about their people or the project.

A CEO's work ethic contributed to his ability to launch a business-university partnership to co-develop and evaluate the value of a technological product for the educational market. This CEO made sure that, as chair of a newly formed partnership committee, he followed up with assignments between meetings (e.g., writing and circulating minutes, calling consultants and potential donors, collecting data, and developing goals and action plans from the committee's recommendations). His work ethic became so contagious that committee members contributed in unprecedented ways, and the partnership began officially 6 months earlier than expected.

Confidence

Confidence, a dimension of self-awareness (Goleman, 1995), refers to our self-assurance about our ability to serve effectively. Personal reflection and feedback from others helps us to become aware of ourselves as collaborative leaders, as reported by Slater (2005), who studied principals in collaborative relationships. Slater's findings are consistent with studies of self-awareness that indicate that our identities come from our own stories or narratives about our experiences and interactions with others (Ashmore & Contrada, 1999; Bracken & Lamprecht, 2003; Wepner, D'Onofrio, & Wilhite, 2008). We become self-aware as a result of testing the meaning of exchanges with others in the workplace.

Experience in a leadership position promotes confidence because of multiple opportunities to interact with others and reflect on such interactions in relation to our sense of self. Confidence is what enables us to do our job because so much of our job requires an ability to "take the heat" from others for all types of decisions.

The ability to handle criticism from others is essential for partnership initiatives because of the change created in the organization and its positive and negative effects on personnel, programs, and resources. A principal was criticized mercilessly by his teaching staff when he rearranged the instructional schedule so that a group of university faculty could come into the school to work with his sixth graders on an innovative science unit on forensic medicine in the world. An education dean took a great deal of criticism from others when she hired a new associate dean who would be responsible for her PDS network because it involved a consolidation of other positions.

Leaders who are collaborative also need to have enough confidence to accept disappointments and use them to regroup. Collaborative leaders must be prepared for disappointments along the way, and use such disappointments to strengthen the partnership concept. Disappointments can emanate from colleagues and external groups. Those who express interest in being involved might not attend meetings and events when they say that they will. Money from constituent groups might not be forthcoming when such funding already has been included in the budget. Grant agencies and donors might decline funding requests. Speakers might turn down invitations, and superintendents and presidents might lose interest because of more pressing matters. These are just some of the many disappointments that can occur as a partnership idea is pursued.

DEVELOPING AS A COLLABORATIVE LEADER

Because leadership is so critical to school improvement, much has been written about leadership in education and the qualities needed to be an effective leader (e.g., Davies, 2007; Jenkins, Roettger, & Roettger, 2006). An important component of leadership is the ability to collaborate with others. Collaborative leaders somehow know how to form relationships with others that are collegial, communicative, egalitarian, respectful, honest, and mutually beneficial. They develop partnerships that focus on clearly established goals that honor the current needs and histories of the organizations involved (Lefever-Davis, Johnson, & Pearman, 2007). Numerous models exist for collaborative leaders to use as guideposts in forming partnerships (e.g., Houck, Cohn, & Cohn, 2004; Ravid & Handler, 2001), but they are almost as dizzying as the many diets that are offered for weight loss. As with dieting, collaborative leaders need to determine the one that works best for them, with consideration given to their own unique challenges. There are some basic strategies that have proven to be effective for collaborative leaders' use in cultivating effective partnerships.

Strategies for Cultivating Partnerships

Make Sure Your Institution Is Ready to Partner. There need to be at least two people within your institution who are interested in partnering with another institution. Within school districts, teachers, principals, and central administration must be willing. Within universities, faculty, deans, and upper-level administration must be interested. See Chapter 3 for a discussion about signals for partnership readiness.

Make Contact with the Right Person. Cold calls to district superintendents, education deans, and CEOs usually do not go very far because these people are inundated with solicitations on a near-daily basis. Find others who might have a relationship with a potential partner. It could be a graduate or member of a civic club or organization. (See Johnston & Armistead, 2007.)

Prepare Before You Approach a Potential Partner. Do research, or have someone else do research, by looking at the potential partner's website to learn about its history and philosophy. If appropriate, be prepared to provide a written plan that reflects what the goals of the partnership would be.

Develop a Relationship. Invest time in getting to know your partner. Let the partner know about your goals for students. Don't ask for money or equipment during the first meeting. Focus on common interests and shared goals.

Make Sure There Is Time to Collaborate. Communicate frequently and meaningfully. Depending on the location and communication interests of the partners, establish a schedule for meetings, email exchanges, or telephone calls. Develop agendas collaboratively so that partners are invested in the discussion.

Keep Your Partner Apprised of Your Responsibilities, and Ensure That All Partners Stay Apprised of Their Responsibilities. Make sure that you are complementing and not competing with your partner's efforts. Divide the labor so that goals are being accomplished. As one partner is taking the lead on developing the written agreement, another might be working on finding space for a special event related to the partnership. If partners are informed of each other's activities, there is less chance for conflicts to arise. (See Brodie, 2006.)

Create an Advisory Board or Leadership Committee. Use an advisory board or leadership committee to help determine the direction of the partnership, establish goals, identify an action plan, and monitor the implementation of the goals and plan. Have one of the collaborative leaders chair the board. Involve key faculty and administrators to ensure a shared vision for the partnership. Establish agendas and take minutes so that there is a record of the discussion and decisions. Meet as regularly as possible, respect different perspectives, and ensure through assignments that as many members as possible have an active role during and between meetings.

Delegate, Delegate, Delegate. Delegate partnership responsibilities to others who are interested and knowledgeable. Remember that, even if the person to whom you delegated will not be able to do it "as good as you do," you still will be helped in accomplishing your goals for the partnership (Emerson, 2008).

Provide Encouragement and Recognition. All of us enjoy a pat on the back for a job well done, especially those who exert additional time and energy to projects and programs that are not necessarily proven entities. By encouraging and recognizing others, we are helping to remind them that what they are doing will provide short- and long-term benefits to their own professional and personal development. Public recognition of others' efforts during meetings and other events enhances "the status and influence of the recipient in the eyes of other organizational members" (Arends, Reinhard, & Sivage, 1981, p. 18).

Support and Participate in Ceremonial Duties. Ceremonial duties such as ribbon-cutting events, end-of-year receptions, agreement-signing ceremonies, and welcoming remarks at important events provide visibility for and communicate commitment to the partnership. Even though such ceremonial duties often require additional time and/or resources, they are important symbolic gestures for conveying support.

Do Your Best to Acquire and Allocate Resources Fairly. Finding resources to support a partnership requires the ability to provide a persuasive rationale for its value and often a bit of luck, especially if funds are sought through grants and other funding sources. In addition to your quest for external funds, work closely with your partner to identify available funds within each institution. If a partner is a source of funding, help the partner understand how the funds will be used. Work closely with your partner to figure out how to allocate funds. While school district faculty might prefer stipends, university faculty might prefer release time from teaching.

Monitor the Partnership's Progress. Be vigilant about keeping track of previous and current partnership activities. Assign someone within your organization to keep a running record of accomplishments and impending projects to ensure that all partnership activities eventually are archived. When issues arise or projects are derailed, communicate with your partner so that, together, you can figure out ways to redirect people and resources. Your knowledge of the partnership's progress protects your ability to influence the partnership's path.

Keep the Concept Alive for Others. Communicate at every opportunity information about and progress with the partnership. While the partnership might be exciting to the collaborative leader, it simply might not be as important to others. Use the formal authority of your position and any bully pulpit opportunities to make your position clear about your support of the partnership. Use print forums—newsletters, alumni magazines, monthly updates—to highlight your institution's involvement with the partnership, and how it is benefiting the faculty and students. Similarly, use your website, any appropriate listserv, and email to do the same.

Along with the use of strategies is the need to reflect on your collaborative leadership abilities and determine whether you have the psychological mindset to serve in such a capacity.

Self-Reflection with Regard to Collaborative Leadership Qualities

Collaborative leaders have the ability to recognize the impact of their behavior and words, and adjust accordingly. They know their natural strengths as leaders and build on their strengths through professional development and practice. They use their strengths to help others become collaborative partners who then know how to provide support.

To help assess one's own ability to be a collaborative leader, there are inventories, checklists, and exercises. For example, the Institute for Educational Leadership, an organization focused on improving preK–12 education through positive and visionary change, developed a Collaborative Leadership Qualities Inventory to assess collaborative leadership skills and capacities (Institute for Educational Leadership, n.d.). This instrument of 26 leadership qualities (items include, for example, "I have in-depth knowledge of school and education reform" and "I manage conflict effectively") enables leaders to think about and take action on their development as leaders who can work effectively in diverse environments. While these instruments do not capture what collaborative leaders actually do, they help one to think about the qualities that contribute to success.

Psychological Components for Success

Critically important to collaborative leadership is a psychological mindset for collaborative work outside our own institutions. We need to be willing to change our usual work patterns so that we have the time and energy to cultivate one or more new partners. We need to have the wherewithal to ingratiate ourselves with new partners and be willing to adjust our usual patterns of interaction to fit with a new set of collaborative partners who operate differently because of the nature of their organizations. We also need to be willing to push members of our own organization to branch out of their comfort zones to serve as collaborative partners.

My colleagues and I studied the leadership dimensions of education deans. In many respects, our findings apply to leaders in general. Leaders' effectiveness reflects a combination of the person and the institutional culture. On a daily basis, leaders determine ways to balance individual, institutional, community, and societal needs with one's own needs. Leaders are called upon to decide quickly and act reasonably while satisfying multiple constituencies. These fundamental responsibilities of the position require leaders to have a strong sense of professional identity that enables them to evaluate how their own decisions impact their constituency, and adjust accordingly (Wepner, D'Onofrio, & Wilhite, 2008). Even with external pressures from state and federal mandates, leaders cannot minimize the impact of their daily decision making on the quality of life within the organization.

Those who have studied collaborative leadership in general (Rubin, 2002) or specific types of leadership positions (Slater, 2005) find that one's psychological framework contributes significantly to one's ability to do the job. For example, Slater believes that those who collaborate need to adapt new mindsets and ways of being because so much of the process requires a leader's ability to recognize, understand, and manage the emotional aspects of the process.

Whether at the preK–12 or higher education level, collaborative leaders call into play a variety of different emotional considerations, that is, a finely tuned sense of appreciation of individuals, groups, and themselves. They anchor their understanding of problems within the context of interpersonal relationships and organizational responsibilities. They recognize the importance of emotion in affecting decision making (Wepner, D'Onofrio, & Wilhite, 2008).

Zahorchak (2008) believes that leaders are made and not born. While there definitely are specific skills and strategies that can be learned for collaborative leadership, the psychological orientation for wanting to serve in this capacity probably is a combination of what a person brings to and learns about leadership. Everyone is not born to lead, just as everyone is not born to be a scholar, an athlete, a physician, or an artist. Vicarious and direct experiences with leadership can help determine whether individuals have the intellectual, emotional, social, and moral capacity to lead organizations. Self-reflection of one's psychological mindset for leadership can help determine the types of skills and strategies that already are developed as well as those that need to be developed to be able to serve effectively in such a role.

CONCLUDING REMARKS

Collaborative leaders are able to reach out to others to pursue new ideas and initiatives, particularly in the form of partnerships. Collaborative leaders are knowledgeable, competent, visionary, and confident. They possess strong interpersonal, entrepreneurial, negotiation, and managerial skills. They have a repertoire of collaborative leadership strategies that they use to promote and sustain partnerships. They also have a psychological mindset for working with others outside their own institution that enables them to push themselves and others to challenge the status quo. Collaborative leaders are born and made to believe that the use of multiple minds and hearts can only strengthen the education enterprise.

REFERENCES

Arends, R. I., Reinhard, D. L., & Sivage, C. A. (1981). The educational dean: An eamination of behaviors associate with special projects. *Journal of Teacher Education, 32*(5), 14–20.

Ashmore, R. D., &Contrada, R. J. (1999). Conclusion: Self, social identify, and the analysis of social and behavioral aspects of physical health and disease. In R. J. Contrada & R. D. Ashmore (Eds.), *Self, social identify, and physical health: Interdisciplinary explorations* (pp. 240–255). Oxford, UK: Oxford University Press.

Bracken, B. A., & Lamprecht, M. S. (2003). Positive self-concept: An equal opportunity construct. *School Psychology Quarterly, 18*, 103–121.

Brodie, C. S. (2006). Collaboration practices. *School Library Media Activities Monthly, 23*(2), 27–31.

Davies, B. (2007). *Developing sustainable leadership*. London: Paul Chapman.

Dewey, J. (1938) *Logic, the theory of inquiry*. New York: Holt.

Emerson, P. (2008, July). *Dealing with stress*. Presentation at the Women in the Deanship Annual Conference, Denver, CO.

Fullan, M. (1985). Change processes and strategies at the local level. *Elementary School Journal, 85*(3), 391–421.

Gmelch, W. H., Wolverton, M., & Wolverton, M. L. (1999, February). *The education dean's search for balance*. Paper presented at the Annual Meeting of the American Association of Colleges for Teacher Education, Washington, DC.

Goleman, D. (1995). *Emotional intelligence*. New York: Bantam.

Gross, T. L. (1988). *Partners in education: How colleges can work with schools to improve teaching and learning*. San Francisco: Jossey-Bass.

Houck, J., Cohn, K., & Cohn, C. (2004). *Preparing to lead educational renewal: High-quality teachers, high-quality schools*. New York: Teachers College Press.

Institute for Educational Leadership. (n.d.) *Collaborative Leadership Qualities Inventory*. Washington, DC: Author. Retrieved July 15, 2008, from http://www.iel.org/pubs/collaborative_leadership_qualities_inventory.pdf

Jenkins, L., Roettger, L. O., & Roettger, C. (2006). *Boot camp for leaders in K–12 education: Continuous improvement*. Milwaukee, WI: ASQ Quality Press.

Johnston, J. H., & Armistead, L. (2007, April). Win-win partnerships. *American School Board Journal, 194*, 42–44.

Kise, J., & Russell, B. (2008). *Differentiated school leadership*. Thousand Oaks, CA: Corwin Press.

Lefever-Davis, S., Johnson, C., & Pearman, C. (2007). Two sides of a partnership: Egalitarianism and empowerment in school-university partnerships. *Journal of Educational Research, 100*(4), 204–210.

Leithwood, E. (1992). The move toward transformational leadership. *Educational Leadership, 49*(5), 8–12.

Leonard, P. E., & Leonard, L. J. (2001). The collaborative prescription: Remedy or reverie? *International Journal of Leadership in Education, 4*(4), 383–399.

Marzano, R. J. (2003). *What works in schools: Translating research into action.* Alexandria, VA: Association for Supervision and Curriculum Development.

Ravid, R., & Handler, M. (2001). *The many faces of a school-university collaboration.* Englewood, CO: Teacher Ideas Press.

Reeves, D. B. (2006). *The learning leader: How to focus school improvement for better results.* Alexandria, VA: Association for Supervision and Curriculum Development.

Rubin, H. (2002). *Collaborative leadership: Developing effective partnerships in communities and schools.* Thousand Oaks, CA: Corwin Press.

Sergiovanni, T. J. (1994). *Building communities in schools.* San Francisco: Jossey-Bass.

Slater, L. (2005). Leadership for collaboration: An effective process. *International Journal of Leadership in Education, 8*(4), 321–333.

Turning Point. (1997). *Collaborative leadership: Self-assessment questionnaires.* Seattle, WA: Author. Retrieved July 15, 2008, from http://www.collaborativeleadership.org/pages/pdfs/CL_self-assessments_lores.pdf

Wepner, S. B., D'Onofrio, A., & Wilhite, S. C. (2008). The leadership dimensions of education deans. *Journal of Teacher Education Deans, 59*(2), 153–169.

Wepner, S. B., Hopkins, D., Damico, S. B., & Johnson, V. C. (2008, February). *From skeletal idea to successful initiative: Four deans' perspectives on using collaboration to develop strategic partnerships in teacher education.* Presentation at the Annual Meeting of the American Association for Teacher Education, New Orleans, LA.

Zahorchak, G. L. (2008). States must take the lead in improving school leadership. *Education Week.* Retrieved August 18, 2010, from http://www.nisl.net/resources/pdfs/Zahorchak-edweek-07-16-2008.pdf

7

How Collaborative Leaders
Cross Boundaries

Jeffrey Glanz

This chapter provides

- research, theory, and practice about developing collaborative leadership competencies;
- examples of crossing boundaries, especially in the principal's role; and
- ideas for developing one's capacity for collaborative leadership.

* * *

The Oakridge Public School District is located in a suburban setting approximately 80 miles north of New York City. The regional population is approximately 250,000. For a suburban area, however, it has attracted a relatively high percentage of industries and commercial establishments, probably due to its lower tax base. Within a 10-mile radius, three institutions of higher learning are available. The Oakridge School District, although not particularly diverse, is committed to preparing students to live in a culturally diverse and global society. The district maintains a strong commitment to educational excellence and community involvement.

After an earthquake and resulting tsunami wrecked coastlines along the Indian Ocean and killed an estimated 250,000 people, James McGregor, principal of Oakridge Middle School, seized the moment by planning a communitywide effort to raise awareness of the tragedy and encourage his students to play an active role in the relief effort. Wanting to use the catastrophic opportunity as a learning experience, Principal McGregor contacted several lead teachers during the Christmas break to solicit their involvement in

145

planning curricular and instructional activities when students returned. Teachers, under his facilitative leadership, planned lessons and assembly programs. Flags at the school were flown at half-staff to honor the dead; plans were made to raise money for relief efforts; and science and social studies teachers engaged students in lessons designed to help them understand the natural disaster and its long-term implications for human welfare.

Susan Fearson, a science teacher at the 900-student Oakridge Middle School, engaged students with such topics as energy transfer, plate tectonics, and the way in which waves travel. "It was an invaluable opportunity to bring science they have learned into events that were happening in the world," she said. She had her students spend a day reading articles she had collected from newspapers and the Internet. The next day, they created a timeline on a world map showing how the disaster unfolded. They also wrote one-page essays on different aspects of the tsunami. In social studies, Chester Esser said the best way to teach about the disaster was to link it to something the students were already learning or already knew. For example, he engaged students in research and discussions about how the natural catastrophe might affect existing conflicts in Sri Lanka and on the Indonesian island of Sumatra.

Principal McGregor, a strong believer in community involvement, invited a local politician to speak to students at the school about the importance of the relief effort. Students were given a larger political and social context for the work they were about to undertake. The principal invited others from the community to share their views on how the community might come together during this momentous and tragic occasion.

These instructional and curricular in-school activities, by themselves, were important means to connect real-world experiences (in this case, catastrophes) to the lived experiences of students in the classroom. However, Mr. McGregor envisioned educational opportunities for his students well beyond the usual instructional and curricular activities other schools might develop. He mobilized fund-raising efforts by calling together student, faculty, and staff leaders, while at the same time he reached out to local businesses and corporations. In-school and community efforts to hold events that would raise substantial monies for the relief effort were rapidly coordinated. Donations were solicited from the entire school community and given to the Red Cross during a major assembly program. The event was covered by local newspapers and other media. One article read, "At Oakridge Middle School, students, teachers, administrators, parents, and the local community rally to support the tsunami relief effort. It shows what whole community involvement can accomplish." Principal McGregor explained, "Community involvement is integral to our institutional mission, so it was natural for us to immediately think 'community' as we began relief efforts and educational planning."

Principal McGregor contacted three well-known relief agencies: the American Red Cross, Save the Children, and Care USA. He requested information about fund-raising activities and solicited their assistance for his work at the school. These three organizations later became the recipients of over $29,000 in collected donations. Several

months later, McGregor was given the Principal-of-the-Year Award by the school dis-
trict in large measure for his school-community leadership that resulted in far more
funds for the relief effort than other schools in the region had collected. (Vignette devel-
oped and adapted from information gleaned from Trotter, Honawar, & Tonn, 2005.)

* * *

Consider the fact that schooling in the 21st century is more complicated than ever. The headmaster or principal of yesteryear who single-handedly was able to monitor, oversee, and manage all school operations is no longer viable or even a possibility (Tyack & Hansot, 1986). The roles and responsibilities of principals have expanded (Sergiovanni, 2009) in the current world of heightened accountability, and they are challenged to manage and lead larger schools with increasing diversity. Many school systems have given over to principals fiscal or budgetary responsibilities. Teachers, too, are required to handle much more than in the past. Teachers and principals by themselves cannot manage the ever-changing educational landscape. The nostalgic notion or image of the teacher (e.g., Nick Nolte in *Teacher*) or the evangelical (some might say maniacal) image of the principal (e.g., Joe Clark in *Lean On Me*) who almost single-handedly combats social and political forces that "win the day" is naïve, at best, given the complexities educators face in today's schools (Schlechty, 1991). The notion of principal as white knight riding in on a white horse to save the day is ludicrous, if not unrealistic. In short, collaboration is more important than ever (Fullan, 2008).

But, have we been taught to be collaborative? Most of us have been raised in a culture that values independence and a go-it-alone attitude. Cultural images of independent leaders are embedded and reinforced through television, film, and other forms of media (see, e.g., Spring, 2004). When we do reach out to others, it is usually because we need something, not because we value the other's viewpoint to better inform our own. While we may realize that no single individual can go it alone, we have not developed the skills necessary to make collaboration work. These skills and/or mindsets might include, among other things, the ability to listen to others' viewpoints, the willingness to let go of a dogmatically held view in order to achieve consensus, the realization that solutions developed collaboratively almost always turn out better than decisions made by just one person, and the ability to negotiate, coach, and problem solve.

Effective school leaders today must cross boundaries. Collaborative leaders cross boundaries for a variety of reasons:

- Problems confronting schools are more complex than ever, and strategies that have worked in the past are no longer viable.
- School leaders realize that, alone, they cannot single-handedly address the plethora of exigencies they face daily.

- Schools today are accountable to the public they serve and are expected to serve their local communities as social resources.
- School leaders realize they and their schools are connected to the ever-expanding global community.
- In an economic environment of declining resources, school leaders must find and create new ways to support their school initiatives.
- Authentic learning can only occur when students are connected with communities and the challenges each faces.
- Schools, perhaps more than ever, realize their obligation to prepare citizens who are committed to civic engagement and service learning.

This chapter discusses ways in which collaborative leaders cross boundaries from their own institutions to other institutions or agencies. Both theory and practice are used to describe the characteristics, impetus, and methods that collaborative leaders use to work both sides of the aisle, so to speak, to develop and move along partnership ideas and agendas. Recommendations for serving as a collaborative leader are embedded in the chapter, rather than reserved as a stand-alone section. Many of the examples provided are generic enough to be applied, with some creativity, in all preK–16 contexts. Suggestions for how leaders negotiate, communicate, and problem solve within and across contexts are explored. Best practices for cross-boundary collaborations are provided. Professional development opportunities to extend personal knowledge of collaboration as well as to establish networks of potential collaborations are enumerated.

A school-community leader

- envisions the school building as nested within a larger community structure;
- considers ways the school may meet community needs, and vice versa;
- realizes that external community factors may influence student learning even more than school experiences;
- spends much time forging and sustaining relations with parents, certainly, but also with local businesspeople, religious institutions, colleges and universities, social and health agencies, and civic groups;
- thinks creatively about different ways of involving others in school matters as relevant;
- shares information with community partners;
- listens to community partners about ways to improve the school or suggestions for further collaborations;
- encourages innovative ideas and thinking by all members of the community; and

- forms committees of internal and external constituents to plan strategically ways to improve the school, in general, and more specifically, ways to better promote student achievement.

BELIEFS ABOUT DEVELOPING COLLABORATIONS

Devoting Time to Building Relationships

Principals cannot afford to ignore the community in which their buildings reside. Today's schools are so complex that inattention to concrete and sensible ways to involve community to benefit the school is shortsighted at best. Certainly, principals are busy with a plethora of demands within the school building. Still, without serious and mindful attention to building school-community ties, the principal will not be able to best and most effectively address the varied needs of learners in the building. Without doubt, a principal should establish leadership practices that consider the importance of involving school district and community resources in order to further the school's mission. Effectiveness as a principal is contingent on one's ability to garner communitywide resources aimed at enhancing the educational experiences of students that directly or indirectly promote student learning. Work in schools does not occur in isolation of the large external school community (Epstein et al., 2002). A principal needs to see the value of crossing boundaries as a means of enhancing the overall educational program in the school.

Working with Teachers vs. Dealing with Community-Related Issues

Certainly some could argue by citing relevant research (e.g., Leithwood, Seashore Louis, Anderson, & Wahlstrom, 2004; Marzano, Pickering, & Pollack, 2001) that working directly with teachers on instructional matters has significant positive consequences for student learning. However, given the complex nature of teaching and learning, combined with many outside school influences on student learning, careful attention to factors beyond the classroom and, even, school door can only bring to bear additional important resources to assist in one's work as a principal. These outside efforts should use community resources that have a direct impact in the classroom. For example, if a local senator's office funds a modest $20,000 grant to purchase a dozen computers with wireless capability and other multimedia items, then teachers have better resources to accomplish their goal of promoting student achievement. Successful principals look for creative ways beyond the walls of the school to enhance instructional and curricular work within the building. These individuals make a difference. They are forward looking, optimistic, and focused on furthering the school mission (e.g., Goldberg, 2001).

Establishing Contacts in the Community

Community relations leadership is a moral imperative for 21st century principals. They must articulate a commitment toward establishing contacts within the community to promote student achievement by reaching out. Developing a strategic plan is essential. Examples of activities that effective school-community leaders can pursue include:

- visits to local business establishments and health agencies;
- involvement with local civic associations;
- participation in nonschool community functions;
- the offering of ongoing parent workshops and student-parent events;
- invitations to parents and community members to volunteer in the school;
- solicitation of partnerships with local colleges;
- celebration of community events;
- circulation of school-community newsletters; and
- hosting of community breakfasts.

Fiore (2002) suggests three kinds of school-community relations plans:

- *Coordinated plan.* Developed by the school with representatives from the community. The principal retains authority in this plan, but the involvement of central office staff and other community nonprofessional educators is vital to its success.
- *Centralized plan.* Initiated and coordinated by central office staff, usually the superintendent or designee. This plan centers on tapping into the vast expertise and resources of central office personnel involving matters of public relations and community involvement.
- *Decentralized plan.* Involves almost no direct participation of the central office; instead, authority for development and coordination rests with the building principal. This plan allows a principal to frame a community effort that meets the specific needs of a particular school.

The principal is ultimately responsible for the success of the selected plan and should address key questions as the plan is developed and implemented (Fiore, 2002, p. 14):

- Does the plan make use of appropriate and varied communication channels for the various audiences involved?

- Do all individuals with responsibility in the school-community relations plan know what the goals and objectives are?
- Does the plan contain strategies for involving all stakeholder groups whenever possible?
- Are the goals, objectives, and desired outcomes of the school-community relations plan consistent with the school philosophy and the state's laws?
- Are the goals, objectives, and desired outcomes stated in measurable terms to the extent possible?
- Has the design of the plan's strategies and activities considered available human resources, funds, and facilities?
- Does the plan distinguish between long- and short-term goals and objectives?
- Are there provisions in the plan for future audits of its effectiveness and results?
- Is the school-community relations plan tailored to the specific needs of the school and its community?
- Does the school-community relations plan take into account the need for inservice education of the staff?

Scheduling Time to Forge Community Relationships

A strong school-community leader cannot sit behind a desk; instead, he or she must pay close attention to the community and its activities. Monthly meetings or luncheons with key community members (e.g., the local Rotary Club or League of Women Voters) are recommended. Membership in local, state, and national associations and involvement with different types of community groups (e.g., museums, galleries, and other cultural attractions; ethnic and cultural groups; health agencies and hospitals; senior citizens; and artists, musicians, and craftspeople) also are important.

Working with Local Politicians

Although community involvement is recommended, caution is suggested when working with local politicians. Interacting with local politicians is wise, but given the vicissitudes of politics and the ever-changing nature of alliances, siding with one politician over another might come back to bite you later. Maintaining friendly relations with all is highly recommended. Consult the superintendent for advice before engaging in a political campaign. Politicians are often willing to assist with school-related projects regardless of one's personal political stance. Seize upon their willingness to help.

Closing the Achievement Gap

Community involvement and awareness does much to dispel the insular approach to raising academic achievement, especially with the Black-White achievement gap. Numerous nonschool-related forces and factors affect student achievement. Remaining cognizant of our responsibilities to promote student learning within direct areas of control, proactive school-community leaders attempt to influence nonschool related factors that also impact student learning. Principals can contribute greatly to the larger effort to narrow this achievement gap by serving as advocates, for example, of "policies to stabilize family housing, school-community health clinics, early childhood education, after school programs, and summer programs" (Levine, 2004, p. xi).

Principals who are effective school-community leaders maintain an optimistic belief that their work makes a difference. They remain committed to the notion that all students can learn, albeit at different rates. They are unrelenting in pursuing ways to help each child succeed and reach potential. Although they realize the limits of their efforts, they remain steadfast to their commitment to close the achievement gap.

FRAMEWORK FOR SCHOOL-COMMUNITY COLLABORATIVE LEADERSHIP

Figure 7.1 illustrates the role of the school leader, in this case the principal, in attempting to facilitate and influence the critical elements of school-community relations (i.e., encouraging wide and diverse involvement, building community alliances with diverse institutions, and influencing out-of-school factors that affect student learning). Effective principals reach out to a variety of community constituents. When these aspects of school-community relations work at their best, a large array of forces, resources, and personnel are brought to bear to positively influence student achievement. Best practices for promoting deep and far-reaching collaborations are presented in the following section.

BEST PRACTICES IN BUILDING COMMUNITY ALLIANCES

Arriaza (2004) frames community as "a source of knowledge that educators need to access in order to understand the cultural, social, and linguistic barriers that separate schools from the communities they serve" (p. 14). Constructivists view the community as the school's natural extension since its students exhibit cultural traits that spring from within their communities. They strongly encourage the school's involvement in the community's social events because they believe that it obligates communities to commit to assisting schools by giving "resources (tangible and intangible) and services needed" (p. 15).

FIGURE 7.1. A Model of School-Community Collaborative Leadership That Crosses
Boundaries to Promote Student Learning

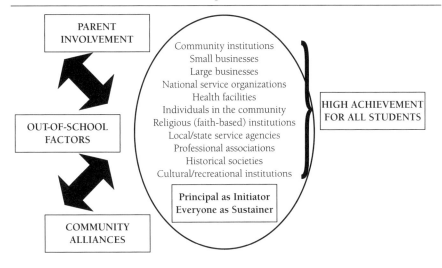

Best Practice 1: Undertake Community Building

It is not easy to convince the community to join the school in partnerships. Of course you will find the irate parent who continually complains or the businessperson who has a vested interest in marketing his product in your school who will get involved. But to encourage community members who truly believe in contributing positively to student growth is not so simple. How do you attract those kinds of individuals or groups? How do you build community support for your school? Reynolds (2002) offers several practical examples of building community support that are mutually beneficial to both the school and the community:

- *Community night.* Teachers and student delegates from the Future Teacher's program teach evening classes to members of the community.
- *Community lock-in.* Teachers, community members, and local police officers volunteer an evening to supervise middle level and high school students who want to spend a night in the school playing games and having fun. Local patrons donate prizes for the students to win.
- *Community betterment project.* Students volunteer after school and weekends to help with various landscaping projects for businesses in the community.

- *Food pantry distribution.* Students volunteer to help unload trucks at a local church to ensure that the community food pantry is well-stocked when people in the community are in need.
- *Share resources.* Schools partner with local chapters of national associations, other schools, and area organizations to promote community goodwill by engaging in the following activities:
  - Staff members and the local police officers produce a Drug Abuse Resistance Education (DARE) graduation program for elementary school students as part of a drug-free program.
  - A neighboring school uses another school's gymnasium and multipurpose buildings for athletic contests.
  - The Future Business Leaders of America organization sponsors a blood drive in a school's gymnasium for the community.
  - The Family, Career and Community Leaders of America organization collects Toys for Tots for families within the community

Best Practice 2: Develop an After-School Program

Although many schools offer after-school programs, very few of these programs have developed a curriculum and learning activities that offer enrichment or remediation to students who attend the school during the day. Successful school-community leaders take an active role in shaping and influencing the curriculum in after-school programs. Here are a few suggestions for getting started:

- *Conduct a need assessment.* What type of after-school program already exists? Was there one in the past? What happened to it? Who controls programming of the after-school program (private enterprise, school district, or the school itself)? What authority might you have to get involved in shaping the curriculum of the after-school program? Who are the students attending the after-school program? What are their educational needs?
- *Seek approval* for helping to coordinate the curriculum in the after-school program and serve as its advocate. Demonstrate why involvement in the after-school program benefits your students academically.
- *Form a curriculum committee.* Involve teachers, parents, and professional specialists to help review after-school curricula and offer suggestions for better matching learning activities in the after-school program with in-school activities.
- *Train teachers.* Offer professional development opportunities for teachers who work in the after-school program. Assist them in providing

appropriate remediation and/or enrichment lessons matched to the special needs of each student who attends that school.

After-school programs may have different purposes and foci, which are not always primarily academic. Still, such programs build strong community alliances that can indirectly affect student achievement. Fashola (2002) describes several successful after-school programs that have a community focus. Any opportunities to visit and observe such programs will indeed strengthen your commitment to building community alliances. Three successful programs are described below:

- *New York City Beacons.* Approximately 40 New York City schools currently have beacon programs. "The main goal of the program is to reduce crime and violence among youth and their families by providing after-school programs for the whole family, to ultimately improve school and community linkages" (Fashola, 2002, p. 45). Educational, cultural, and recreational activities, workshops, and programs are available for the whole family. Social welfare, language acquisition skills, family counseling, and health-related services are provided. Youth participate in decision-making activities to help eliminate violence, substance abuse, juvenile delinquency, and teenage pregnancy. Parents are encouraged to help in the after-school program and participate in adult education, cultural, and recreation classes during the nonschool hours. The Beacons staff accompany parents to meetings with school staff, and host parent-teacher Beacons meetings. The school serves as a hub for creating a network of youth and adults, school staff members, and minority communities to increase school attendance and improve community problem-solving capabilities.
- *Child First Authority (CFA).* The Child First Authority is a Baltimore community-based, after-school program that seeks to improve the quality of life in low-socioeconomic communities. Funding comes from the mayor's office, the governor, and the city council through a local Industrial Areas Foundation branch named Baltimoreans United in Leadership Development (BUILD). During the first year of funding, in 1996, the CFA established community-based learning centers in 10 schools. The program serves public school students and their families in school-based, extended-day centers. The program uses the schools as hubs of activity in which parents, staff members, administrators, church members, students, and other community members get together. CFA programs are not all the same and depend on the needs and goals of the program planning teams.
- *Big Brothers Big Sisters of America.* Big Brothers Big Sisters of America was created specifically to provide young children from single-parent

families with adult mentors. The organization is mainly funded by the U.S. Department of Justice. The goal of this program is to provide young, inner-city children with role models who will teach them to make healthy decisions and help them strive for the best in life. Children participate in Big Brothers Big Sisters of America by connecting with local agencies. Adults who sign up to be a big brother or big sister are screened and, if selected, asked to spend at least 4 to 6 hours every month with their little brothers or sisters.

Best Practice 3: Avoid Barriers to Implementation

Leaders committed to school-community leadership inevitably encounter obstacles to implementing school-community collaborations. Remaining aware of these obstacles is critical to success. Proactive school-community leaders take affirmative steps to build and sustain community alliances.

Sanders (2001) suggests that schools expand their database of potential community partners. Principals might solicit interest among universities/colleges, health care organizations, government agencies, volunteer organizations, faith organizations, senior citizen groups, and/or agencies outside their geographic neighborhood. Sanders and Harvey (2002) provide a more detailed array of possible collaborations with the community, described, in part, below:

1. *A nonprofit health organization.* This type of organization, possibly affiliated with a school of medicine, can assist in the prevention of hypertension and diabetes in high-risk communities. The organization can work with the school to survey families about their knowledge of health care issues. In addition, the organization can sponsor a good nutrition poster competition and a healthy cooking competition for students and their parents.
2. *A collaboration between a community-based initiative and a local church.* The collaborating organizations implement an after-school program with academic, cultural, and behavioral objectives for students. Students are assisted with homework, attend field trips, and engage in recreational and cultural activities. The program begins immediately after school and ends around 5 p.m., Monday through Friday. This type of after-school program has a predesigned parent/community involvement component, which includes a 4-hour per month volunteer requirement. Parents can volunteer or have representatives, such as older siblings, grandparents, and other family members, volunteer for them. The program is offered free of cost to its participants.

Reaching Out to University Faculty to Create a Math Night for Parents at a Low-Performing School

Christine L. Marroquin

Lamar Elementary School, Corpus Christi Independent School, Corpus Christi, TX

A year ago I was given an assignment in an inner-city school rated unacceptable by the Texas Education Agency. One of my first thoughts about my new assignment was how to replicate the collaboration system that had been established at my previous assignment. Would individuals be willing to invest time in a low-performing school?

During the first semester the priority was clear: We would have to change the culture of the school from a "behind closed doors" mentality to one of cooperation and affiliation with others. Until collaboration was visible inside the school, inviting those from outside to work with us would be difficult. Before we could cultivate collaboration among the staff, we would have to learn to trust one another. Team building activities, professional development, and familiarizing staff with the benefits of collaboration were essential components in our course of action. This culture change took time; however, the rewards have been immense based on data collected.

To help staff conceptualize how partnerships help schools achieve, we reached out to Dr. Elaine Young, a Texas A&M University–Corpus Christi math professor recognized by our community for her eagerness to work with preK–12 schools. Collaborating with our teacher advisor, Dr. Young helped us create and implement a math night that involved her university students and our Lamar staff. Student and parent attendance was less than expected; however, our faculty participation was 100%. This was a significant milestone in our efforts to build staff collaboration. The synergy observed gave us hope and led to other collaborative events that data have proven to have positively impacted student achievement.

A year later Dr. Young and her university students helped us hold a second family math night. The results were phenomenal. Attendance was triple that of a year before. Comments from the university students who participated included "the teachers loved our activities . . . I was a part of something that will contribute to the classroom" and "it was pretty cool to teach a teacher." Our staff gained new knowledge from these aspiring teachers. Our walls are coming down; teachers are reaching out; and a new culture is emerging.

Whether internal or external, collaborative efforts help initiate progress. Sustaining those efforts necessitates being visionary and having a willingness to abandon the status quo. Lamar Elementary, now rated academically acceptable, is flourishing due to the partnerships founded through collaboration.

3. *A health care facility.* The facility provides health information to staff, students, and parents through workshops and classroom presentations. Topics can include cholesterol management, HIV prevention and treatment, Attention Deficit Disorder information, parenting skills, diabetes management, and CPR certification. The organization can provide refreshments and volunteers to help implement school events such as family fun and learning nights, father and son banquets, and an end-of-year picnic. The organization can also sponsor a student academic recognition program, which honors academically successful students at quarterly awards breakfasts.

4. *A local church.* A local church can have an outreach committee that provides school supplies to students in need, and also provides refreshments for school parties, including Valentine's Day and Christmas parties. Members of the outreach committee can work as volunteers in the student cafeteria.

Best Practice 4: Become Part of a Professional Development School (PDS) Initiative

A professional relationship with a local college or university is not easily formed. Too often principals are unaware of the possibilities, too busy with other matters, or are dissuaded by school district officials. Colleges and universities too are apt to isolate themselves from the actual realities of public school teachers and administrators. Exceptions are professional development schools (PDS) that provide unique ways for schools and colleges to collaborate. Schools and colleges share in the responsibility of preparing future teachers and preparing school children to succeed academically and otherwise.

Many PDS models are possible, allowing schools and colleges opportunities to create relationships that make sense to their particular situation and needs. See Chapter 3 in this book for a description of different PDS models. Principals, as school-community leaders, should engage in the following activities to get started in forming a PDS:

- Take the initiative to reach out to and call meetings with college and university faculty in the school or department of education to develop a PDS model. Work closely with the college dean or chair to ensure the successful implementation of a PDS.
- Identify school personnel and college faculty to help in planning and developing the PDS.
- Offer on-site classroom space for college classes so that courses might be held at the school during the day.

- Provide opportunities for college students to observe, tutor, and teach in classrooms, as appropriate, during the school day.
- Co-plan professional development opportunities for both teachers and professors. Encourage college faculty to offer in-school workshops, and encourage school teachers to attend professional development sessions at the college. Offer incentives to teachers who engage in the PDS model (e.g., release time or stipends).
- Encourage colleges to offer on-site graduate courses or programs for teachers and suggest that senior teachers teach graduate courses at the college or university.
- Encourage school teachers to mentor teacher education candidates.
- Share the research about the PDS model with parents and other community members and solicit advice and assistance from them.
- Hire a PDS consultant.
- Seek opportunities to foster student learning and achievement by encouraging professors and teacher candidates to work with teachers and students.

BEST PRACTICES IN USING COMMUNITY RESOURCES AND REFORMS TO CLOSE THE BLACK-WHITE ACHIEVEMENT GAP

One in eight children never graduates from high school. Two in five never complete a single year of college, and every 9 seconds a public high school student drops out of school. We spend more money on prisoners than we do to educate our children. Barriers to learning include increased levels of violence, teen pregnancies, depression, eating disorders, sleeping disorders, and absentee family members. Good teaching is certainly necessary, but it is not enough.

Research has demonstrated that social class differences affect student achievement (Rothstein, 2004). Rothstein explains that "parents of different social classes often have different styles of childrearing, different ways of disciplining their children, different ways of communicating expectations, and even different ways of reading to their children" (p. 2). Although he admits that these social class differences "do not express themselves consistently or in the case of every family" (p. 2), patterns or family tendencies on the average can be noted.

Rothstein (2004) explains that these social and economic realities can impact student learning. "Lower-class children, on average, have poorer vision than middle-class children, . . . have poorer oral hygiene, more lead poisoning, more asthma, poorer nutrition, less adequate pediatric care, [and] more exposure to smoke" (p. 3). Other social class characteristics also affect student achievement. For instance, inadequate housing facilities is an important social factor to consider (lower-class children are more likely to live in transitory housing accommodations that can lead to poorer attendance rates in school).

Good teaching, high expectations, rigorous standards, accountability, and inspiration are not enough to close the Black-White achievement gap because of social and economic factors that affect achievement. Although these in-school factors can go a long way to close the gap, by themselves they are inadequate. Teachers cannot go it alone. Despite best efforts, some students will not succeed. They will not succeed, in all likelihood, due to social and economic forces beyond the immediate control of a school.

What role does the principal play in the school and community to narrow this gap and help ensure that all students achieve at a level that corresponds to their academic potential? Of equal importance is the principal's influence on factors external to the school via school-community relations that might also contribute to narrowing the achievement gap. In other words, school-community relations may play a critical role in assisting school officials (principal, teachers, and counselors) to help each child learn to the best of his or her ability. Clearly, principals cannot influence certain factors such as parental income levels or access to adequate living quarters. But, through the use of effective school-community relations, a principal can bring to bear the resources of a number of social agencies through partnerships. The following two best practices are based on Rothstein's research and suggestions:

Best Practice 5: School-Community Clinics

Adequate health care for lower-class children and their parents is needed to help close the achievement gap (Rothstein, 2004). Principals can assist by making connections with local health care facilities to establish a health clinic at the school to serve children from disadvantaged homes. Information about health services in general can be found at http://www.mayoclinic.com/; http://www. narhc.org/; and http://www.1-800-schedule.com/. Visit a local health clinic, establish rapport with local officials, and reach out to local politicians for assistance. Also, provide family health support in your school to contribute to the health of students and families attending your school. Health clinics associated with schools in lower-class communities should include obstetric and gynecological services, pediatric services for children through their high school years, physicians to serve parents of all school-age children, nurses to support these medical services, dentists and hygienists for both parents and children, optometrists and vision therapists, social workers, community health educators, and psychologists or therapists to assist families and children who are experiencing excessive stress and other emotional difficulties (Rothstein, 2004). Rothstein asserts that schools might get a bigger test score jump, for less money, from dental and vision clinics than from more expensive instructional reforms.

Best Practice 6: Early Childhood Education Centers

Research demonstrates that formal educational experiences for low-income children that begin at 6 months of age and continue throughout the preschool years can play a significant role with student achievement in later years of schooling (Rothstein, 2004). School-community principal leaders who are forward thinking will reach out to parents of the community to make them aware of such early childhood programs that may exist in the community. Affiliations or collaborations with local churches, civic associations, or health centers will give you access to parents of preschool children. Whenever possible, serve as a guest lecturer to help parents learn about the impact of toddler and preschool experiences on academic achievement in school. Explain that daycare settings do not offer the necessary enrichment their children will need to succeed. Instead, they need formal early childhood programs that are more content rich and usually staffed with licensed teachers. Urge local politicians to support such early childhood programs.

BEST PRACTICE CASE STUDY IN HIGHER EDUCATION

While this chapter focuses on the need for school leaders to forge deep and meaningful relationships with the community, this responsibility is equally relevant and necessary for those in higher education. Students attending institutions of higher education must develop the requisite knowledge, skills, and dispositions to interact intelligently in a global economy. Given this need, institutions of higher education cannot afford a silo mentality. Below is one such institution that readily sees the importance of such collaborations.

Provost Devorah Lieberman, academic leader in a small liberal arts college in New York City, aims to infuse civic engagement throughout the curriculum. "We believe that offering students opportunities to engage with the larger community will serve not only to deepen learning for students, but will make significant contributions to the communities serviced by our students" (personal communication, January 9, 2009).

Miranda, a junior, attests to her experiences with Wagner's civic innovations project. She is currently enrolled in a civic innovations course on health policy taught by government and politics faculty. She and her classmates were invited to a breakfast at which area residents testified to the lack of available and affordable care on Staten Island, New York. Miranda works as a tutor in the community and sits on a community board to discuss ways to maintain health services in a worsening economic climate.

Provost Lieberman looked at her college's curriculum to determine the extent to which service-learning programs and experiences were offered. She discovered that her college's nationally known curriculum, the "Wagner Plan," which integrates experiential learning and civic engagement with curricular requirements for majors, did not go far enough. Linkages between academic departments and community organizations that hosted student practica were not strategically and developmentally organized. While faculty members suggested community venues for service learning, collaboration between the community organizations and the professors were cursory at best.

To address this disconnect, Wagner addressed two questions: (1) How do we ensure that all students receive community-based experiences that are truly meaningful in the context of their academic preparation and career aspirations? and (2) How do we use our human and intellectual resources to achieve sustainable social improvement for the residents in the Borough of Staten Island?

After much campuswide deliberation, it was decided that Wagner's new civic engagement initiative would

- create partnerships that engaged an entire department with a single community service agency;
- establish courses within the department that fulfilled desired student learning outcomes as well as needs of the community partner; and
- commit to sustainability to provide continuity for the community partner, participating students, and partnering academic departments and their faculty. (Thanks to Cassia Freedland and Devorah Lieberman for the material in this case study that they are preparing for publication in a more extensive study.)

PERSONAL PROFESSIONAL DEVELOPMENT OPPORTUNITIES FOR SCHOOL LEADERS

Collaboration is not instinctive for many individuals. Learning to collaborate, however, is imperative. There are numerous professional development opportunities available to help with collaboration across contexts and the establishment of professional networks.

K–12 Professional Development Opportunities

Summer Leadership Programs. The Harvard Graduate School of Education's Programs in Professional Education are probably the most renowned programs for preparing leaders. In-depth summer institutes are offered, but also year-round opportunities. Go to http://www.gse.harvard.edu/ppe/k12/ for information about this program.

Professional Organization Opportunities. The following organizations offer superb opportunities to develop professional networks with colleagues on a national and an international level. Attend at least one major national conference yearly, and encourage faculty to attend as well. Obtaining funding to support these conference opportunities is admittedly more difficult than ever. The rewards, however, for attending are enormous. Try to seek grant support from philanthropies, foundations, and school boards:

- Association of Supervision and Curriculum Development
- National Association for the Education of Young Children
- Teachers of English to Speakers of Other Languages
- National Council of Teachers of English
- National Council of Teachers of Mathematics
- International Reading Association
- National Science Teachers Association
- National Council for the Social Studies
- Council for Exceptional Children

District-Based, Professional Development Opportunities. School leaders often do not capitalize on district-based services. Many opportunities for professional development exist at the district level. For instance, in one school district, several important training opportunities in technology are available. In their efforts to cross boundaries elsewhere, school leaders should not neglect opportunities in their own backyards.

Visitations to Other Districts (in and out of state/country). Just as we recommend that teachers visit others who teach, so too school leaders would gain greatly from observing innovative practices elsewhere. Opportunities for such visitations should be seized when they become available.

Web-Based Activities. Johns Hopkins University offers a cutting-edge approach to reaching out to community schools and offers a wide range of professional development opportunities. Other universities offer similar programs. This particular one is offered as an example because it offers excellent opportunities for students and school personnel at all levels. For information about this program, go to www.jhu.edu/news_info/educate/alpha/. The University of Washington K–12 Resource Guide is an excellent website that addresses the Black-White achievement gap. Valuable leadership training is offered to grapple with the issue. Go to the following website for additional information: www.outreach.washington.edu/k12guide/resourcepage.asp?ProjID=426).

Higher Education Professional Development Opportunities Summer Leadership Institutes. Summer is a special time for renewal. Administrators in higher education should avail themselves of invaluable training opportunities listed at http://www.k-state.edu/provost/academic/leadership/index.htm and http://peabody.vanderbilt.edu/x3332.xml?id=13 at Peabody College.

Professional Organization Opportunities. The following is a partial list of organizations for those in higher education to establish networking opportunities:

- American Association for Higher Education
- American Council on Education
- American Association of Colleges for Teacher Education
- Association for the Study of Higher Education
- Council of Independent Colleges
- National Association of State Universities and Land-Grant Colleges
- Society for College and University Planning
- Society for Research into Higher Education
- National Resource Center for Higher Education

CONCLUDING REMARKS

This chapter has underscored the too-often, taken-for-granted role of school leaders as visionaries who are wise enough to cross boundaries for the benefit of their schools. I reviewed best practices for building community alliances and discussed the importance of addressing the needs of those who are often left behind academically by using community resources to strengthen opportunities for all children and community members. Each of these best practices helps in direct and indirect ways to support student learning and achievement.

Strategic and collaboration-minded leaders want to transform their work in schools. Doing so takes time and effort within a collaborative and empowering paradigm. Our work in this area is fundamental and morally imperative.

REFERENCES

Arriaza, G. (2004). Making changes that stay made: School reform and community involvement. *High School Journal, 87*(4), 10–24.

Epstein, J. L., Sanders, M. G., Simon, B. S., Salinas, K. C., Jansorn, N. R., & Van Voorhis, F. L. (2002). *School, family, and community partnerships: Your handbook for action* (2nd ed.). Thousand Oaks, CA: Corwin Press.

Fashola, O. S. (2002). *Building effective after school programs.* Thousand Oaks, CA: Corwin Press.

Fiore, D. J. (2002). *School community relations.* Larchmont, NY: Eye on Education.

Fullan, M. (2008). *The six secrets of change: What the best leaders do to help their organizations survive and thrive.* San Francisco: Jossey-Bass.

Goldberg, M. (2001). *Lessons from exceptional school leaders.* Alexandria, VA: Association for Supervision and Curriculum Development.

Leithwood, K., Seashore Louis, K., Anderson, S., & Wahlstrom, K. (2004). *How leadership influences student learning.* St. Paul: University of Minnesota: Center for Applied Research and Educational Improvement.

Levine A. E. (2004). Preface. In R. Rothstein (Ed.), *Class and schools: Using social, economic, and educational reform to close the black-white achievement gap* (pp. x–xi). New York: Teachers College Press.

Marzano, R. J., Pickering, D. J., & Pollock, J. E. (2001). *Classroom instruction that works: Research-based strategies for increasing student achievement.* Alexandria, VA: Association for Supervision and Curriculum Development.

Reynolds, M. (2002). Bringing your school closer to your community. *Principal Leadership* (Middle Level Ed.), *3*(2), 81–82.

Rothstein, R. (2004). *Class and schools: Using social, economic, and educational reform to close the black-white achievement gap.* New York: Teachers College Press.

Sanders, M. G. (2001). The role of 'community' in comprehensive school, family and community partnership programs. *Elementary School Journal, 102*(1), 19–34.

Sanders, M. G., & Harvey, A. (2002). Beyond the school walls: A case study of principal leadership for school-community collaboration. *Teachers College Record, 104*(7), 1345–1368.

Schlechty, P. C. (1991). *Schools for the 21st century: Leadership imperatives for educational reform.* San Francisco: Jossey-Bass.

Sergiovanni, T. J. (2009). *The principalship: A reflective practice perspective.* Boston: Pearson.

Spring, J. (2004). *Images of American life: A history of ideological management in schools, movies, radio, and television.* New York: State University of New York Press.

Trotter, A., Honawar, V., & Tonn, J. L. (2005, January 12). U.S. schools find lessons in tsunami. *Education Week, 24*(18), 1,2.

Tyack, D., & Hansot, E. (1986). *Managers of virtue: Public school leadership in America, 1820–1980.* New York: Basic Books.

8

How to Become a Collaborative Leader

Shelley B. Wepner

This chapter

- uses examples from collaborative leaders and collaborative initiatives to provide ideas for succeeding in both preK–12 and higher education,
- discusses reasons for successful and unsuccessful collaborations, and
- uses ideas and recommendations from previous chapters to offer guidelines for becoming a collaborative leader.

* * *

When Lenora Boehlert became assistant superintendent of human resources in the White Plains School District, New York, in 2004, she discovered that her district was in need of substitute teachers for the entire district. Even though the state was fairly lenient on qualifications for substitute teaching, Lenora wanted to develop a pool of substitute teachers who actually knew how to teach. The White Plains School District is very diverse, with a student body that is approximately 42% Hispanic, 34% White, 20% Black, and 3% Asian. Almost half of the students are economically disadvantaged.

Lenora knew from her predecessor that White Plains enjoyed a positive relationship with its neighboring college for student teaching placements but was not certain about other previous collaborative initiatives. When the college's director of field experiences contacted her, she agreed to meet with her and see if she could develop a plan for hiring teacher candidates as substitute teachers. A series of meetings with the director and the dean of the school of education led to a three-part partnership agreement that enabled her to establish a mechanism for getting substitute teachers and helped the college obtain student teacher placements. The partnership also enabled the college to establish a professional development school (PDS) with one of the elementary schools to prepare teacher candidates, provide teacher development, enhance student learning, and conduct inquiry and research.

Lenora had learned that the success of the PDS depended on having a principal who had a strong teacher following and would be positive and committed to bringing new ideas into a building. She arranged to have those principals interested in the PDS idea meet with the college dean and director to identify the principal who seemed to have the most potential to succeed. Lenora then worked with the principal to ensure that the district's administrators and school's teachers were interested in pursuing such an initiative. Seven years later, the PDS is thriving, with many teachers and college faculty transformed in the way that they teach. The other parts of the partnership— substitute teaching and student teaching—continue to operate with success.

Lenora's success in collaborating with the college and her own administrative team stems from her view of herself as one who thrives on working with others to help an idea move forward. She does what she can to promote an idea. For example, she makes presentations at the college about the benefits of substitute teaching in her district. She also has had the dean of the School of Education present to members of her board of education so that they are aware of the benefits of the partnership agreement with the college.

* * *

Lenora is a collaborative leader. She knows who she is and what she stands for. She is honest, fair, and respectful of others (Canada, 2000). She works well with both her district and college colleagues. She is fortunate to be surrounded by an administrative team that supports her efforts to form partnerships with the local community. This administrative team, from the superintendent to the principals, legitimizes her efforts by engaging the teaching staff and parent community with partnership opportunities and following through on the most trivial requests. Her college colleagues are equally enthusiastic about working with their stakeholders to initiate new ideas for the partnership and assume responsibilities.

Not every leader with collaborative tendencies is as fortunate as Lenora in getting sincere and unequivocal support from colleagues, both internal and external. There might be overt or covert resistance from K–12 central office administrators and principals, teachers, or parents and/or higher education administrators and faculty; issues with state approval, accreditation, and resources; or an inability of critical partners to follow through because of other more pressing matters that simply take precedence over a collaborative initiative.

This chapter discusses how leaders can address such challenges while forging ahead to develop collaborative initiatives, primarily between school districts and higher education, that actually work.

FORGING AHEAD WITH A COLLABORATIVE PARTNERSHIP

There needs to be a reason for leaders to collaborate, whether to acquire something new, different and/or needed for one's institution, share something of potential interest to others, respond to an external mandate that requires collaborative work, or claim available funds. Collaborative leaders do not necessarily have to be administrators. There are a number of successful administrators, that is, deans, superintendents, and principals, who are not strong collaborative leaders. Many manage their institutions effectively, but they do not exhibit the traits we have identified. They may or may not be able to envision the new possibilities that partnering could make possible. Regardless, they choose not to explore opportunities for collaboration. This could be due to their perception that a partnership will be additional work; that it is easier to do business as usual; or that their capacity for risk taking is not sufficient to lead a partnership.

The collaborative leader can be a teacher, faculty member, or community or business leader who is motivated to lead an initiative. Such persons appreciate that partnering with one or more persons or entities leads to improved problem solving, efficient and effective use of personnel, new allies, budgetary support, and capacity building (Russell & Flynn, 2000). Our research on collaborative partnerships between preK–12 and higher education indicates that most relationships originate from higher education institutions rather than preK–12 institutions. Reasons include time constraints, varying mandates from local and state agencies to form partnerships to accomplish local goals, and fewer opportunities to learn about the benefits of collaborative work with local universities.

CHALLENGES WITH UNIVERSITY-INITIATED COLLABORATIVE PARTNERSHIPS

Partnerships that originate from higher education institutions often have faculty and their students going into a school or several schools to "help" with the curriculum, instruction, or assessment. A major concern from preK–12 partners is a one-way flow of activities from the university to classrooms with little reason for teachers to take ownership of a project or to consider using the activities that have been developed by others not directly involved with the curriculum (Tomanek, 2005). Little regard seems to be given to what the teachers in the classroom want and need. As a result, the services offered by a university usually do not last longer than the time that university faculty and students are in a school. Partnerships are not sustained because there often is a mismatch between the professional practices of the university faculty and the preK–12 teachers, and time has not been devoted to developing a culture of professional learning and improvement. There also is not enough consideration given to demands on preK–12 teachers' time, especially within the current climate of accountability and high-stakes assessments (Moreno, 2005).

Universities that create collaborative partnerships with school districts need to be acutely aware of how to develop projects and programs that come from the teachers. The following four university-originated projects demonstrate how individuals and groups collaborated successfully with others to help with instruction, professional development, student achievement, and teacher preparation.

Project-Based Collaborations to Reach Out to Teachers

Middle and Secondary School Math and Science. A project at North Dakota State University (NDSU) involving STEM (Science, Technology, Engineering, and Math) places graduate students from the STEM disciplines in yearlong fellowships with practicing middle or high school science and mathematics teachers to increase collaboration between NDSU scientists and mathematicians and area middle and high schools. The project is working because teachers, rather than faculty or graduate students, originate the ideas for the curriculum enhancements because they know which units of instruction need improvement. Moreover, the graduate student fellows are physically present in the middle and high school classrooms and are serving as conduits between the teachers and university faculty in interpreting what is needed (Tomanek, 2005).

Hispanic Student Preparation for College. With funding from the U.S. Department of Education for the Platte River Corridor Project, the University of Nebraska at Kearny was able to work with eight local school districts to better prepare Hispanic students for college. The university, with a 96% White population, realized that it needed to do something to change its demographics. Both the university and local schools worked collaboratively to address biases and systemic barriers impacting Hispanic students' achievement and to identify ways to adapt instruction and programs to meet students' needs (Hof et al., 2007).

Secondary History Teacher Professional Development. University research historians formed a collaborative with secondary school history teachers to improve the way in which history is taught. Of particular note is the attitudinal and instructional transformation of Karen Halttunen (2008), a history professor at the University of California, Davis. She went from being a "missionary" who sought to share her intellectual capital with secondary school history teachers to being a collaborator with other secondary research historians, because she realized that her secondary counterparts had as much, if not more, to share with her. She also began taking responsibility for her students' learning instead of just focusing on teaching students.

Field-Based Literacy Course. Nancy Steffel, a teacher education professor, knew that her college juniors majoring in elementary education needed to be in the schools, and the teachers in the public schools needed her students to promote authentic teacher development (personal interview, May 4, 2009). She worked with a local principal to schedule her literacy course on site, and worked with her college colleagues to change the requirements for one of the literacy methods courses so that her students could spend a full year in the school to practice the methodologies learned in class. Teachers are motivated to receive the teacher candidates because they can observe and critique teacher candidates' use of new strategies with their students, have more time to observe their own students' responses to different strategies, and get to keep the materials that the teacher candidates create.

Improvement of instruction is at the center of each of these collaborative initiatives. Even though the target student population and specific content area varies, each university-initiated collaborative strives to bring together school district and higher education faculty to improve their instructional capacity on behalf of student achievement.

Partnerships Originating from School Districts and the Community

The following three examples describe how a principal, a countywide executive, and a superintendent initiated projects with their local universities and/or the community to acquire something needed for their institutions and stakeholders.

High School Students Attend College. The high school principal at McLane High School in Fresno, California, created Turning Point Academy (TPA) to counter the low graduation rates and even lower college attendance rates at his school (Ward, Daughtry, & Wise, 2007). With the understanding that high school students who are introduced to college life end up completing high school and attending college at higher rates, he sought out California State University (CSU) at Fresno to develop a partnership that would enable his high school sophomores to attend CSU each spring for one semester to take courses and enjoy expanded academic and social opportunities. Targeted students are those who need extra support to stay in school.

TPA students attend classes at the high school in the fall so that their teachers can establish the expected behaviors/attitudes for college, and teach study-skill strategies. TPA students then take entry level courses taught by college professors during the spring semester. Teachers and administrators discovered that this program requires constant maintenance because of the maturity levels of high school students and the attitude of some professors toward what they consider "teenage invaders." Yet, the data indicate that more than 80% of the TPA students attend either 2- or 4-year colleges and graduate at higher rates than non-TPA students. The university has benefited because of increased applications and additional opportunities to place university students in the high school for class assignments and fieldwork.

Helping High School Students Transition to College. A director of a countywide school board association worked closely with the president of a local college and determined that she should work with her school board presidents and superintendents to identify countywide needs that could involve the college. When the director convened a representative group of school district presidents and superintendents for breakfast meetings during the year, she found out that they were concerned with their high school seniors' lack of preparation for handling the psychological, social, and financial challenges of their freshman year of college. This task force recommended that they work together with the college to develop and offer a transition-to-college conference to have experts present ideas for addressing this challenge and showcase districts that are offering preparatory coursework and workshops. They also determined that they should create a transition-to-college curriculum database for their districts to use.

The college representatives realized that the more they did with the local high schools to prepare the high school seniors for college, the easier it would be to help these students acclimate to college life. A subcommittee of the original task force group planned the conference. Each participating school district at the conference was required to bring a team that included the superintendent, school board president, high school principal, a high school guidance counselor, a parent, and a high school senior. Teams were given time during the conference to work together to determine what their districts needed to pursue, based on what they were learning. The teams then gave their ideas to the task force to develop recommendations for all high schools in the county, including a way to track college retention rate. The countywide director who initiated this collaborative relationship prompted her school district stakeholders to finally address the unspoken challenge of transitioning from high school senior to college freshman.

Promoting Safe and Healthy Schools. The superintendent of the Salinas Union High School District, California, stepped forward as the lead local education agency for the federal Safe Schools/Healthy Students (SS/HS) initiative. This $8 million grant enabled collaboration between schools, law enforcement officials, mental health experts, social-service providers, county agencies, parents, and students to make schools safer, increase healthy childhood development, and identify factors of youth violence. An agricultural community, Salinas, California, is plagued with unemployment, poverty, drug use, and crime. The superintendent saw this grant as an opportunity to provide needed services that would help students with both prevention and intervention. He helped to form a 24-person grant project team from all sectors of the community, which has become the infrastructure for policy makers and service-delivery systems to ensure that students who attend targeted schools are able to learn in a safe, disciplined, and drug-free environment (Elizondo, Feske, Edgull, & Walsh, 2003). At the center of these three initiatives is the desire to seek optimal conditions for K–12 student learning so that students have the opportunity to achieve to capacity.

CONSIDERATIONS FOR COLLABORATIVE LEADERSHIP IN PRE-K–12 AND HIGHER EDUCATION

As these examples and the examples from previous chapters indicate, collaborative leadership works when a person has a purpose, takes the initiative, has the charisma to energize and excite others, interacts effectively with people, and follows through with tasks and responsibilities. Collaborations truly are as effective as the leaders who take charge from each institution, department, office, and/or area. Effective collaborative leaders seek and maintain support and approval from all constituencies through regular communication and reporting of the collaboration's progress. They work effectively with their partners to generate, implement, and evaluate agreed-upon goals and plans. Effective collaborative leaders also work independently and together to get others to motivate others to generate and advance new ideas.

Two principals, both excited about having their schools become professional development schools with a local university, had very different levels of success because of their own collaborative leadership capabilities. Principal A approached her local university almost a year before the PDS would become official. She had received permission from her supervisor to proceed and had worked closely with the university to put together a formal agreement. Three months later, the agreement still was not signed by her district because she was unable to convince her superintendent of the benefits of forming a PDS. She also began to question the university about ways in which her school would benefit and stalled the entire project for another 3 months. The university's PDS coordinator tried to contact Principal A numerous times, but was unsuccessful in connecting with her to help her understand the benefits for her school, the processes she could use to garner administrative support, and ways to develop a leadership team. The partnership never happened.

In contrast, once Principal B determined that she wanted her school to become a PDS, she initiated meetings that included lead teachers, her vice principal, the university's PDS coordinator, and two other university administrators. She had this group identify goals for the PDS in relation to her school's goals, delineate benefits for each institution, and develop a process for getting the PDS started in her building. Between meetings, she wrote and electronically distributed notes so that everyone had the same information. The PDS began officially 3 months after the first meeting.

Principal A did not know how to bring the right people together to help her conceptualize and formalize a PDS partnership. She did not take the initiative to convince her superintendent of the PDS benefits for her school and did not follow through in communicating effectively within her own organization or with her partner institution. In contrast, Principal B communicated her commitment by taking action to bring stakeholders together, worked through perceived challenges, and developed a useful and doable plan that excited and energized the stakeholders. She also assumed responsibility for moving the idea along and made sure to keep her stakeholders involved with the plans.

Even though these two principals had the same opportunity for their schools, one succeeded and one did not because of collaborative leadership abilities. As discussed in Chapter 6, everyone is not born to be a collaborative leader. However, there are certain general guidelines that can be followed to strengthen one's ability to collaborate productively with others. The following four guidelines synthesize recommendations from previous chapters and other research to promote collaborative leadership.

Have a Purpose and Take the Initiative

Collaboration for the sake of collaboration obviously does not make sense. As stated previously, there needs to be a purpose for reaching out to others who will help to accomplish something that ordinarily could not be accomplished. For example, the superintendent of a statewide education agency responsible for providing educational services to schools learned from his constituents that the county needed a doctoral program in educational leadership for practicing and prospective administrators so that they would not have to travel 2 hours to the closest university. This superintendent reached out to the dean of education of a local university to encourage him to develop such a program. In return, the superintendent would guarantee students, resources, and facilities for the program. The dean saw this offer as a golden opportunity for the university and worked with the superintendent and his own constituency to develop such a program.

One leader's purpose has to become a shared or common purpose with at least one other leader so that together they are addressing a need, a challenge, a problem, or an idea that either leader alone could not resolve (Callahan, Schenk, & White, 2008). Collaborative leaders need to care about the purpose of the collaboration and believe that something bigger and better can occur.

Someone needs to take the initiative to start the collaboration. While it is understood that collaborative leaders cooperate on an equal footing and will receive equal recognition (Callahan, Schenk, & White, 2008), at least one of these leaders must come forward as the "silent director" of the initiative. The person responsible for directing a collaborative partnership can change, based on the phase or facet of the collaboration that is being emphasized. However, there always must be someone pushing, prodding, and promoting the collaboration, in other words, committed enough to the collaboration to see it through.

What it means to "take the initiative" varies with situations and people. It could mean sending the first email or initiating the first telephone conversation; scheduling a virtual or face-to-face meeting to bring stakeholders together to discuss the purpose of the collaboration and how to proceed; conducting research about the potential of the collaboration; writing a grant application; or drafting an agreement for the collaboration. Taking the initiative can be a one-time-only responsibility or, at the other extreme, it could be expected throughout the collaboration. Those involved need to figure this out. The need to take the initiative depends on the other leaders' excitement and interest in the collaboration, the urgency for the collaboration (e.g., grant application deadline), and time availability. My colleagues and I have both badgered partners to respond to our emails and telephone calls and have felt badgered by other partners to respond to their requests.

Regardless of the interest in or desire for a collaborative partnership, unless one of the prospective partners takes on the responsibility to get things moving, the partnership will not materialize.

Conduct Environmental Scans

Since the basis for most partnerships is some shared purpose or need, a collaborative leader's analysis of how well his or her organization is functioning and what it needs to improve is an important starting point. An analysis yields information about directions that an institution needs to pursue. Lenora Boehlert from the introductory vignette learned that her school district could not function effectively if it did not increase its pool of substitute teachers to cover for teachers' absenteeism. The high school principal from Fresno, California, discovered that he needed to do something to counter the low graduation rates and college attendance rates at his school.

Superintendent's Perspective on Developing a University Preparatory High School Program

Julie Carbajal

Flour Bluff Independent School District, Corpus Christi, TX

Flour Bluff's University Preparatory High School Program, affectionately called University Prep, began in 2005 when the education dean at Texas A&M University–Corpus Christi approached me as superintendent of Flour Bluff Independent School District to see if we were interested in partnering with the university to establish an early college–high school. The opportunity, supported by a Gates Foundation 4-year planning grant, was administered by the Communities Foundation of Texas. Using the model, Challenge Not Remediation, their goal was the launch of early college–high schools throughout Texas.

We signed the first memorandum of understanding between our two educational entities in October of 2005. The name University Preparatory High School Program was selected early in the collaboration and emphasized the university connection. Our motto became, "Building a Learning Legacy for a Lifetime." Planning was fast and furious.

The dean and I saw leadership as crucial and immediately hired a principal, Mr. James Crenshaw. School location was also critical. We finally chose a building within the district but separate from the main high school campus. Dr. Audra Ude, assistant superintendent for curriculum and instruction, the principal, the dean, and I began establishing budgets, dialoging with district and university instructors, and developing criteria for student acceptance. An advisory committee of public school and university administrators and instructors was formed. Planning discussions were intense and passionate. Concerns centered on readiness, rigor, and maturity of high school students. After lengthy planning sessions regarding course sequencing, tuition and fees, schedules, grant guidelines, transportation, and university services, the University Prep program enrolled approximately 80 inaugural students in August 2006.

Fifty-two of the initial students are still active in the program and each will obtain between 10 and 62 college credits before graduation. Currently, 293 ninth, tenth, eleventh, and twelfth graders are in the program. Student exits are due to procrastination, lack of interest, moving out of the district, choice of extracurricular activities, or poor performance. All, however, benefited from the opportunity to understand the expectations and make choices.

The Communities Foundation of Texas continues to gather qualitative and quantitative data for their evaluation purposes. Other measures of student accomplishment and achievement that we use include tests, grades, attendance, college hours earned, confidence gained, and graduation.

(continued on next page)

(continued from previous page)

The collaboration between the university and our school district has strengthened alignment of curriculum and fostered relationships. The most difficult obstacle has been overcoming the operational rules and requirements of the multiple entities involved in this mission; however, the success of students is the substantial return on our investment.

Conducting environmental scans, whether formally or informally, helps leaders to determine strengths and weaknesses of an organization. Environmental scans consider the factors that will influence the direction and goals of an organization. They are a process of gathering and analyzing both factual and subjective information about the internal and external environment to identify opportunities and threats (Cool Avenues, 2000; Pashiardis, 1996; Popovics, 1990).

One type of scan is a SWOT (Strengths, Weaknesses, Opportunities, Threats) analysis, which is a framework for analyzing a community's strengths, weaknesses, opportunities, and threats. Developed by Albert Humphrey at the Stanford Research Institute, SWOT analysis enables a leader to use a readily available inventory of contextually based needs to plan strategically for an organization.

A SWOT analysis of a teacher preparation program probably would reveal the need to develop partnerships with school districts to better prepare the next generation of teachers to increase student achievement (Vandal & Thompson, 2009). These partnerships offer substantive field experiences for teacher candidates, customized professional development for teachers, and continuous feedback mechanisms about student achievement so that university faculty and administrators know what they need to do to improve their candidates' preparation (Vandal & Thompson, 2009).

A SWOT analysis for a school district might indicate the need to become increasingly dependent on colleges and universities to help its teachers become better prepared to meet state requirements with student assessment. Many states have created data systems to track the impact of individual teachers on student achievement, or value-added assessment systems, and teachers' evaluation for tenure, salary increases, and other forms of compensation might ultimately depend on their students' achievement. Strong partnerships between school districts and teacher education programs can lead to continuous improvement in teacher quality (Vandal & Thompson, 2009). A key element to the success of such partnerships will be the ability and interest of collaborative leaders to reach out to prospective partners in response to findings from their environmental scans.

Communicate and Collaborate with Different Constituencies

Successful collaborative leaders understand the importance of communicating with different constituencies (Callahan, Schenk, & White, 2008). They communicate that their heart is into the collaboration and that they are committed to making it work. They do this by meeting regularly with their partners, being prepared at meetings, and working hard on assignments related to the collaboration. Collaborative leaders are honest about their interests, their availability, and their ability to follow through. A change in leadership can result in a partnership's rise or fall because of the differences between two leaders.

The original leader of one partnership concept worked with his constituents on a regular basis. His successor gave lip service only to both the concept and the people. The original leader, a superintendent in a very diverse school district in a suburban town, began a consortium with other school districts with similar student populations to develop community health clinics. This superintendent arranged to have the consortium members meet bimonthly with other community officials, developed committees to conduct research and write grants, and organized special events to raise funds for the clinics. At the time that the superintendent retired from his position, his consortium group was on the verge of opening two of the five planned clinics. Even though this superintendent spent a great deal of time mentoring his successor, who pretended to be committed to the project, the new superintendent had his own secret agenda and plans for his district and community. While he continued to hold consortium meetings, he did not spend enough time learning about the project, cultivating his constituency, planning meetings appropriately, or following through on the essential details. The clinics did not open and, after a year, the project fell apart. Since then, a superintendent from another district has appealed to community officials and other superintendents to allow his district to take responsibility for the project.

Collaborative leaders see value in a community of people working together to address challenges. They make sure that team members have their own clearly defined roles with an explicit process for getting things accomplished. They admire the skills and abilities of their team and provide the necessary resources for their team to accomplish its goals. They also provide opportunities for interaction to build trust among team members (Callahan, Schenk, & White, 2008).

Institutional Culture Clashes. Collaborative leaders have a unique understanding of potential institutional culture clashes that can exist within and between groups and the ability to communicate effectively with different constituents so that they can coexist. An institutional culture clash speaks to a set of differing principles by which different groups operate, for example, how one's day is scheduled, how one is compensated for one's work, how one is evaluated for job performance, how one's work environment should be managed, and how one defines professional development.

Institutional culture clashes are particularly obvious between the preK–12 and higher education worlds, especially as preK–16 partnerships are formed. Classroom teachers are directly involved with their students most of the day. They use the end of the school day to catch up on the day's events, review student work, and prepare for the next day. They are not necessarily "psyched" for someone outside their immediate environment to tell them what or how to do their business. University faculty spend their days differently, with less time interacting with students and more time involved in committee work and scholarship that contributes to their understanding of specific academic disciplines. Their daily pressures are different, thus, creating a different set of expectations for themselves and others (Wepner, Bettica, Gangi, Reilly, & Klemm, 2008).

Collaborative leaders recognize institutional differences and help those within each type of organization come to acknowledge, appreciate, and work within and around each other's operational habits. For instance, collaborative leaders will use a mix of communication methods such as face-to-face meetings, telephone conversations, printed material, and electronic tools. They will then determine their constituency's tolerance level for each type of communication. If they find that face-to-face meetings yield disappointing rates of attendance, they will depend on the telephone and email to communicate. On the other hand, if they find that their group thrives on face-to-face meetings because of the social networking benefits, they will capitalize on this communication method. I have worked with groups that enjoy face-to-face meetings and groups that abhor such meetings, with both groups accomplishing great things.

Use of Technology. Technology's use is dependent on the tools available, the availability and expertise of those who oversee such tools, and the expertise of the stakeholders. Email and relevant email distribution lists help to disseminate information. However, as Callahan, Schenk, and White (2008) explain, we need to exercise caution with the volume of material sent and the relevancy of the material sent. Creating a website for participants is helpful if someone ensures that the website is current and relevant. Blogs and wikis are great for sharing ideas and creating content together. Blogs are a type of website, usually maintained by an individual, that contain information about a topic, event, or issue that is generally in reverse chronological order. Wikis are websites designed for users to make informational additions or edits to any page. Facebook and Twitter are useful for fast updates. Facebook is a social utility that connects people, friends, and others about personal and professional interests and events. Twitter is a social messaging utility for staying connected in real-time through the exchange of quick, frequent answers to a simple question.

Generate Enthusiasm and Excitement for the Collaborative

Collaborative leaders understand and make use of a variety of techniques for generating enthusiasm about and for the collaborative to get things done. They know how to get their team members to value and support interdependency (Callahan, Schenk, & White, 2008). They are constantly seeking ways to have members of the partnership share knowledge, responsibilities, and the limelight. Strategically, they often begin by getting pledges of support from a select group of individuals critical to the partnership, and then use that success to generate more success. Collaborative leaders use every growth spurt to acquire the necessary resources to maintain quality control.

Collaborative leaders celebrate those involved, yet are careful about the reward structures that are put in place (Callahan, Schenk, & White, 2008). They know that, while extra money and time are important, collaborative leaders recognize that their team members must take pride in doing something beyond their own situations rather than simply taking part to accrue personal recognition or bonuses.

Big-Ticket Events. Big-ticket events provide visibility so that others beyond the immediate partnership members become aware of the partnership's importance in relation to institutional, teacher, and student growth. Such events include conferences, symposia, ribbon-cutting ceremonies, dinners, luncheons, receptions, and award ceremonies. These events honor and celebrate the partnership itself and those who have had direct and indirect involvement. Formal ribbon-cutting ceremonies for each new PDS, for instance, with the superintendent and college president speaking and jointly cutting the ribbon, convey bona fide support from each institution's top leader. Conferences focused on the themes and purposes of collaborative initiatives, with keynote speakers to set the tone and workshops to showcase the accomplishments of individual partners, publicize to others the usefulness of such work. Award ceremonies enable collaborative leaders to bring public acclaim to those who have dedicated themselves to the partnership's success.

These big-ticket events are symbolic gestures that generate positive feelings toward and from those responsible for the work and financial resources. These events also help those on the periphery or in opposition to be more supportive of an institution's decision to donate personnel and material resources to such an initiative.

Publicity and the Media. Use of publicity to entice the media to cover a collaborative partnership is usually quite helpful. Publicity by the local and mass media outlets provides free and independent coverage regarding the partnership. This publicity may appear in print media (newspapers and magazines), electronic media (television and radio), and new-age media (email and websites) (Manohar, 2008). Media coverage can be sought through press releases (brief documents that set forth the newsworthy angle of the initiative), pitch letters, telephone calls, emails, or faxes. Accessing media coverage usually means providing something new, distinctive, or relevant to a current trend or problem (Yudkin, 2009).

Although desired, positive media coverage alone is not sufficient to sustain a partnership. One collaborative project aired on a major television network. The project was using a new type of technology for developing science literacy across the grades. Students were interviewed about their response to it. Two months after the technology project was aired, it died because the teachers did not think that the product was useful for their students and stopped using it. Nevertheless, media coverage about collaborative initiatives, especially when it is positive, can help to generate excitement.

Sustaining Momentum. Challenges abound to keep collaborative partnerships active and functioning well. Successful collaborative leaders know that it is better to convince others to take on the responsibilities of the partnership rather than to do too much of the work themselves (Center for Community Support and Research, 2008) so that if they disengage from the partnership, the remaining members are not lost and unsure of which way to turn. A successful partnership will continue to be viable regardless of a change in leadership. Collaborative leaders also know that, to sustain momentum, they must hold others accountable for their commitments. Realistic, relevant, and doable commitments keep participants engaged and energized, and collaborative leaders recognize that.

Collaborative leaders conduct productive, goal-oriented meetings that provide for the meaningful exchange of information. They ensure regular participation from all group members by drawing out less vocal members, balancing the contributions of more vocal members, and following up on members' absences from meetings (Carter, 2006). They keep the partnership alive by managing the collaborative team effectively. They constantly communicate that the partnership is important for the participants, their constituencies, and their organization.

At the same time, collaborative leaders work with their partners to constantly revisit and refocus the partnership so that it continues to be purposeful and productive. If they suggest changes, collaborative leaders base them on assessment data and anecdotal reports that reveal issues that might not be readily observable (e.g., a drop in participation of the third-grade teachers in professional development activities). To reverse trends and sustain momentum, collaborative leaders might work intensively on the problems that surface, bring in new partners and volunteers, hold retreats to request recommendations for improvement and renew each institution's commitment, or conduct seminars to remind participants of the partnership's vision and design (Learning Point Associates, 2004).

Sustaining momentum requires that leaders have their finger on the pulse of the partnership's participants and activities so that interest does not wane. When Principal Fran Barber discovered a bit too late that her three teacher volunteers were not attending the leadership team meetings for a school-university-community partnership that she had co-created, she had to quickly find other teachers to attend. Although she later discovered that the three original teachers had legitimate reasons for not attending, she already had embarrassed herself and her school because of their lack of participation in one of the partnership's key events. As Fran Barber and other experienced collaborative leaders have learned, partnerships require constant monitoring and maintenance.

REFLECTIVE COMMENTS ABOUT COLLABORATIVE LEADERS

As my coeditor Dee Hopkins explained, collaborative leaders are as varied as the partnerships they serve. To varying degrees, collaborative leaders share some of the same traits. Most are creative visionaries with the ability to see new and different ways to solve problems. They take risks and enjoy the challenge of finding solutions, often by drawing on expertise from multiple sources. Positive in their approach, rather than worried about why something cannot be done, they brainstorm ways to get it done. Sometimes those ways strike others, even other administrators, as far-fetched or beyond the boundaries of the proverbial box. Collaborative leaders do not even see the box most of the time. Instead, they visualize connections others would never think of or would miss. Collaborative leaders have the ability to help others see the connections that are obvious to them, using enthusiasm and a can-do attitude. Big-picture thinkers, collaborative leaders not only see the benefits of partnerships but also thrive in those environments, recognizing the strength of many minds to share ideas and solutions.

As we explored partnerships and the collaborative leaders within them, we wondered whether someone could develop a talent for collaborative leadership. What makes one person more persuasive than another or more willing to go out on a limb to try something new and different? We did not find a definitive answer except to note that many of the characteristics of collaborative leaders described throughout this book can be developed.

CONCLUDING REMARKS

Collaborative leaders are more than leaders with followers. Collaborative leaders bring many people to the table to create goals and action plans, share ownership of the process, build and sustain hope, and keep the participatory flame alive as teams forge ahead to achieve goals (Center for Community Support and Research, 2008). They are able to do this because they are willing to take risks, are eager listeners, are passionate and optimistic, and are able to share knowledge, power, and credit (Carter, 2006). Collaborative leaders of partnerships understand that, because they are working with more than their own institution, they are there to guide rather than control and to motivate rather than direct. They have a purpose that is based on their understanding of the needs of their own institution and work with their collaborative partner(s) at other institutions to develop and delineate shared purposes and identify relevant stakeholders and community resources to develop the partnership. They know they must have the support of their own constituency (e.g., administrators, faculty, and board members) and include their own constituency in collaborative partnership activities They are aware of the many roadblocks that can occur (institutional culture clashes), yet exude excitement for the possibilities so that others are naturally drawn in to participate.

As the examples in this chapter and other chapters have shown, collaborative partnerships have succeeded because of the qualities and skills of effective collaborative leaders. They know enough about themselves, their environment, and their colleagues to know what they can and cannot accomplish with others. They also have the capacity to work with others to build consensus, manage teamwork, build trust, and manage the workload (meeting agendas, partnership activities, and communication mechanisms) to help a collaborative partnership attain its goals. Unlike hierarchical leadership, collaborative leadership requires a unique set of qualities and skills because the focus is on the success of a cross-institutional team rather than the success of an individual (Carter, 2006). With today's focus on the achievement of a diverse preK–12 student population, collaborative leadership across educational institutions should be a top national priority.

REFERENCES

Callahan, S., Schenk, M., & White, N. (2008, April 21) Building a collaborative workplace. *Anecdote: Putting stories to work.* Retrieved June 1, 2009, from http://www.anecdote.com. au/whitepapers.php?wpid=15

Canada, B. (2000, September). What kind of leader are you? *School Administrator.* Retrieved February 26, 2009, from http://findarticles.com/p/articles/mi_m0JSD/is_8_57/ ai_77204834

Carter, M. M. (2006). *The importance of collaborative leadership in achieving effective criminal justice outcomes.* Silver Spring, MD: Center for Effective Public Policy.

Center for Community Support and Research. (2008). *What makes a collaborative leader.* Retrieved June 25, 2009, from Center for Community Support and Research, Wichita State University website: http://www.ccsr.wichita.edu/assets/library/381_whatmakesacollaborativele.doc

Cool Avenues. (2000). *Marketing glossary: Environmental scanning.* Retrieved June 29, 2009, from http://coolavenues.com/know/mktg/ee.php3

Elizondo, F., Feske, K., Edgull, D., & Walsh, K. (2003). Creating synergy through collaboration: Safe schools/healthy students in Salinas, California. *Psychology in the Schools, 40*(5), 503–513.

Halttunen, K. (2008). *From K–12 outreach to K–16 collaboration.* Center for History and New Media. Retrieved March 5, 2009, from National History Education Clearinghouse website: http://teachinghistory.org/tah-grants/lessons-learned/19347

Hof, D., Lopez, S., Dinsmore, J., Baker, J., McCarty, W., & Tracy, G. (2007). The Platte River Corridor Project: A university/K–12 collaboration to meet the needs of Latino students. *Equity and Excellence in Education, 40*, 321–330.

Learning Point Associates. (2004). *Maintaining momentum in collaboration.* Retrieved July 13, 2009, from http://www.nerel.org/sdrs/areas/issues/envrnmnt/css/ppt/chap6.htm

Manohar, U. (2008). *Different types of media.* Retrieved July 13, 2009, from http://www.buzzle.com/articles/different-types-of-mass-media.html

Moreno, N. (2005). Science education partnerships: Being realistic about meeting expectations. *Cell Biology Education, 4*(1), 30–32.

Pashiardis, P. (1996). Environmental scanning in educational organizations: Uses, approaches, sources and methodologies. *International Journal of Educational Management, 10*(3), 5–9.

Popovics, A. J. (1990). Environmental scanning: A process to assist colleges in strategic planning. *College Student Journal, 24*, 78–80.

Russell, J., & Flynn, R. (2000). Commonalities across effective collaboratives. *Peabody Journal of Education, 75*(3), 196–204.

Tomanek, D. (2005). Building successful partnerships between K–12 and universities. *Cell Biology Education, 4*(1), 28–29.

Vandal, B., & Thompson, B. (2009, May). *State partnerships for quality teacher preparation.* Washington, DC: Educational Commission of the States and National Center for Teacher Transformation, U.S. Department of Education Fund for the Improvement of Postsecondary Education.

Ward, J., Daughtry, J., & Wise, D. (2007). A turning point for inner-city youth. *Leadership, 36*(4), 12–14.

Wepner, S. B., Bettica, A., Gangi, J., Reilly, M. A., & Klemm, T. (2008). Using a cross-curricular learning experience to promote student engagement through a school-college collaboration. *Excelsior, 3*(1), 27–45.

Yudkin, M. (2009). *The publicity FAQ: Frequently asked questions about getting media coverage.* Retrieved July 13, 2009, from http://www.yudkin.com/pubfaq.htm

About the Contributors

David M. Byrd is the director of the School of Education at the University of Rhode Island. He has a long-term professional and research interest in programs for beginning teachers and teacher professional development. Dr. Byrd has authored or coauthored over 30 articles, books and chapters, including chapters in both the *Handbook of Research in Teacher Education* (2nd ed.) and the *Handbook of Research in Supervision*. He has served as coeditor of the Association of Teacher Educators' Teacher Education Yearbook Series. David is a graduate of the doctoral program in teacher education at Syracuse University.

Jeffrey Glanz holds the Raine and Stanley Silverstein Chair in Professional Ethics and Values in the Azrieli Graduate School of Jewish Education and Administration at Yeshiva University. He formerly served as dean of graduate studies and chair of the education department at Wagner College in New York City. Prior to that, he served as executive assistant to the president at Kean University where he was also a professor of education and director of the Holocaust Resource Center. He was named Graduate Teacher of Year and earned the Presidential Award for Excellence in Scholarship, both in 1999. He has authored, coauthored, edited, and coedited 20 books. He currently is coeditor of *PRISM: An Interdisciplinary Journal for Holocaust Educators*.

Dee Hopkins has been a primary and junior high teacher, school library media specialist, professor, and administrator. As dean of West Virginia University's College of Human Resources and Education, she is the primary editor of *It's All about People: Case Studies in Higher Education Leadership*. Her chapter, "To Dean or Not to Dean: Personal and Professional Considerations," appears in *Dean's Balancing Acts: Education Leaders and the Challenges They Face*. Raised in southern Indiana where tall tales are an art form, she frequently uses them to make a point, provide a laugh, or represent a culture. She still likes visiting classrooms to share a good story.

David Hoppey is an assistant professor in the Department of Special Education at the University of South Florida. David spent 11 years working in public education as a middle school teacher, inclusion specialist, and district special education administrator before moving to higher education. He has collaboratively developed and implemented professional development school partnerships in Florida and West Virginia that emphasize inclusive teacher preparation. David's research is intricately woven and closely tied to his work with professional development schools. His research has focused on inclusive teacher education, school reform, and ongoing professional development for inservice teachers.

D. John McIntyre is a professor in the Department of Curriculum and Instruction at Southern Illinois University Carbondale. His research interests include design and practice in teacher education, supervision, and school partnerships. He is the recipient of both the Distinguished Research and Distinguished Teacher Educator awards from the Association of Teacher Educators. Dr. McIntyre has published more than 75 articles, books, and chapters in the area of teacher education, including as coeditor of the *Research in Teacher Education Yearbook* and the *Handbook of Research on Teacher Education*, 3rd edition. He is a graduate of the doctoral program in curriculum at Syracuse University.

Ted Price is an assistant professor in the Department of Educational Leadership Studies at West Virginia University. His research work is focused on leadership, change management, strategic planning, and school reform. Dr. Price received his Ph.D. in Educational Administration from the University of Southern California in 1985. Prior to his move to the East coast, Dr. Price served in numerous educational administrative positions (director, principal, assistant principal, and coordinator) in California and most recently as the assistant superintendent of education for the Orange County (California) Department of Education, where he was responsible for programs for alternative education students.

Lee Teitel has been a researcher, writer, consultant, speaker, and professional development school (PDS) advocate since 1989. His work focuses on PDS start-up, sustainability, and impact assessment issues; new leadership roles in PDSs for teachers and principals; and the development and implementation of national standards for PDSs. He is author of *The Professional Development Schools Handbook: Starting, Sustaining, and Assessing Partnerships that Improve Student Learning* (Corwin, 2003), as well as numerous articles and monographs. He directs the School Leadership Program at Harvard's Graduate School of Education, where he teaches about partnerships and other approaches to improving teaching, learning, and leadership.

Shelley B. Wepner is dean and professor of the School of Education at Manhattanville College, Purchase, New York. She has been in educational leadership positions and involved with collaborations for nearly 25 years. She has published more than 120 articles, book chapters, and books related to connections between K–12 education and higher education, leadership skills for effectively supporting teacher education and literacy development, and literacy and technology. She has published award-winning educational software for literacy development. Her most recent coedited book (with Dorothy Strickland) is *The Administration and Supervision of Reading Programs* (4th ed.), published by Teachers College Press.

Jerry Willis was a professor and associate dean for education in the School of Behavioral and Social Sciences at Marist College in Poughkeepsie, New York. He has published widely on methods of applied research in education and on approaches to supporting organizational change and the diffusion of innovations, particularly innovations that creatively use educational and information technologies to enhance student learning. He has written more than 60 books including *Foundations of Qualitative Research* (Sage, 2007), *Qualitative Research Methods in Education and Educational Technology* (Information Age Publishers, 2008), and *Constructivist Instructional Design (C-ID): Foundations, Models and Examples* (Information Age, 2009). He has also served as a founding editor for several journals.

Diane Yendol-Hoppey is a professor and chair of the Department of Childhood Education/Literacy Studies at the University of South Florida. Diane spent 13 years as a public school teacher in Pennsylvania and Maryland recognizing the power that teacher leadership has in enhancing student learning. Since joining higher education, she has collaborated with others to create and sustain nationally recognized professional development schools in Pennsylvania, Florida, and West Virginia. Diane's research focuses on job-embedded teacher professional development and teacher leadership. Specifically she has explored numerous vehicles for enhancing teacher professional development that support school improvement, including teacher inquiry, professional learning communities, and coaching/mentoring.

Index